FOLLOW ME III

The author, Maj. Gen. Aubrey S. "Red" Newman, U.S. Army, Ret. (left) listens as Maj. Gen. James J. Lindsay, Commandant of The Infantry School (as Chief of Infantry), reads the inscription on the 1983 DISTINGUISHED DOUGHBOY AWARD, which was conferred in Washington upon the retired soldier and longtime ARMY Magazine writer.

The Award is presented annually on behalf of all infantry officers to a man or woman who has made outstanding contributions to the morale and effectiveness of infantrymen throughout the years.

Other recipients of the award have been: Entertainer Bob Hope (1980), business leader and Philanthropist Ross Perot (1981), cartoonist Bill Mauldin (1982), Senator John Tower, Texas (1984), and Gen. Matthew B. Ridgway (1985).

FOLLOW ME III
Lessons and the Art and Science of High Command

Maj. Gen. Aubrey S. "Red" Newman, USA (Ret.)

PRESIDIO

> This book was originally published with the title
> *What are Generals Made of?*

This edition printed 1997

Published by Presidio Press
505 B San Marin Drive, Suite 300
Novato, CA 94945-1340

Library of Congress Cataloging-in-Publication Data

Newman, Aubrey S., 1903–
    What are generals made of?

    1. Leadership. I. Title
UB210.N484   1987   355.3'3041   86-17079
ISBN 0-89141-268-9 (hardcover)
ISBN 0-89141-614-5 (paperback)

Printed in the United States of America

TO
Private Harold H. Moon Jr.
34th Infantry
MEDAL OF HONOR
(Posthumous)
21 October 1944

Contents

Author's Foreword

Military organization and operational procedures rest on the fundamental idea: "Ten good soldiers, wisely led, will beat a hundred without a head"—and that principle applies at all levels of command. Those at the apex of the command pyramid are called generals.

In the world situation today the average American has more peacetime interest in things military than in the past, and military rank seems to hold a sort of disapproving fascination for the average citizen that positions in authority in civil life do not generate. This is particularly evident in their attitude toward generals. However, for some reason not clear to me, most people seem to consider themselves born as good poker players, and as fine General Officer material.

From a military lifetime of service with star wearers of varied ranks, viewed from many angles, in my opinion they do require some of the qualities of successful poker players.

The question arises: "Who are these wise leaders...and how do we find them?"

In four years at West Point, and nearly 35 years on active duty as a commissioned officer, the human element in uniform has held an ever increasing fascination for me. So I began to write about it. Eventually, in retirement, I progressed to my column in ARMY Magazine—now completing its 20th year. The chapters in this book (except Nos. 1, 46 and 63) were selected from my column, *The Forward Edge*. The primary focus is on the human element in military service as the foundation for professional success.

However, leadership annd organizational ability in controlling and organizing the work of others are as important in civil life as in uniform. Since human nature is the same everywhere, in my view the same qualities and principles lead to success in civil life as in military service.

So come with me, in retrospect, for a look at the habitat in which potential generals were nurtured and developed. It is my hope this conducted tour of my back trail will be of some value to soldiers and civilians alike—and help civilians understand and empathize with their nation's armed forces.

Aubrey S. "Red" Newman
Major General, US Army
Retired

Company Grade Officers

Lieutenants and Captains

Experience is an essential element in the composition of generals, since with experience comes a certain *understanding* of things as they are that can be acquired in no other way. While experience cannot in itself raise a man to high rank, it does more than serve as a catalyst—it provides the kind of empirical knowledge that books and classrooms can never produce.

It is not possible to arrange the chapters here in any precise manner, since each theme is developed to stand alone in its own right. However, the chapters in *Part One* were selected as bearing primarily (but not exclusively) on the first third of a career officer's service, with particular reference to the human element in uniform.

CHAPTER 1
Who Gets the Stars, Why and How?

"Generals are curious people," is the way my lieutenant aide expressed an idea that seems to be widely shared in military and civilian life. After I retired a civilian neighbor said to my wife, "I can't imagine how Aubrey became a general because he is so quiet and polite." In my defense Dorothy explained, "But you do not know him very well."

Apparently most people have ambivalent convictions about the composition of star wearers. One recent phone call from a reader wanted to know how "bad generals" reached that rank—another version of the curve ball query, "When did you stop beating your wife?"

A widely held view about the nature of generals is revealed by an experience of the late great battle leader, Major General Ernest N. "Old Gravel Voice" Harmon. It happened when he commanded the 2nd Armored Division during World War II, camped at Fort Bragg, N.C., before they went overseas and became famous together.

One rainy night he was returning to camp in an official car when his headlights picked up a soldier slogging along the muddy red clay road, bottle in hand and weaving. When Ernie told his driver to pick him up, and put him in the front seat, the driver protested—saying the soldier was drunk, dirty and probably disorderly. However the soldier was obviously from their command (thus "one of our own" as Ernie expressed it), so they picked him up—seated in front with the driver.

He proved to be a friendly fellow, oblivious of his surroundings, alcoholically loquacious, and anxious to share his bottle—which turned out to be French champagne. When this offer was refused from the back seat, the soldier did not turn around—and began to express incisive opinions about his superiors.

Some of them he liked, some he disliked—and said why, in detail.

Eventually he rose in rank to the commander of the 2nd Armored Division, and paused.

"Well," he said finally, "he is a general and, I suppose, some kind of a son of a bitch."

About this time the car pulled up at the soldier's company street. When he opened the car door in getting out, the dome light came on, which illuminated the rear seat—and he saw the glitter of his commanding general's two stars.

"Jesus Christ!" he said, straightening up.

"No, son," General Harmon replied, "just your division commander."

That soldier's idea about generals seems to be a popular conception, and supports the lieutenant's view they are curious people. Another angle was contained in a cartoon that showed a multi-starred general in the Pentagon, pounding his desk and shouting angrily at a cowed-looking staff officer:

"There is no reason for it, I tell you—it is just our policy."

But enough of these esoteric views about the composition of generals, and on to the more balanced question: Who gets the stars, why and how? The best broad answer to that question was stated by the respected military analyst and Pulitzer Prize winner, Hanson W. Baldwin:

"The shaping of a general, like the making of a soldier, is a complex process involving both heredity and environment. It is a process that defies definition or consistent pattern. Like the miracle of man, it can be examined but never analyzed."

He then adds, "Great generals, like great writers, poets, or artists, are born, not made, yet the influences that touch their lives unquestionably shape their careers."

Now we are getting somewhere, "... *the influences that touch their lives unquestionably shape their careers.*"

History is replete with records of how background and experience lead to success in military command. Consider these examples:

- Alexander the Great's father was King Philip of Macedon who built the army and trained his son for the command and leadership role he was later to play in conquering the known world of his day.
- Similarly, Hamilcar Barca of Carthage played an analogous role in setting the stage for the great campaigns of his son, the matchless Hannibal of Cannae fame in his Italian years.
- In our own time we have General of the Army Douglas MacArthur,

born on an Army post as the son of Arthur MacArthur, Medal of Honor winner, who reached the top authorized rank of his day, lieutenant general. As in the cases of Alexander and Hannibal, the son eclipsed the father.

Of course these are exceptional cases and (as Hanson Baldwin pointed out) the truly great ones are born—yet situations and influences that lifted them to stellar greatness also had to be there. So what about "the general run of generals"? How did they get where they did, under what influences?

That is something I know about, having lived all those years in uniform subject to the same influences that resulted in the selection to General Officer rank of uncounted hundreds of generals over more than half a century—including contacts with the active Army from the vantage point of objective observation in retirement.

In another book* my focus was on the American soldier, accenting the human element in uniform, and how to get the job done below star level. In this book, however, the focus is on qualities and factors leading to star rank, ending with some conclusions about *What Generals Are Made Of*—and how to function in that estate.

Small incidents can have large implications, whose significance is often unnoticed at the time. When I was a Plebe at West Point our Superintendent was already world famous from World War I: Brigadier General Douglas MacArthur. He was a remote and legendary figure to me and my fellow cadets until one small action gave us a new insight into the many-faceted character of our "Supe."

It happened when he got married, and *every cadet received a piece of his wedding cake* individually packaged in a small silver-trimmed cardboard box. Although I did not realize it then, this was a unique demonstration of one of his great leadership characteristics: a "reaching out" for contact in a personal touch manner. In World War II, some twenty-three years later, I was to see him exercise this characteristic in unforgettable fashion in a critical situation.

The basic theme threading these pages is this: What men do reveals who and what they are—and that the human element pervades all levels

---

*FOLLOW ME, *The Human Element In Leadership*, Presidio Press, Novato, CA of military service. Further, as officers advance in rank they become more complex and sophisticated—personally and professionally—because they are the sum of their experiences in the lower grades as they progress upward.

The chapters which follow limn this unique development process in action.

CHAPTER 2
New Lieutenants Must be Seen and Heard

My indoctrination into the Army began when I reported to my first company commander, a hard-nosed middle-aged veteran of World War I commissioned from the ranks. His cold gray eyes gauged my military potential and his thin-lipped scowl indicated an unfavorable prognosis.

I'm sure I had something to eat that evening in the bachelor officers' mess, but one thing I remember about the meal was the disconcerting discovery that my scowling company commander sat at the head of the table. My West Point classmates—Ernest Wilson, Eddie Mack and Wayne Smith—sat with me at the other end. The other thing I recall is that we were finishing coffee when a telegram was delivered to the captain.

He looked at the yellow sheet, his scowl darkened and he rose to his feet in sudden irritation. Before stalking from the room he flipped the telegram on the table and snarled, "Hell, no! What do they think I am, a doctor?"

After the captain had gone a first lieutenant picked up the telegram and whistled. "Listen," he said and read it aloud: "Come home at once mother very ill your loving sister signed Alice."

At the foot of the table the four of us had no comment. The captain's reaction so matched the image he projected that we had no idea it might be staged.

The next day the first sergeant delivered a sealed envelope to me. The paper inside, under the heading of regimental headquarters, began:

Special Order No. GYP
Reference: Army Regulations 1,000-1 and 2,000-2
The following officers are detailed as a board to examine into the fitness of newly joined second lieutenants to remain in the service:

Until that moment I believed my West Point class had been commissioned without limitation or reservation or maybe as second lieutenants in the Regular Army. So that order was a shock.

The president of the board was Major (future Lt. Gen.) Oscar W. Griswold, my battalion commander, who from my cadet days I remembered as a stern tactical officer. Among four more names was that of my hard-nosed company commander. A trial judge advocate and a defense counsel were also designated—an unsettling touch. The order was signed by the regimental adjutant and crimped with the regimental seal, but none of us noticed the special order number or discovered there were no such AR.

Our defense counsel, Lt. Joe Hussing, was a heavy-set balding former football player. He bustled around to interview us, complained bitterly about the "unfair" selection of "stone faces" for our board and borrowed a West Point yearbook to check our cadet activity records. The only added evidence I could offer Joe to support my claim to be officer material was two years at Clemson College—the first year in agriculture, the second in architecture.

We were "arraigned" at a public hearing at 8:00 P.M. in a large assembly room over the bachelor officers' mess. When we marched in—complete with knee-length boots, yellow gloves, jingling spurs and dangling sabers—all officers of the regiment were there, seated on folding chairs around an open area where we could stand with our backs to them as we faced the board.

Our counsel announced this was really just a formality and proposed we be "examined" as a group. This drew instant fire from the judge advocate—a small first lieutenant of acid tongue and exceptionally obnoxious manner. He demanded we be "tried" singly, that it was the board's duty to insure the Army got men competent to command as officers, not fancy-pants schoolboys.

Our conscientious counsel objected in anguished tones against such malicious innuendo and appealed to the president to stop it. We four uniformed pawns stood trembling in our Peel boots from London, seemingly forgotten, as the president entered fray. In deadly level tones he warned them both of disciplinary action unless they substituted facts and evidence for unsupported verbosity.

By this time the Army had turned into a tougher place than I ever imagined it could be. They finally agreed to take us singly (planned in advance of course), and picked me as the juiciest victim to start on.

The JA called for a test of my hearing, having learned of a mastoid operation on my left ear. My thin-lipped company commander stepped forward to test me (though he had probably never seen the inside of a college, much less of a medical school).

"Close your right ear with a finger, Mistuh Newman," he said in his sandpaper voice. After checking to be sure I had done so he walked off behind me.

Concentrating hard on listening, I announced, "Sixty-six!"

Then, after more strained ear effort, I said, "Cincinnati!"

That ended my hearing exam, as I obviously had better ears than others present for, as I learned later, nobody else had heard anything.

My counsel then offered the West Point yearbook as evidence, open to my graduation picture, and pointed to the entry "President of YMCA" as proving my leadership ability. In reply the JA singled out another item, "Senior Hop Manager," and demanded to know if I had engaged in pushing dope.

My outraged counsel explained heatedly that that meant I was chairman of the dance committee. Whereupon the JA tilted back his head, looked down his nose and said, "I'll leave it to the experienced officers who sit in judgment here to decide whether or not this gentleman, who chooses to spend his time as a YMCA worker and dance organizer, is the kind of man we want as a combat leader of infantry."

Eventually, after a brief recess, the JA announced the board had decided the action in my case. "In view of your YMCA interest, agricultural experience and architectural knowledge," he said, "your duty assignment will be: assistant to the post chaplain, assistant to the post gardener and assistant to the post engineer."

As I collected my wits to assimilate that one, my "defense counsel," good old Joe Hussing, whispered urgently in my ear, "Tell 'em you joined the infantry to be a soldier, not to understudy the chaplain or grow vegetables—and you want a combat soldier's assignment!"

So help me, I did just that.

Now it was the board's turn to collect its wits. The first to recover was my scowling company commander. "Mistuh Newman," he said, "what you want and what you get may not be the same thing."

Major Griswold pushed his chair back, walked around to face me, and his face creased into a quiet smile as he held out his hand. "Welcome into our regiment, and to my battalion."

Others crowded forward including my company commander, who even managed to unfreeze his eyes as he said, "Glad to have you in the company, Newman."

Of course I discreetly withdrew while my classmates were put over their jumps. Then all of us assembled for a pleasant and lively coffee call. Pertinent comments are:

- This was not just an idle practical joke but served to bridge age and rank gaps to get better acquainted. Thus the four of us had a new sense of "belonging," with the self-confidence to make us better officers than if we had been widely ignored.
- Today hundreds of officers are commissioned each year, including many serving on limited tours who we'd like to keep as career soldiers. The comedy gambit of my first regiment will not fit the tempo of modern times as a greeting for them.
- But human nature has not changed. Nobody wants to be ignored, especially young lieutenants arriving on an Army post for the first time, uncertain of which way to turn or what to do next. If they are greeted with a common-sense informal briefing and orientation geared to their needs and the local situation, their superiors will be setting an example of human understanding and efficiency for them to emulate. These first days can be an important influence either for or against the Army as a career.

CHAPTER 3
Understanding Reaches Beyond Facts

One morning during my plebe year at the U.S. Military Academy, after returning to the barracks from a gymnasium period, I found roommate Clarence H. Smith looking in the mirror on our mantel. Good old Smitty was turning his head from side to side, examining his face in careful detail.

"Do you like what you see?" I asked.

"That sucker hit me with his right hand!" he replied.

The final half of our gym period had been boxing instruction, including sparring *with the left hand only.* Seeing Smitty's critical examination of his face, and hearing his announced conviction about an assailant's "right hand," I put these facts together and concluded that Smitty had caught a surprise good one on the kisser in that boxing sparring and had reached his own understanding, based on the way his nose was pointing, that the blow had been delivered with the outlawed right hand.

The principle involved here serves as a basic guideline for any profession, military or civilian: It is not enough to know the facts in any given situation—you must understand the implications derived from those facts. While this illustration may seem strained, it portrays the principle in action.

My second year in the Army, on the rifle range at Ft. Benning, Ga., in 1927, I gained an understanding of how to aim the rifle: that placing the front sight under the bull's-eye was relatively unimportant, unless it was also centered in the rear sight. On the rifle range that year I also experienced another, broader facet to understanding of far greater and more fundamental importance.

I was shooting comfortably at the expert level on arrival at the 300-yard firing line for slow fire—five shots sitting and five kneeling. The sitting shots went off fine. However, on the second kneeling shot I gave out of breath before my trigger squeeze activated the firing pin. So I stopped the squeeze, exhaled and began to inhale again—and the rifle fired. Down went the target, then up again with a spotter at the edge, but out of the scoring area. The red flag signaled a miss.

Of course this discombobulated me but was not fatal to my Expert Badge aspirations. On my next shot I was extremely careful and knew it was good, but my target did not go down. However, the target to my right went down and the soldier there complained loudly that he had not fired, which his scorer verified. Then I realized my shot, a nice bull's-eye, was on his target—and so did he and both scorers.

"Hey, lieutenant," the soldier called to me, grinning widely, "I'll shoot on your target!" And the two scorers looked at me too, also with wide grins.

There was nothing for it but to call for a mark on my target, get another red flag and a second miss on the record. When the scores were totaled on the chart behind the firing line later, my total was under Expert by one or two points.

"Lieutenant," my neighbor on the 300-yard firing line said, "you should have let me shoot on your target. I could have gotten at least a deuce."

There was a murmur and more smiles at my miscues, but the tone was sympathetic and amused, not jeering. In fact, I realized in an indefinable way that this seemed to make me more one of them and that there was no adversary relationship between enlisted and commissioned ranks.

This rifle range incident and uncounted other details of shared service in my first years in the Army brought me a certain understanding of how I fit into the scheme of things among soldiers of all ranks. It is expressed this way in an extract from my files:

No career is more fascinating than that of the professional soldier. Before the end of my tour at [Ft.] Benning any lingering doubt about leaving the Army was gone. I was proud to serve with the fine soldiers I had come to know, to like and to respect. This was the life I wanted.

From peacetime Georgia (1927) to World War II in New Guinea (1944) is a long hop, especially from second lieutenant platoon leader to wartime chief of staff, 24th Infantry Division (Reinforced) on Goodenough

Island—actually an amphibious task force scheduled to land in Tanahmerah Bay for the Hollandia invasion. It was my responsibility to coordinate the planning for this operation.

A war-room-type facility was needed so orders were issued to establish one, including selecting a fine young officer to operate it. The primary coordinating and organizing method of control was a layout on the vertical wall surfaces of the operations order, and the supporting administrative order, showing who would prepare each part and where the drafts would be posted on the walls, and by what date each draft would be posted.

Once this system for each draft was completed, it was up to individuals and agencies indicated to get the drafts finished and posted for all concerned to see. But it still remained my responsibility to get it done ultimately. I therefore understood that the danger that remained, on which timely completion of the order depended, was this:

Some drafts could not be completed until certain other drafts supplied the necessary planning information. So it was crucial to timely completion of task force orders that the schedule for subordinate parts be met, not only by my staff sections, but by the major units involved—especially the artillery and the three infantry regiments, all of whose commanders were senior to me in age and rank.

On reviewing my understanding of how things get done, I realized one way to avoid such possible delays would be to require each of the major units to pitch a planning tent for a planning staff at task force headquarters near the war room. Further, when any draft from a unit was due on the war-room walls, that unit's planning staff would continue working in their planning tent on the due date until the draft in question was, in fact, posted.

Finally, my understanding enabled me to realize that the task force commander would not be too enthusiastic about approving such a didactic order to his major unit commanders, but he would approve it (and did) for the same reason I was requesting his command backing—that it is better for people to be a little unhappy about how things are done, than to have the resulting overwhelming unhappiness if those things are not done.

Another example of the varied nature of understanding, this time at the five-star level, is detailed in *The General: MacArthur and the Man He Called 'Doc'* (Hippocrene Books Inc.), by his aide-de-camp (1944-45), Roger O. Egeberg. How an official letter that the then-Major Egeberg wrote in New Guinea almost got him court-martialed (yet later was instrumental in bringing him to Gen. Douglas MacArthur's attention) is something that must be read to be believed and understood.

The book also cites the part understanding played in a climactic battle when the great American armada sailed up the west coast of the Philippines, well out to sea and headed for the amphibious landings on the beaches of Lingayen Gulf in northern Luzon. The ships were attacked by Japanese *kamikaze* pilots. With General MacArthur watching the attacks from his command ship, Rear Adm. J. B. Oldendorf's flagship was hit on the bridge, with murderous effect. Other large warships were hit as were some smaller ones. Several of them sunk but the landing proceeded as planned. When this selection of targets for the *kamikazes* became clear, General MacArthur said: "Thank God they're after our men-of-war. Most of them can take a number of hits, but if they attack our troop ships so ferociously, I think we would have to turn back."

That, it seems to me, is the ultimate illustration of the value of understanding: both the Japanese and American commanders had the same factual knowledge of the nature and type of targets available. Fortunately for the Americans, the Japanese commanders were lacking in the capacity to understand the significance of the vulnerability of the relatively defenseless troop ships. Besides, it was the troops, not the warships, which were the real threat in an amphibious landing.

Two comments:

• It is a matter of history that the Japanese continued to fail to understand the proper targets for *kamikaze* pilots in the Okinawa Campaign. But the larger question can never be answered: if there had been no atomic bomb, and we had launched an invasion of the Japanese mainland, where thousands of *kamikaze* planes and pilots were waiting, would they have failed to understand, for the third time?

• Great commanders have always had the irreplaceable attribute of understanding, as Gen. George S. Patton Jr. demonstrated so brilliantly in Africa, Sicily and Europe. But it is not just on battlefields that understanding is vital to success. It applies in every aspect of life and career, so that its potential in things great and small must be recognized and applied to the facts available, even to the direction your nose may be pointing, or in a young lieutenant's decision to make the Army his lifetime career.

So how is your understanding?

CHAPTER 4
The Spirit that Drives the Infantry

All branches of the Army are vital to our military strength, but there is a vast difference in the nature of duties in each of them. That's why selecting the branch you prefer is a major decision. In our modern Army the infantry offers the same tough test it always has, but there is a special lure in that challenge too.

Analyzing the infantry as a career is too broad a task to do here. So we'll look backward to 1932, when I was a student in the company officers' course at the Infantry School at Fort Benning, Ga. This famous school is founded on the battle principle best stated by Euripides centuries before the birth of Christ: "Ten good soldiers, wisely led, will beat a hundred without a head."

Even in the atomic age our organization for battle begins with the infantry squad, which is nothing more or less than those "ten soldiers, wisely led." This is symbolized by the Infantry School's crest: a bayonet, point up, on an infantry blue shield, and above it the words "Follow Me."

The will to "close with the enemy" must be there but, in addition, an almost unbelievable array of skills is required. It is not enough for a unit leader to have the courage and stamina to lead the way. He must also have a broad base of professional knowledge and know-how; hence, the Infantry School, to develop and teach principles and techniques of close combat.

While the arts of command and leadership become more complicated as the units you head grow larger, that special quality of mind and heart called "the spirit of the infantry" must permeate the ranks of men and officers alike to spark their will to go: a combination of "what are we waiting for?," "shoot the works," "get your butt under you," "I can lick you any time," "blood and guts," "follow me" and others, all rolled into one. The Japanese have a word for it: "Banzai!"

In that class of 120 carefree yet professional young officers were many who would meet an infantryman's destiny in battle. Some would give their lives; others would know the violent feel of maiming steel; some would rise to distinguished rank. Two became four-star generals in vitally important international posts. That these young men had that special spark is clearer to me now in retrospect than it was then. This often showed in small ways having nothing to do with military knowledge, especially on field exercises.

Once, on a wooded ridge line, when a major finished his instruction and got in his car to leave, it failed to move because the rear axle had been tied with a rope to a tree. The major got out, found the trouble, then looked with speculative gray eyes at the grinning class.

"Mistuh Soandso," the major finally said to a lieutenant, "step over here, please." The lieutenant did. "Now untie that rope from my car."

The lieutenant did that, too, without argument. For he was the one who had tied it there.

How the major picked him out nobody is sure. The point is that the major was an infantryman too and did not accept defeat, but launched a successful counterattack. In later years the major became a much respected general, and so did the lieutenant.

Another time on a field exercise, the instructor noticed an inattentive lieutenant. "Mistuh Soandso," the instructor said, "the corporal of that squad over there has just been killed. You are the second in command. What are you going to do?"

"Well," the lieutenant said, coming down to earth, "are you sure he's dead?"

"Yes, he was shot through the head."

"In that case," the lieutenant said with sudden inspiration, "I'm going over and steal his watch."

A laugh from the class got the lieutenant off the hook. But everybody got the message, too, and gave the exercise close attention thereafter.

Of course, many hours were spent in lecture halls also, but these were not arid sessions where, to gain academic credit, a captive audience endured the sound of a droning voice. We were young professionals listening to older, more experienced professionals. And it was a two-way exchange, for a major feature of the course was encouragement of questions by students.

In the lecture hall, as in the field, however, there were minor unscheduled incidents that revealed the restless energy and high spirited mettle so vital to battle leadership. Like the time when our last-hour-of-the-day session neared its end, and the instructor said, "Let me think a minute to see if I have left out anything."

As the major paced the platform in a huddle with himself, a lieutenant named Red in the seat ahead of me noticed his neighbor on the right dozing. So he poked him sharply in the ribs with an elbow, saying in an urgent whisper, "Stand up, you dope. He asked you a question!"

Coming awake with a jerk, the drowsy lieutenant pushed his chair back with a scraping sound and rose to his feet. The instructor halted his pacing, and the two stood looking at each other in silence, until the standing lieutenant said in his deep bass voice: "Sir, I didn't understand the question!"

The instructor looked at him in amazement for a moment, until a sudden belly laugh from the class broke the spell. The major said, smiling, "Class dismissed."

Before you decide that this happening was meaningless, let me add that the humorously imaginative lieutenant named Red (Col. Russell P. Reeder, Jr. USMA 1926) later commanded a regiment with great valor and distinction in the invasion of France, until he suffered a serious battle wound in the furious fighting among the Normandy hedgerows that forced his retirement.

The image of the Army most Americans have comes from street parades and ceremonial functions: ranks of marching men in inspection uniforms, shiny helmet liners and colorful scarves, polished field boots rising and falling in rhythmic unison to martial music.

However, as I once heard a battle-wise general say at a spit-and-polish marching ceremony, "It's beautiful, it's brave, it's glorious. But it's not the face of war!"

At the Infantry School it was the seamed and scarred, smelly and deadly, exhausted and explosive face of war that was portrayed with remarkable clarity. The weapons are different now, but that special professional skill and esprit are unchanged.

For the face of war is close combat, and the infantry—the Queen of Battles—still leads the way. This was concisely stated by Gen. Maxwell D. Taylor (an artilleryman, then Army chief of staff, later chairman of the Joint Chiefs): "To those who would say 'The Queen is dead,' I would reply, 'Long live the Queen!' "

The old queen with her outdated weapons is indeed dead, but a new queen with new arms and new methods sits on the throne that commands the battlefield.

The brilliant combat record of U.S. armed forces in two world wars is directly attributable to our marvelous system of military schools and colleges. We have technical schools for all branches, as well as specialized schools such as the airborne, rangers, special forces and Army aviation. But for pitched battle, none holds quite the place of the Infantry School.

Benning's teaching methods have been developed over the years into a high art form. Often the action is played out physically on the ground in front of the class, with live ammunition and a great variety of weapons, vehicles and sophisticated equipment. The money cost of such a program is high. But the skill and sure professional knowledge of Benning graduates have paid off with blue chip dividends on the battlefields of the world—in victory, at low cost to American lives.

Now, back to our original point: should you choose the infantry as your branch of service? That's a decision only you can make, but here are three observations from this lifetime infantryman:

- While I stood high enough in my class at West Point to have my choice of branches, I've never regretted making the infantry my career. And I would do it again.
- If you are technically inclined, and your natural choice is some other branch of service, I would be the last to try to recruit you in the infantry, for the infantry would be in a bad way without the best possible supporting branches.
- If your inclination is to the command and leadership of men, rather than manipulation of the latest innovations in military hardware and equipment, then the infantry offers you the greatest challenges and the broadest opportunities.

CHAPTER 5
Reviewing and Renewing Old Principles

A famous line can be paraphrased "Old soldiers never retire, they just serve on in their memories." That is what this old soldier is doing now, looking out the window where blue sky meets green water—and soldiers of other years pass in retrospective review.

Old principles never die either, they just need reviewing and renewing. However, there must be some way to condense teeming memories into some useful form. Then the idea came: suppose some military school asked me to talk to a graduating class of 200 brand new second lieutenants. What would I say—*in not over 15 minutes?*

After looking out the window some more, that 15-minute talk came out like this:

Gen. Stargazer, Col. Bonebreaker, graduates of this fine school, ladies and gentlemen:

It is a unique privilege to address you today because I reported as a brand new second lieutenant to my first duty station more than fifty-nine years ago. The question is: after twenty-four years in retirement, what can I say of value to you as you wear your gold bars out to meet the challenges and responsibilities of officers?

Time is short, so I'll narrow my comments to one great intangible that permeates all levels of command and leadership. This fundamental was identified years ago in a study at the U.S. Military Academy at West Point, to discover the personal qualities required for successful leaders. Of course many qualities are necessary, including intelligence, initiative, mental and physical courage, judgment and common sense. But one simple, fundamental quality stood out—all successful leaders had it to a marked degree.

What do you think that quality is?

The study found that all successful leaders had *the quality of human understanding.* That should have been evident at the outset. How can you be a successful leader of soldiers unless you understand them? The Army today, like the Army in my time, is full of people who act and react like people—and, in your service, you must deal with this human element in uniform.

As an officer, you assign tasks and tell the right persons to do each of them. This applies at every level of authority. The skill with which you apply this principle in working with others will, in large measure, govern your success as an officer.

When I was deputy commandant, Army, at the Armed Forces Staff College in Norfolk, Va., we sent a query to major headquarters around the world asking for suggested changes in our curriculum. The only meaningful reply was this: *Teach them how to get along with people!*

To issue the right orders to the right people is not enough. You must do it in the right way, too, considering the nature and special situations of the individuals. In the exercise of military authority, the human element in the first soldier you must deal with is yourself. If that sounds like a co-nundrum within an oracular pronouncement, let me cite this case history of my first experience in responsibility to and over others.

In September of 1919 I put on my first uniform (age 16 years, 8 months) as a Reserve Officers' Training Corps (ROTC) cadet at Clemson College, S.C. This was a fully uniformed regimental unit, living in bar-racks complete with mess hall, latrines, reveille and taps. A year later, as a sophomore, there was a slight change in my uniform, the two stripes of a corporal were now on my sleeves. It did not take long for circumstances to impress on me the nature of my new status.

The special learning situation for Corporal Newman involved his first exercise of authority and responsibility as corporal of the guard, marching a squad-size unit to place sentries on post at night in the old barracks area of that time. As we marched militarily along a hallway it would soon be necessary for my squad to make a right angle turn down a stairway to the basement level, a little matter to which I gave no thought until the need was imminent. At that moment I saw the imposing figure of the commandant of cadets, Lt. Col. (later Maj. Gen.) Joseph M. Cum-mins, ahead by the stairwell.

With no planned-in-advance command ready, my mind went blank—while my squad marched inexorably along. Suddenly panic and responsibility coalesced in my shouted command, "Down the Stairs!" And that is what my squad did, with me, my chevrons and red face following.

That was an unforgettable lesson on the need for advance thinking about what you, personally, will have to do or say to meet the responsibilities of authority. This becomes increasingly important and complex as you advance in rank.

I wish I could tell you more command and leadership incidents, and lessons learned from them. But we have time for only one, which happened in my first command: Co. G, 26th Infantry, at Plattsburg Barracks. Veteran 1st Sgt. James S. "Big Jim" Redding taught me more about the Army and how to exercise command than any officer of any rank.

During my second year in command, he came into my office one day and said, "Sir, three of the new men want to see the captain." He referred to a recruit platoon of seventeen men undergoing special training. All were just out of high school. The first sergeant had a sign on his desk that read: "The Buck Stops Here." Knowing that sign meant what it read, I said, "Send them in."

The three young soldiers presented a petition signed by all the recruits. They wanted a new platoon sergeant because they did not like the one they had. I looked in silent surprise at the petition and collected my wits. Then I referred to the court-martial manual, mentioned mutiny and sedition, thumped the desk and told them to "scram," or words to that effect. They saluted snappily, appearing fully satisfied now with Sergeant Stinson and left.

I summoned the first sergeant. "Sergeant, why did you let those recruits get in here with a petition?"

"Oh, captain," he laughed, "it's been too quiet around here lately. It's not good for the company. It was time for the Old Man to blow his stack again."

The more I thought about that, the better I understood that there was a sound command principle involved. Also, let me add, this little byplay could not have taken place without a firm foundation of mutual respect, understanding and trust between the company commander and the first sergeant.

There is no simple formula for commanding soldiers, and no two officers exercise command and leadership the same way. A general rule can be stated like this: "Pat them on the back when they deserve it, kick them in the behind when they need it—but not too much of either—and never forget that every soldier is a very separate and unique individual."

There has been time to touch on only a few primary points, so I've said nothing about fundamentals like these: to be a good officer you must look like one, always well groomed; know your soldiers by name, work at this; establish a money-saving plan (like ten percent of your pay each month)—financial security adds an indefinite something that makes you a better officer. And you could not have a better start than by graduating from here today.

However, there is one key fundamental I must mention before closing. All too often I've heard young officers complain, "They don't give me enough to do, not enough responsibility." These young officers never seem to realize they have confessed their failure to meet the one responsibility of an officer that cannot be delegated, and that responsibility is to be a *self-starter*.

If you find yourself with nothing to do, and you will on occasion, start thinking: "What among all the things I can do, should I do now that I have the time?" Read regulations, prepare instruction for drill, check company mess arrangements, study supply procedures and orderly room administration. The list is endless, and the choice will be yours.

When you do this, an interesting change will take place in your professional life. The more you know, the more you will want to know. The better officer you become, the more duty assignments will come your way. The more pressing the demand on you as an officer, the happier you will be. So remember, be a self-starter. Do not expect somebody else to program the computer that is your brain—program it yourself.

No career is more fascinating than that of a professional soldier; being a good officer is not a trade, it is an art with never-ending facets to discover and study. I was proud to serve with the fine soldiers I came to know, to like and to respect. And it will be the same with you, too.

Two comments:
- That is the best I can do in 15 minutes and is modeled on my talk to a graduating class of the Infantry basic course, all second lieutenants, at Ft. Benning, Ga., on 8 November 1983.
- There is no better way to gain detailed knowledge and understanding of command and leadership than from happenings at company level—especially if you are the company commander and have the right first sergeant to share and discuss them with you.

CHAPTER 6
Sergeants Add Spice, 'Tone and Tint'

Certain words cast up instant pictures in your mind. For me "flag" materializes Old Glory in technicolor, flaunting in bright sunlight atop a tall pole. Say "apple" and a large juicy red one appears; mention "Maude" and there is the gentle old horse of my barefoot horse-and-buggy years. And when I hear "girl" my mental T.V. screen gets all cluttered.

But announce "sergeants" and a wonderful composite picture looms out of memory's mists, of three stripers and rocker men like Fugate and Old Man Brown, Big Jim Redding and Long John Smith, Doc Dougherty and Bosco—and so many others. This composite is weathered by sun and years, neatly uniformed and soldierly, with eyes that can be professionally impersonal, smile or frown, or light with interest and empathy.

Behind this visualized image are intangible characteristics. These involve humor and force, professionalism and human understanding in ways that only anecdotes and happenings can limn. Consider this little experience from my files of more than thirty years ago.

"Take your hands off your hips, colonel," the sergeant said.

The sergeant was a slender man of medium height, who stood erect and looked straight into my surprised eyes. In twenty-five years as a commissioned officer this was a new experience. But I dropped my hands without a word, and the sergeant walked away, also without a word.

That makes more sense than you might think. It rests on the foundation that when a man jumps out of an airplane—well, the law of gravity does not salute. This is one of the first things you discover as a student paratrooper at the Airborne School at Ft. Benning, Ga.

Our first hour was a vigorous exercise period. It was during the break following this hour that the sergeant instructor so tactfully informed me, in seven words, that in this business you do not stand around with a hands-on-hips mental attitude. That back-on-the-heels posture is *verboten* at jump school (or was in my day).

In the second hour, we reported to wooden replicas of airplanes for Mock Door training: practice in details of how to get out of an airplane in flight, doing everything the way the sergeant said. "Go!" and the sergeant slapped the man in the door across the rump. The jumper leaped out in space, as others automatically shuffled forward and poured out of the door.

"Hold it! Stop where you are!" the sergeant roared.

He walked up to one scared looking youngster, took his hand from the static line and made him grasp it the right way.

"Listen," the sergeant said, "in this business you do what you are told, exactly the way you are told."

There was a pulsing silence.

"You had that line under and over your wrist, when you have been told to have it over and under.

"Now," the sergeant continued, "I don't give a damn what happens to a guy who can't do what he is told. What would happen to you is that line would tangle around your arm when you jumped out the door, and maybe pull the arm off. That's okay with me, except I got to kick your arm outa the way (this was illustrated graphically with a violent kick) before the next man can jump. While I kick your arm outa the way, the rest of the stick is crowding forward—so you risk the lives of good soldiers because you can't do what you are told."

The sergeant spat disgustedly out the door, gave another lusty kick at the imaginary arm on the floor, and we continued with our practice, each mentally resolved not to ever get our hand the wrong way around that static line. To lose an arm would be bad, but to suffer the sergeant's public scorn would be worse.

The first time we really sweated was in the Mock Tower.

While a Mock Door is only two feet above ground, a Mock Tower practice plane stands on top of thirty-four-foot-high telephone poles. That may not sound high, but it is easy to confuse a Mock Tower with the Empire State building—if you are looking down with the idea of jumping off.

There is a door to jump out, with a harness that allows you to fall about ten feet. Then you dangle in the air on a cable that delivers you to a sawdust landing pile. This is the place where the men are separated from the boys—and I'm glad I'll never have to do *that* for the first time again.

It was not until my third jump from the tower that the sergeant said, "That was satisfactory, colonel."

In every practice jump, Mock Tower or Mock Door, each man counts loudly, "One thousand, two thousand, three thousand."

Why? Because a parachute jump is normally at a height of 1,200 feet or lower. Figure it out yourself: after you have fallen for three seconds, and your main 'chute has not opened, there is not much time left to pull your reserve. Or to express it the way one of our sergeants phrased it: "So you don't like to be in no hurry . . . well, you better like it. In this business seconds mean life or death. Either you pick up your 'chute and walk away, or they pick you up in a shovel. You guys better get that straight."

If the wind is blowing, your inflated 'chute will drag you over the countryside unless you know how to collapse it. So we learned how. As usual, any new activity opened with one of our sergeants giving us the hot oil about how to do it.

"This here is a parachute," one instructor explained solemnly, holding up the folds of the mottled, greenish sky umbrella.

"These 'chutes are made of nylon." He shook out the folds of the soft fabric in front of us. "And nylon is smooth and nice to touch—in case you didn't know."

He looked around at us, deadpan. We all looked back at him, also deadpan, because nobody wanted to be told, "This ain't funny. You men wearing smiles, hit the dirt and knock out ten."

That *knock out ten* was with us all day. It meant any culprit who had in some way incurred the sergeant's displeasure must execute ten pushups. That is, drop full length face down on the ground, then chin yourself ten times.

This was not punishment, according to the Airborne School, just a quickening exercise that keeps you alert (to avoid it) or (if you don't avoid it) the pushups develop muscles that cushion the "points of contact" when you make a landing fall.

One day, I stopped at my training company orderly room for a brief chat with an old-timer, the first sergeant. A sign on his desk read:

> Your story has touched my heart.
> Never have I met anyone with
> More troubles than you have.
> Please accept my sincere sympathy.

"Well, sergeant," I said, "I guess you hear a good many reasons why they haven't got what it takes."

The sergeant gave me a quick look and said feelingly, "I sure do, colonel. Would you like to see the 'quit file'?"

When a would-be paratrooper failed he was required to fill in a "quit slip," stating in writing that he wanted to quit. He was also called on to answer two questions:

Question: Why did you volunteer for airborne?

Answers: "I wanted to be a trooper," "A bunch of fellows said it was a good idea," "I was talked into it by friends," "I could use the money," and so forth.

Question: Why are you quitting?

Answers: "I gave it what I could, but can't take it," "Parents are against my jumping," "I froze in the 34-foot tower, and have not got the nerve to jump," "I am too nervous for the training," "I don't like this place here," and the like.

When I handed the file back to the sergeant it was time for dinner. He went to a microphone connected to loudspeakers, and his vibrant voice penetrated every corner of the barracks:

"All right, glamour boys. Outside, and line up for chow."

Of course, the time comes when they take you up in an airplane, and expect you to jump out of it. That's when you ask yourself, "Well, you dumb so-and-so, why in hell did you get yourself into this fix?" But you jump.

When you hit the ground, find yourself all in one piece and rise to your feet, it is more than worth the effort. The air feels good in your lungs, the earth feels good under your feet and you are proud to be a paratrooper.

As I was experiencing this feeling for the first time, there were footsteps behind me, and I turned to find an erect and soldierly figure walking toward me. He was smiling, and held out his hand with obvious pleasure.

"Congratulations, colonel," was all the sergeant said. But Sergeant Wey conveyed a welcome beyond words with that direct look in his sergeant's eyes that accepted me into his part of the Army.

Two comments:

- Every rank in our Army plays its own indispensable role, each with its specialized responsibilities and missions. But the word "sergeants" goes beyond their image of efficiency and toughness, and their demanding ability to get things done. They bring a special aliveness to military service, like that in my experience as a student paratrooper.

• Of course, it's not only in the airborne that sergeants add their special spice to training and duty. Early retirements today have somewhat reduced their average age, but their irreplaceable yeast perpetuates the "rise and shine" in our modern Army. Two words made famous by Gen. Douglas MacArthur in his farewell talk to West Point cadets say it best: Sergeants add a unique "tone and tint" to life in uniform.

CHAPTER 7
Lieutenants Have Other Missions

Not long after I pinned on eagles, in July, 1942, as a division chief of staff, an unavoidable obligation faced me. The chief clerk in my office was an outstanding master sergeant who, obviously, should be commissioned under existing wartime regulations. Therefore, I initiated the paper work to, as the Navy says, "make it so."

In looking for a replacement, one of my requirements was that he not be in line for promotion out of the job and a forty-six-year-old warrant officer seemed to fit my needs. The only trouble was that I soon decided he ought to receive a direct commission as a captain.

When I approached him with this idea he said, "No, colonel, that can't be. I hold a reserve commission as a second lieutenant, so would have to come on active duty as a second lieutenant—and I can't do that!"

I then pointed out that this would open the door to further promotion and asked him why not take the opportunity.

"It is this way, colonel," he replied. "As a senior warrant officer I can walk down the street and hold my head up with professional pride. But if I put on the gold bars of a shavetail, everybody will laugh at this baldheaded old bastard."

So I promised that after he was activated as a second lieutenant, I would personally hand carry a letter to the Hawaiian Department chief of staff that would explain the technicality involved and recommend accelerated promotion in view of his age, length of service and proved ability. He finally agreed, with great reluctance. He eventually retired as a much-respected lieutenant colonel.

The point of this footnote to the vagaries of wartime promotion policies is to call attention to the place of lieutenants in the scheme of things, especially second lieutenants. When I was a lieutenant, this subject—to use the current vernacular—began to bug me. As a result, my first article on a professional military subject was published in the May-June, 1935, issue of *The Infantry Journal,* titled "Why Lieutenants?"

That article, edited slightly to reduce its length, follows:

Why Lieutenants?

I am a doughboy lieutenant, have been for ten years, and will be for some years to come. (Actually, a new law promoted me several months later.) During those ten years this question has often troubled me: what is my real job?

I have formulated answers to my questions from time to time, but none satisfied me.

Some aspects of my job as a platoon leader of foot troops have been clarified as time provided the background against which to evaluate and understand the responsibilities of a junior company grade officer. Each field maneuver, each correction by a superior, has painted another highlight in my mental picture of what is expected of me. But still the answer did not stand forth.

As a shavetail in Company A, 29th Infantry, fresh out of West Point, the importance of a thorough knowledge of drill regulations loomed large. Proper voice inflection in giving commands was a matter of concern.

Then as sweat stains marred the newness of my Sam Browne belt and my drill shoes lost their squeak, problems of supply and mess management reared their heads; the comfort and well-being of my men commanded consideration and attention. Balanced meals and cubic-feet-of-air-per-man in barracks were puzzles to be solved, and a correctly fitted shoe became more important than the Saturday-morning surface shine.

Five years passed, and the bars on my shoulder changed color. As I moved from Army post to Army post, command and leadership techniques were added to my growing list of gradually understood duties and responsibilities. I realized that field maneuvers as preparation for actual warfare were deadly serious matters. Thus, a lieutenant must learn from them to avoid errors that, under whining machine-gun bullets and bursting shrapnel, would be paid for in the dear currency of torn and crumpled bodies on the battlefield.

But still, somehow, my job was not yet defined and separated from those above and below me. Drill regulations have a place, so do squad-room air space, mess management, tactics, troop leadership and supply. But all of these can be taken care of by higher-ups, or by the sergeants.

Why, then, lieutenants? What, in the event of war tomorrow, is their true function, if any?

Only yesterday this story of a cockney noncom's reply to a similar question gave me my answer.

An American lieutenant on leave in England was observing British troops at drill. He saw noncoms giving commands, handling everything; the English lieutenants strolled out and said simply, "Carry on, sergeant," and disappeared. Inquisitive, the lieutenant cornered a grizzled old Tommy, a World War I veteran, wearing ribbons for service in other wars.

"For several days now I have watched your drill," the American said. "Always the noncoms are in charge. The lieutenants walk up and say, 'Carry on, sergeant.' If that is all they do, what are your lieutenants good for, anyway?"

The old fighter considered the question. He appeared to think back to days when the air was full of screaming death and ground saturated with the blood of his comrades. Then, with pride and respect in his voice, he said:

"Sir, when the time comes, they show us how to die."

I suppose that answer satisfied me, at the time, because it was the one area of my job as a lieutenant in which I wondered about my competence. That was a duty, if and when a battlefield situation called for it—but I shared that grim possibility with sergeants too. The preponderance of sergeants among those awarded combat decorations in all our wars makes this self-evident.

So we come back again to the question: why lieutenants? What is the special job of a lieutenant that is peculiarly his own, that he does not share with the experienced sergeants?

Lieutenants do have the responsibility to learn and carry out all aspects of their grade-level duties. But the one special requirement each lieutenant faces over and above those, is to begin preparing himself to meet the added demands of higher rank. To be thoroughly knowledgeable on his job, while a platoon leader, is the basic foundation, but only the foundation, for those higher and more complex responsibilities he will face later.

In brief, the primary duty that he cannot delegate is this: he must prepare himself to *grow*—not just be ready to take on the next higher rank, but to keep advancing in knowledge and capacity. Just as all sergeants start as recruits, then build on that basic training, so all senior officers begin as second lieutenants and must start the process of *growing*—not just punch the drillschedule time clock.

These comments seem pertinent:

- An officer should begin, as a lieutenant, to think of his career like a tactical situation. He must, of course, deal effectively with the location that lies within his sight and hearing. But also, in his mind's eye, he must anticipate and prepare himself for the larger challenges of higher rank that lie further down the road of the future.

- One of the most effective ways to help you see a long way down that future career road is to look at the past by reading military history, including biographies of great military leaders. This is far more fascinating than reading fiction.

    Besides, instead of just the memory of a good story you retain lasting professional knowledge. There are so many fine books it would require a book to list them, but here are sample titles from my library: *Patton Ordeal and Triumph* (Farago); Bruce Catton's great trilogy: *The Army of the Potomac: Mr. Lincoln's Army, Glory Road* and *A Stillness at Appomattox; Nelson as Military Commander* (Lewin); *The Military Staff: Its History and Development* (Hittle); *Bloody River: Tragedy at the Rapido* (Blumenson); *Panzer Leader* (Guderian); *Combat Command* (Harmon); *Born at Reveille* (Reeder) and others, which have given me wonderful hours of fine military reading.

- Two especially interesting books are *Hannibal* (Lamb) and *Alexander the Great* (Green). Both of these peerless battle leaders were trained from youth by their great military fathers, Hamilcar Barca of Carthage, and Philip of Macedon. Unfortunately, not many second lieutenants can have famous battle-leader fathers like those of Hannibal and Alexander to point them at a young age toward preparing for future high rank. But any lieutenant can point himself in that direction by reading, studying and observing, thus doing that part of his job that nobody else can do for him.

- There is no need to buy books. Libraries are nearly everywhere, so you can scan the shelves with hungry eyes like a kid in a candy store. Also, newsstands offer a plethora of paperbacks at moderate prices, which is where I found my copy of *Hannibal.* No one man can read all the good military books available but if you start as a lieutenant—which, sadly, I did not—you can go a long way toward stimulating your professional thinking to meet the new, varied and complex problems of senior officers in command, leadership and high-level staff duties.

CHAPTER 8
Travel in the "Old Army"

Many things in the Army are bigger, better and more efficient than they were in my time, but not necessarily more interesting or pleasant to live with. Take modern overseas travel on airplanes or great ocean liners, compared to "going on foreign service" on U.S. Army Transports (USATs) in the 1920-40 era.

Sadly, the old USAT *Somme* and her sister ships *Château-Thierry* and *Cambrai*—along with the queen of the line, USAT *U.S. Grant*—are gone with the years like the horse, the wrap legging, and the Springfield rifle. But they live in the memories of senior citizen sunset watchers who traveled on them. To say they were small creates a false impression; they were smaller than that. But for our time they were ideal. How could the little U.S. Army of that era have found enough passengers for larger transports?

My first overseas trip was from Brooklyn on the *Somme* through the Panama Canal to San Francisco, thence on the *Grant* by way of Honolulu to Manila—a memorable six-week vacation cruise with pay. It was a nice, sociable, two-week trip around to Frisco—with three good meals a day besides morning, afternoon and evening coffee calls in the dining salon. Also, I began my career as a bridge player.

One fringe benefit of those coffee sessions was the variety of stories about the Army you would not otherwise have heard—especially those related to USAT travel. Like the time one more family was ordered on a transport than there were staterooms. Since the three junior officers were newly married second lieutenants, this resulted in the three bridegrooms in one four-bunk cabin, and their brides in another one. But the problem did not prove unsolvable. The lieutenants prepared a drill schedule for the use of available facilities.

In San Francisco we boarded the *Grant,* a rakish, dashing-looking ship compared to the *Somme.* Also more versatile, for the *Somme* just rolled, while the *Grant* added an exceptional ability to pitch and yaw as well as roll. But, to us, she was a grand ship. In fact, scuttlebutt had it the *Grant* was the German Kaiser's yacht until the United States acquired it after World War I.

There were many more passengers than on the *Somme,* but the *Grant* was still small enough to be friendly and clubby, so everyone was soon acquainted with everybody else. Perhaps its yacht personality lingered on, for out-of-routine things seemed to happen and a more lively atmosphere prevailed.

In my stateroom there were three double-decked bunks and a couch, occupied by five infantry second lieutenants, an old warrant officer with 29 years of service, and a young ensign of the Coast and Geodetic Survey. When a costume party was announced for the main salon, one of the other infantry lieutenants named John teamed up with me to go as diapered babies. As our nurse, from another cabin we recruited an infantry friend of ours with the forbidding name of Ovid.

John and I folded sheets for our basic costume, borrowed safety pins from Ovid's wife and other young mothers aboard, and added T-shirts as a bow to convention. The young mothers manufactured baby caps for us, complete with under-the-chin tie-ons, and contributed nippled bottles. Our nurse, Ovid, wore an ankle-length dress, long-sleeved, high-necked, frilly blouse and sunbonnet—and a tight-lipped, harassed look and querulous manner.

It so happened that when we left Honolulu a couple of bottles of Hawaiian Mule—better known as Okolehao—had somehow followed us on board. This was not only against one of the Army's most rigid taboos—especially on transports—but was also against the law, as Prohibition was still in force. So the Hawaiian Mule was carefully sequestered for an appropriate occasion—and this costume affair offered unique opportunities.

When we arrived in the main salon, with Ovid fussing at us as John and I sucked on our milk-filled bottles, we were the hit of the show. But nobody guessed our milk was spiked with a nice kick from the Hawaiian Mule. After a time, when John's bottle got low on milk, he began to cry, so Ovid rushed over and checked his pants then flew into a rage, dragging John out to be "changed."

Of course, the "change" consisted of refilling John's milk bottle, with the proper spike in it—also for Ovid to absorb a good kick from the Hawaiian Mule before going back. When they returned, with Ovid mumbling and carrying on about drastic measures to get John and me "housebroken," it was my turn to cry. The routine was repeated, Ovid going into a real tizzy as he dragged me off to be "changed"—so we could get mule-kicked again.

Everybody got a bang out of us, but laughs from some of the older generation looked forced. Obviously, they wondered what the Army was coming to when three young officers would make such fools of themselves. But we didn't think we were such fools—not when we could pitch a private three-man cocktail party right under their noses, and get away with it.

In our next enterprise, however, we did not come off so unscathed.

You could hardly blame us, though, because the situation invited action to relieve the tedium of keeping the bridge game going in our seven-man stateroom. That's when one of our more imaginative minds realized there were potentialities in the way the old warrant officer with 29 years of service got up and took a walk down the corridor to the head about 0400 each morning.

Our cabin was 303, and 301 next door was occupied by five Army nurses. Since numbers over cabin doors were of brass, attached with screws, they could be moved with little effort. So the imaginative mind decided that if the last digits were interchanged around midnight, the results could be interesting—maybe even ease the tedium a little.

Well, it did—twice as well as planned. At about 0400 next morning, a little while after the old boy had gone for his usual promenade down the corridor, there was a subdued commotion next door where the nurses lived. Then the old-timer came scuttling back into our cabin in a dither, and popped himself into his bunk.

Half an hour later the curtain on our cabin door was pushed aside, and the oldest nurse among the five next door—who was nearing the old biddy stage—entered our cabin, head down. Then she looked up, emitted a little gasping squeak, and retreated in disorganized disorder. Like our warrant officer, she had taken an early morning stroll, for the same reason. Also, like him, she trudged back in a sleepy fog looking only for the right number over her cabin door.

Our antiquated warrant officer then got the idea, went out and verified it before we could change the numbers back, and returned to berate us loudly as "damned graceless whippersnappers." If that had been the end it would have been just nice clean fun—but it wasn't the end. The oldest nurse also discovered what had happened, decided it was a plot to humiliate her, and took off in high dudgeon to report the matter to the transport commander, a tough cookie. Apparently she gave him quite a pitch, because the colonel got real hostile with us.

This is only a quick look at selected scenes from one U.S. Army transport ship, but maybe it backlights a little why those of us from that time do not envy you your modern computerized travel on transocean planes and big-ship transports—or blocked space on commercial luxury planes and ships. The same principle applies in some measure for all phases of military life.

The time will come when you will sit where we are now. We hope when your years go where ours have gone you'll feel as we do: that to be retired but not tired of living is a wonderful thing. We've had our fling, and each can say, "I do not repent how I spent the sunrise and bright skies, nor wonder where they went. In the glowing embers of sunset my heart remembers . . . and is content."

CHAPTER 9
Promotion Ball and How it Bounces

The rank structure of our stratified military society is divided by sharp lines, and diverse personal facets and chance circumstances can affect promotions. The longer a man stays in the service, and the higher he goes, the more tensions swirl around duty assignments and higher rank. Backtracking my own rank trail may bring these special angles into clearer focus.

In 1925, I was commissioned second lieutenant. From behind the World War I "hump" on the promotion list, I would serve about seventeen years before making captain. After five and a half years my gold bars turned to silver, but nobody seemed to care much. Then, in 1935, a new law authorized promotion to captain after ten years of commissioned service.

At that time I was returning from Hawaii aboard the Army transport *Grant,* sharing a cabin with a major and another first lieutenant who ranked me two years. The first two nights, when the major crawled into his bunk, he said to one of us, "Turn out the light before you turn in, Lieutenant."

On the third day, a radiogram to the ship heralded my promotion to captain. Fortunately, the PX had captain's bars in stock. When I returned to our cabin the first lieutenant who ranked me two years was not happy to see my new bars, and promptly concluded his name must have been left off the radio by administrative error; thus, he would still rank me in an emergency requiring exercise of authority.

Naturally, I couldn't let such insubordination go unchallenged, so I mentioned the possibility that I might rank him out of his lower bunk. When the major climbed into his berth, I climbed into mine and leaned out to say to my erstwhile superior, "Turn out the light before you turn in, Lieutenant."

His loud and acrimonious reaction was most gratifying. At last, when I got promoted, somebody cared!

In early 1941, a War Department order reached my in-basket (as G2, Hawaiian Division) with "p. 3" penciled on the cover by the adjutant general's clerk. On page 3 my name was among those promoted to major.

Several ideas trickled through my mind. First, sadly, that I could never be a company commander again. Then, not so sadly, as a field grade officer, my days on guard as officer of the day were over. Next, since a copy of that order was being circulated to the chief of staff and commanding general, one of them might decide to pin on my new leaves. So I rose from my chair and left headquarters.

At the Schofield Barracks PX I got a pair of gold leaves, then went to Company D, in the 19th Infantry quadrangle, where I had been company commander just months before. 1st Sgt. John Christopher, one of the truly outstanding soldiers in the Army, was at his desk. After we exchanged greetings, I said: "This was the last company I'll ever command, and you were the last first sergeant I'll ever have. You helped me get these major's leaves, so will you pin them on for me?"

World War II erupted in December with the Japanese attack on Hawaii. One side effect was my promotion to lieutenant colonel in January 1942; another was my designation in July as division chief of staff. Eight days later, the division commander pinned on my eagles—a wartime spot promotion. I was in the right place at the right time, so the ball bounced my way.

The next morning, in a fresh uniform and wearing my eagles, I met our division artillery brigadier. After returning my salute he stopped to say, "You can always tell recruit colonels. They don't know whether they are coming or going."

That's how I discovered eagles come in pairs: one looking to its right, the other to its left. With the left-looking eagle on your right, and the right-looking eagle on your left, both will look in the direction you are facing. So the brigadier was telling me I had them reversed: my eagles looked where I had been, not where I was going.

In 1952, ten years later—my longest service in one grade—I was president of a general court, trying a soldier for murder. At noon recess, when I returned to the 505th Airborne Infantry, which I was privileged to command, the executive officer handed me a pair of stars, with the information that I had been nominated for brigadier general. After lunch, I again presided over the general court which found the accused guilty of first-degree murder, and we sentenced him to death.

There may be symbolism in that coincidence, though I've been unable to decide what. For some reason, it reminds me of the story about a colonel in Napoleon's army who received word he was to be promoted to brigadier general. When the courier delivered the message the colonel was being treated for a head wound in a field hospital. In fact, the surgeon had just opened his skull and removed his brain.

On hearing the message, however, the colonel jumped off the operating table and headed out of the hospital tent. The surgeon called, "Come back here, you're going off without your brains!"

The former colonel replied, as he continued on his way, "I'm a general now, and don't need any brains!"

Anyway, the Senate approved my promotion and my division commander (and West Point classmate), Major General Charles D. W. Canham, held a small ceremony in his office. He pinned a star on one side, while my wife Dorothy pinned the other side. The stars were a custom-made sterling silver pair that Chuck Canham himself had worn as a brigadier.

My second star, in Germany in 1954, was a turning point—in the wrong direction. It moved me from duty with troops to a staff assignment in headquarters of U.S. Army Europe, and I was never assigned to command or duty with troops again.

President Lincoln is said to have told a story about a ragged and sad-eyed little boy who stood in front of a bakery, looking through the window at a large chocolate cake on display. When asked if he liked chocolate cake, the boy said, "Ain't nobody loves chocolate cake like I do—and gets less of it!"

In my last 17 years of service, I had much duty with troops, including jobs as general staff officer, chief of staff, assistant division commander and deputy commander—but barely one year in actual command. Since command is the chocolate cake of assignments, for the last half of my service I was a charter member of the club with that small boy.

The emotional aspects of promotions on relatives—especially on wives of officers—are too fundamental and far-reaching for analysis here. My ten years as a colonel gave me a clear insight into these tensions, so that when reaching up and touching my first stars I remember thinking: "These are just little pieces of metal, cold and hard to the touch. Not at all the kinds of things worth the heartbreak and needless bitterness that failure to wear them so often brings."

Of course, this hardly touches the surface of the circumstances related to my case. Nor does it reveal how the labyrinth of human relations and personality quirks entwine military rank and assignments in the same way that the serpents in the world-famed Laocoön sculpture enmesh human figures. Hopefully, however, others may read between the lines and see a little clearer these factors about military rank:

- To people concerned, the rank each reaches does matter, but should never matter too much.
- The more an officer avoids letting emotions affect his professional life and guards against "personality conflicts"—especially with his superiors—the better his chances for selective promotions.
- Your family life and professional career should each complement, not complicate, the other. Both impose obligations, but neither can be done justice without reasonable consideration of the other by you, your relatives and superiors.
- There are always more top-quality officers than vacancies in the higher ranks or choice assignments for them. Thus, much depends on what kind of cards Fate deals you, not just on how well you play them. But, to mix a metaphor, how the ball bounces is only one factor; how much you've *got* on the ball is and will remain the basic element.
- "When the Great Scorer pens your name," He'll write what kind of soldier you were, not how much you were touched by fame.

CHAPTER 10
To Lead Well Takes Heart and Head

There are no more magic words in our military profession than "command and leadership"—and these allied functions have been euphemistically classified as "many-splendored things." But when you try to isolate and delineate the "splendors" involved, the glow and glitter of that high-priced word are dulled by reduction to prosaic facts, acts and functions of military life. Only in the aggregate do those intangible words become magic.

Command and leadership are two quite different functions, yet they are inextricably interrelated, each supplementing and strengthening the other. I think of them as Siamese twins, each essential to the life of the other, joined at the head and heart—with the head symbolizing command and the heart denoting leadership.

But enough of evanescent generalities. It is time to flesh out those magic words with some concrete facts of military life, and there is no more fundamental area to do this in than at company level. Forty years ago, after more than 15 years' service at company level (in nine companies, commanding three of them), I took a retrospective look backward and drafted a little study of one specialized facet of command and leadership.

It was published in the December, 1941, *Infantry Journal* and again in December, 1948. But this last was thirty-nine years ago, so here it is for another look:

And Assume Command Thereof
No two men take over a command in exactly the same way. The canned language of orders runs like this: "Capt. Dustcloud is this date transferred to Co. Q, and will assume command thereof."

But just how does Capt. Dustcloud go about "assuming command thereof"?

First, he blows into the orderly room enveloped in a haze of brusk efficiency which somehow conveys the idea he has been sent down to straighten out the outfit. You kind of get the impression he instantly sees a lot of things that need changing and that he thinks Capt. Considerate, the former company commander, was perhaps a good fellow but not so hot as a commander.

After a critical look around, Dustcloud sits down at his desk—and doesn't like the way the desk light is arranged. So he has that changed.

In the kitchen, he tells the mess sergeant to shift the meat block. In the supply room, Dustcloud asks Sgt. Noshortages how he runs his temporary receipts. This is changed, too, although it was a system that worked.

Now that he has made his presence felt, Capt. Dustcloud sits himself down at the desk where the light has been changed to suit him. He is satisfied with Co. Q—he has "assumed command thereof."

Yes, he has. No argument about it; everybody from the first sergeant to the KPs knows Capt. Dustcloud is there. But they're not very happy about it.

Capt. Considerate's method was different.

He walked into the orderly room, shook hands with the first sergeant, looked around until he saw what was obviously a new organization chart on the wall.

"Sgt. Bustle," he said, "that's a nice-looking chart. It's the kind of thing I like to have."

When he inspected the kitchen, Capt. Considerate found the coffee was good and said so out loud. He saw several things he wanted to change later but said nothing about them. There was no hurry.

In the supply room, Sgt. Eveready was busy checking out laundry, so Capt. Considerate said, "Go ahead with your work, sergeant. I'll be in to check property tomorrow."

After talking to the first sergeant about the current training program, Capt. Considerate assembled all the sergeants in the orderly room. His talk to them lasted about 30 seconds, something like this:

"I have assumed command of this company. It looks like a fine outfit, and I am glad to be here. I expect you to give me the same loyalty and support that I can see you have given to your former company commander. For the time being, I want you to go ahead just as you have been doing. Later on if there are any changes I want to make I'll let you know. That's all . . . Thank you."

Both Capt. Dustcloud and Capt. Considerate have very definitely "assumed command thereof"—but if you were a soldier which one of those two company commanders would you rather have?

Stone Borealis

Notice that Capt. Dustcloud was not inhibited by leadership (heart) considerations, but was content just to exercise command. On the other hand, Capt. Considerate included the heart angle (leadership), yet he had just as completely (and more effectively) "assumed command." He understood the fundamental principle of the Siamese twins idea: command and leadership are mutually interrelated and supportive.

There are unending variations in situations and personalities, thus unending variations in how to apply the Siamese twins principle. Here is the situation I faced in assuming command of Co.G, 26th Infantry, at Plattsburg Barracks, N.Y., circa 1936.

I had been a lieutenant for over ten years, most of the time as a company lieutenant, but this was my first command (and your first command is like your first kiss, never duplicated). Further, I knew Co.G was completely outstanding, a tribute to its nine sergeants: six of them (including 1st Sgt. James S. "Big Jim" Redding) were combat veterans with an average of 20 years' service (also with three Distinguished Service Crosses, four Silver Stars, four Purple Hearts, one Croix de Guerre with Palm, and 20 battle stars among them).

Conversely, I had never been in combat, and knew that Big Jim Redding had been first sergeant of that company on that post for 11 years, before I had even been commissioned. On top of that I knew when my predecessor in command walked down the street with that wonderful old first sergeant the word was, "There goes Capt. Easy, and the company commander of Co.G."

Obviously, this was a special situation, and I gave some thought to what procedure to follow in "assuming command." So on arriving at the company for the first time I introduced myself to 1st Sergeant Redding, asked him into my office, invited him to have a seat, then said, in summary:

- That I had just over ten years' service, in six companies, but this was my first command.
- That I knew of the great combat record and long service of the outstanding NCOs in our company. Also, that I realized the great reputation of the company had been won by their skill, efforts and leadership—and that I knew he was the central figure in establishing this high standard in Co. G.
- Finally, that there were two things I expected from him: keep me out of trouble, and remember I was the company commander. (Maybe this was crossing a bridge before coming to it, but in command and leadership there are times to do that; it's called anticipation and foresight.)

As for the rest of my assuming command, I followed the procedure of Capt. Considerate. There must have been something right about that procedure, because no captain in any army ever had a more rewarding and pleasant three years in command of "the best damned company in the Army."

This was an unusual situation requiring an unusual solution, and assuming command of my second company (at another post, in a new regiment) was totally different. There, the existing situation called for harsh disciplinary action on my first day, soon followed by replacing the mess sergeant and supply sergeant—and only then could I (gradually) become Capt. Considerate.

Also, assuming command of my third company required a new approach. I had been in this regiment a year and a half, thus was no stranger to the company, nor they to me. This was a machine-gun company, hence I needed a refresher course in machine-gun techniques. So I asked the first sergeant, as part of my takeover, to arrange for a school for me on the front lawn, with a gun commander (corporal) to be my instructor. You can't fool soldiers, because there are too many of them, but you gain rather than "lose face" when you ask to be instructed in the specialized knowledge you need.

Some comments are:

- Military service is a profession, not a craft or a job, but it goes beyond that. Command and leadership are an art, not a skill or technique that can be circumscribed within rules and rigid regulations. Just as a painter must integrate perspective and color to produce his picture, so a military commander must balance and merge, push and pull to become a leader.

• Time and politics and the world situation have made tremendous changes in military service since my day, but human nature remains unchanged. Thus, when you "assume command" you are assuming authority over animate human beings, and accepting responsibility for weapons and other inanimate appurtenances of your new command. The inanimates have undergone great changes, but not the animates.

• Note the Siamese twins principle in my first talk with Big Jim Redding: ". . . keep me out of trouble" (heart), and ". . . remember I am the company commander" (head). I assumed command of three companies, three regiments, and one division (briefly), and each was a special situation requiring a different solution. But all involved "head and heart" considerations—and so they will for you, too. That's the art of it.

CHAPTER 11
Bonaparte Knew His Maxims

As an *aide-mémoire* I leafed through my shoe-box-size file of three-inch by five-inch slips of paper: pages from old pocket notebooks, small clippings and memos to myself on any scrap of paper handy at the time. Here are some ideas about command and leadership from that file which, considered as a whole, support one of the most basic of all military maxims.

A memo, on a yellowed slip of paper from my first days as a company commander nearly 40 years ago, reads:

"Be interested, be thoughtful. A company has the same feelings and the same reactions as a human being. This is not strange, for a company is made up of human beings—a fact all too often overlooked."

Another little note contains the basic definition of discipline: ". . . instant and willing obedience to orders and, in the absence of orders, to what you think those orders would have been." Nowhere is this more important than at company level, especially among combat troops who operate in the forefront of battle.

Another slip of paper reads: "When in danger, when in doubt, run in circles, scream and shout." Followed by this one, "In the exercise of command, be the hub—not the center of a hubbub!" This last is a way of saying that, in an emergency, the good commander of a well-trained unit gives prompt and clear orders that are instantly obeyed.

A related item (attributed to Mark Twain) says, "It is noble to be smart, but even nobler to tell someone else how to be smart—and is much less trouble." Actually, this is the primary duty of a commander: to tell others what to do.

A small clipping from a magazine gives these quotes: "The eye of the master will do more work than both of his hands."—*Ben Franklin's Almanac*, 1757. Also, "Touring thy plant with a critical eye can do more for the health of thy business than a trip to Washington."—*Acme Steel Notebook,* 1951.

Commanders at all levels will recognize these as stating, in different words, the old command principle that "A unit does well those things the boss checks."

On the other hand, there is this experience by a friend of mine when he was a cocky young second lieutenant. As Buck told me, it happened like this:

One day (Buck said), when I was harassed and busy trying to get a job done, I said to my battalion commander, "Sir, if you would just relax and stop breathing down my neck, I can think better and get this job done right."

So the battalion commander walked quietly away, leaving Buck worried about what he had said. But at the next battalion officers' call the battalion commander said to his assembled officers. "For the first time in my life, I have been bawled out by a second lieutenant. And he was right, so I want you to know about this and be guided by it." He then told them what had happened.

A word of caution might be added here. If other second lieutenants try my friend Buck's approach, they do so against my advice and at their peril—because, in 15 years as a company level officer, I did not see a battalion commander who was that broad-minded and tolerant.

A piece of an airmail envelope from my file reports the time General Charles P. Summerall made an inspection and noticed freshly cut flowers in one dayroom. Later he sent the unit commander a letter of commendation.

On another post, one of the officers who knew of this informed the post commander, because Gen. Summerall was due for an inspection there. So they had cut flowers all over the place.

On his arrival, Gen. Summerall looked at the lavish display of cut flowers, sniffed the air and said, "All these flowers are not appropriate for a military unit. It makes the place look and smell like a funeral." And he inspected hell out of the post.

You might say this just proves generals are cantankerous, which is not exactly a new idea. But the moral comes clear: some things that are good in moderation will, when carried to excess, defeat their own purpose.

Another note reports that Sir Winston Churchill said on TV in April, 1956, ". . . in the long history of diplomacy, suspicion has done more harm than confidence . . ." For military commanders this relates to the indefinable air they exude toward subordinates.

The moral: cultivate the attitude that you trust and believe in those under you, and expect the best from them. When failures occur correct them with simple direct orders, not with the snide attitude that this was what you expected. (But, of course, when the occasion warrants, nothing replaces a good hell-raising bee.)

As to wartime notes, consider this one headed "Anecdote from the Battle of the Bulge." It quotes Gen. George S. Patton saying to his staff when issuing the order for his famous attack: "It is logistically impossible—but you SOBs are going to make it work anyway."

It is interesting to see how clearly Gen. Patton's order is in line with these two quotes from my files: "They conquer who think they can." Also, "for errors of rashness there might be indulgence. For overcaution there can be no mercy."

A summary note to myself reads: "Mobility is dependent on the state of mind of the commander, the state of training of his units and the availability of suitable equipment."

Then there is this reminder on command and staff procedure: "The staff provides details and recommendations. The commander goes into details of essential and material things only—then makes his decision. Finally, the commander's responsibility for planning should not be separated from his responsibility for ultimate execution."

Of course, my file would not be complete without some Confucian note like this item: "Do not begin vast project with half vast ideas." Somebody should have told Hitler and saved the world the agony of World War II.

One of the most revealing true incidents (whose source is not given and is not now remembered) records an exchange during World War II in Italy between division commander Maj. Gen. (later Lt. Gen.) John W. "Iron Mike" O'Daniel and one of his regimental commanders, Col. (later Gen.) Ben Harrell. After Gen. O'Daniel issued a verbal order for a night attack, this conversation took place when Ben Harrell demurred, and was asked to state his reason.

"Sir," Col. Harrell said, "if you will send a man to the latrine without a flashlight, he can tell you the reason when he returns."

Whereupon Iron Mike said, "I'll go myself." So he did, and called off the night attack.

This little exchange is a clear indication of why these two great combat soldiers reached multistar rank. One of the most important elements for success in battle is the ability of commanders to establish a working relation of mutual trust and respect with those above and below them.

A great name in our military history, Gen. Anthony C. ("Nuts") McAuliffe, cited an illustration of the importance in combat of knowing your subordinates. To do this he referred to two regimental commanders, whom we will call Col. Bravo and Col. Serene. Col. Bravo was a personally brave man who hated to take casualties. Col. Serene was quiet and never wanted to ask for help.

So one day when Col. Serene called and said, "Say, it is getting a little rough down here," Gen. McAuliffe immediately sent all the help possible—and just in time to keep Col. Serene's unit from being overrun.

There seems no end to the variety, complexity and importance of the mental side of command and leadership. Here are two general comments:

- Let no one think this mental side of the military profession is limited to officers, for the principle applies with equal force to all enlisted ranks. Gen. Patton said it this way:

  "It is not the point of the questing bayonet, but the cold glitter in the attacker's eyes that breaks the line. It is the fierce determination of the driver to close with the enemy, not the mechanical perfection of the tank that conquers the trench."

- Adequate logistics, training, weapons, administration and other necessary tangible things must also be there. But modern history since Napoleon's day has continued to prove that Bonaparte was right when he stated his great and enduring military maxim:

  "The mental is to the physical as three is to one."

CHAPTER 12
Are Morale and Esprit Alike?

Last week I saw a cartoon based on an old theme, but switched to give it a military angle. It showed a master sergeant holding a small boy by the hand and facing a two-star general also holding a small boy by the hand. The master sergeant's boy was shouting something at the general's boy, and the caption under the cartoon read: "My father can lick your father!"

Unknown to the cartoonist, his sketch illustrates the fact that morale and *esprit de corps* do not mean the same thing. Morale includes a strong element of feeling good and being happy, which that shouting kid does not appear to have. But he sure has a high *esprit de corps* in the unit to which he belongs.

There is a tendency in our armed forces to use morale and *esprit de corps* interchangeably, often using morale as an all-inclusive term. But in my view there is a basic difference. To examine the distinction between morale and *esprit de corps* I consulted my *Reader's Digest Great Encyclopedic Dictionary,* with these results:

- Esprit de corps—French. A spirit of enthusiastic devotedness to and support of the common goals of a group to which one belongs.
- Morale—A state of mind, especially of persons associated in some enterprise, with reference to confidence, courage, hope, zeal, etc.: the high morale of workers.

These definitions are couched in general terms and thus do not bring out the differences, in a military sense, that I was looking for. Nor were my books of quotations any help. In one book there are 51 quotes about a rose, 19 more about roses—and none about *esprit* or morale. So I mixed a cup of strong coffee, looked out my picture window toward Sarasota Bay and asked memory to inquire into the matter.

My initial contact with military *esprit de corps* was at West Point. In my plebe year I was a lot like that master sergeant's son: long on prideful *esprit,* over and above any morale involved.

Then as an upperclassman my day-to-day living was a bit easier and the resulting increased morale made the *esprit de corps* stronger.

Now, having looked at that cartoon and remembered my first years in uniform, it seems to me the definitions above do not include the essence of *esprit de corps* as we in the military know it: pride in our unit in a combat sense, with high, ready-to-fight standards and shared confidence in each other.

Another element not included in those definitions is the place of the chain of command in *esprit de corps.* However, more than 2,000 years ago it was said of Hannibal and his army during their incredible campaigns in Italy: "They were soldiers who had confidence in their general, who in turn relied on them."

That statement also applied to the U.S. Third Army in World War II under General George S. Patton. To this day, officers and men who served under "Old Blood and Guts" will tell you proudly, "I was in Patton's Army."

They say that in the sense of hard-fighting success, in which they were proud to share. This is a feeling over and beyond morale. Even pigs in a pen with all they can eat and plenty of mud to wallow in can be said to have good morale—but never *esprit de corps.*

Conversely, the famed French Foreign Legion was known for its high combat *esprit.* They were admired for and proud of their tough fighting reputation under the most difficult conditions. But it seems unlikely they had that sense of well-being and good feeling that go with high morale.

In the last two years I have been privileged to see *esprit de corps* in action at several widely separated places. At Fort Bragg, N.C., I visited my old unit, the 82nd Airborne Division. In the field I witnessed the briefing held for a senior general from the Pentagon. What made it truly memorable was the obvious *esprit de corps* of the briefing officers.

Each man's field uniform fit him in that undefinable way that professionals achieve. As each briefer talked of airborne you felt that special pride in unit and confidence in himself that are the signs of a professionalism over and above that sense of well-being we call morale. It is this extra quality that we call *esprit de corps.*

Several months later it was my good fortune to be the guest speaker at a "dining in" held by the Rangers at Fort Benning, Ga. (although, regretfully, I had never been a Ranger). This was a special occasion, the 30th anniversary of the great amphibious landings in Normandy during World War II, in which Rangers played such a gallant role on Omaha Beach.

This was a dress-uniform, stag gathering with a formal receiving line. Thus, it was my privilege to shake hands with as elite a group of young combat officers as were ever assembled. All were qualified paratroopers, all had won the prized Ranger tab by graduating from the most physically testing of our military schools and (except for a couple of young second lieutenants) all wore combat ribbons and battle stars.

Before the cocktail bar was opened there was a special Ranger ceremony honoring their lost comrades. After dinner we remained seated for a unique briefing, including pictures of the historic landing on Omaha Beach projected on a wall for all to see. One of these pictures showed an almost vertical cliff that had to be scaled to get out of the beach area.

As we looked at this tremendous obstacle, one of the veterans present told us how it had been there on D-Day when Brig. Gen. (now Maj. Gen., deceased) Norman D. Cota pronounced the words that live in Ranger history. He said, "Rangers, lead the way!" And they did.

It was not just high morale that I felt all around me that evening; there was this added deep pride of combat soldiers that we call *esprit de corps*.

One of the finest demonstrations of *esprit* known to me existed in the 21st Infantry (of the 24th Infantry Division) during World War II in the Pacific. *Esprit de corps* must permeate a unit from the lowest private up—and down. That is the way it was with the 21st Infantry and Col. William J. Verbeck (now Maj. Gen., deceased), their regimental commander.

His record gives silent testimony to the kind of combat leader he was, with eight battle decorations: three Silver Stars, three Bronze Stars (two with V device) and two Purple Hearts.

At the other end of the rank structure, this extract from the posthumous Medal of Honor awarded PFC James H. Diamond (Company D, 21st Infantry, 8-14 May, 1945) gives its own silent testimony:

> He voluntarily assisted in evacuating wounded under heavy fire; and then, securing an abandoned vehicle, transported casual-

ties to the rear through mortar fire so intense as to render the vehicle inoperable and despite the fact he was suffering from a painful wound. The following day he again volunteered, this time for the hazardous job of repairing a bridge under heavy fire. On 14 May 1945, when leading a patrol to evacuate casualties from his battalion which was cut off, he ran through a virtual hail of Japanese fire to secure an abandoned machine gun. Although mortally wounded as he reached the gun, he succeeded in drawing sufficient fire upon himself that the remaining members of the patrol could reach safety.

As it was so long ago in Hannibal's army and more recently in General Patton's Army, there was a special feeling in the 21st Infantry toward their commander and by him toward them. I know because, as the division chief of staff at the time, I visited Bill Verbeck and his regiment in battle. It was over and above morale. They shared that wonderful, inspiring intangible military phenomenon we call *esprit de corps*.

Two comments are:

- I read and hear publicity about the importance of "building morale" in various ways: no draft, no reveille, no KP duty, more hair, beer in barracks, modern housing and a pay scale beyond anything imaginable in my day. The idea always seems to be that everybody must be happy so we will have good morale in the Army—like Omar Khayyám, in the shade of his tree with that "jug of wine, a loaf of bread and thou."

- Of course I am in favor of good morale in uniform of the Rubáiyát type too, including the "thou" referred to (if I understand Khayyám correctly). But that is not enough, unless there is also *esprit de corps*—which requires pride in self and unit. Even a grove of trees, loaves of cake, magnums of champagne and a bevy of "thous" cannot produce that special quality we call *esprit de corps*.

  It takes military pride for that—to be battle-ready in a fine outfit and proud of it. Good morale, to feel good and be happy, is not enough.

CHAPTER 13
Good Timing is the Secret of Success

It is reported that Sir Winston Churchill illustrated an important command and staff operating principle with this story about the manager of a zoo who decided to give his sick bear a dose of aspirin.

First, the zoo keeper computed the proper dosage in relation to the weight of the bear, then pounded the tablets into a fine powder. Next he rolled a sheet of bond writing paper into a tube a bit larger than a lead pencil, poured the powdered aspirin in the tube and was ready for the final phase.

The bear was gentle but he was also large, so the keeper cautiously approached him where he sat on his haunches in a corner of the cage. "Nice bear," the keeper said soothingly, "very nice bear," and carefully inserted the paper tube between the bear's lips.

After breathing a sigh of relief that things were going so quietly, the keeper put the other end of the paper tube in his own mouth. He then began to draw in a deep breath, preparatory to blowing the charge of powdered aspirin down the bear's throat.

But the bear blew first.

The operational principle is clear: making the right decision of what to do and preparing a good plan to carry it out are not enough. The plan must be properly implemented. Even the best plan may fail unless the timing is right.

When I commanded Company G, 26th Infantry, at Plattsburg Barracks in the all-volunteer Army of my day, company messes operated on a money allowance. Our mess sergeant, wonderful old Long John Smith, used the commissary for basic foods but shopped for fresh vegetables, fruits and other specials.

We had a fine mess and one secret of this was timing. When the men had money in pocket after payday, Long John figured absentees in the supper chow line and cut corners. But as the end of the month neared, with its empty pockets, he would run specials for supper, even individual steaks when he could manage.

I was initiated into this timing principle soon after assuming command. As Saturday approached, a week before payday, 1st Sgt. Big Jim Redding came into my office.

"Captain," he said, "this is Sad Saturday coming up—the week before payday. Sergeant Smith says he knows where he can make a good buy in oysters. If the captain will go for beer from the company fund, we can swing a Saturday night beer bust with fried oysters in the company mess hall."

So we did. Thus, by timing, we eliminated Sad Saturday that month. There were other ways to do this, too.

One month we managed to get boats and stage a Sunday picnic on a small island in Lake Champlain (our barracks fronted on that lake). In addition to the picnic dinner (with beer and soda pop) we had other activities, including horseshoe pitching competition, a softball game between privates and a team of officers and NCOs (umpired by 1st Sgt. Big Jim) and fishing contest (biggest, smallest, most fish).

So another Sad Saturday weekend before payday was alleviated. The same program, the week after payday, would have fallen flat—even on the monthly pay scale in effect during the period 1922-41: private, $21; private first class, $30; squad leader (corporal), $42; sergeant, $56; and the two-rocker first sergeant, $96.

This timing principle is all-pervasive in the military service. One aspect of this is *when* to inspect. In my view, more positive beneficial results stem from preparing for announced and regularly scheduled inspections, than from the negative approach of being "caught" unawares. It is a matter of timing but, of course, there are special cases; to check on alert readiness or a fire drill it is inherent that the inspection be so timed that no advance warning is given.

One of the most frequently encountered errors in timing concerns visits to another officer or headquarters. Usually, first thing in the morning or last thing in the afternoon is not a good time to visit a busy person or unit—although, again there are exceptions.

One instance of poor timing comes to mind from my student days in the company officers course at the Infantry School. A senior general officer from Washington visited Fort Benning and asked to talk to all officers. So all students and post officers were assembled in the gymnasium at noon—and the speaker used up most of our lunch hour.

Also consider this case from my days as G1, U.S. Army, Europe, in Heidelberg. A high-ranking politically appointed civilian executive from the Pentagon visited Heidelberg. He arrived in my office at about 1600 and, after initial discussions, he asked that a teletype conversation be set up for him with a lieutenant general in the Pentagon. When a phone call notified me that the lieutenant general was on his way to the Pentagon teletype facility and would be on the line by the time we could walk to our signal installation, I relayed the message to the visitor.

"Well," our visitor said, "let him get on the line first. Then we can walk over there."

That is the kind of "one-upmanship" secretaries play, using timing as a gimmick to establish whose boss is the biggest fish in the pond. What our high-level civilian visitor thought he proved by deliberately timing his trip to the teletype to insure that the lieutenant general waited five or ten minutes, was not clear to me. But it was clear what he did prove.

We then returned to my office, and at 1645 he suddenly directed me to have three or four mess sergeants report to him. When I pointed out this would make them miss their unit supper hour, he said, "That is all right. The cooks can save supper for them."

The discussion with the mess sergeants was prolonged. When I presumed to remind him we were committed to a dinner engagement, this appeared to lengthen his conversation with the mess sergeants. So we were more than half an hour late for the dinner given in his honor at a private home.

The higher you go, the more important it is to consider the timing of what you do. And one of the most important aspects of timing is to evaluate how it will affect others.

Of course, timing in combat operations, from a squad to a theater of operations, is vital to success. One of the basic principles of war is surprise which is another way of saying that timing your operations is an important element of success. History records many examples like these:

- The Japanese attack at Pearl Harbor, early Sunday morning, 7 December, 1941, was devastatingly successful because of its timing: complete surprise. But their follow-up at Midway Island in June, 1942, ended in disaster, largely because it came too late and our intelligence correctly forecast its place and timing.

- Adolf Hitler failed to have his plans for invading England ready in time, so the opportunity passed. On the other hand, his unexpected attack toward Antwerp was timed perfectly to catch the Allies by surprise, and produced the "Battle of the Bulge." This dislocated massive allied preparations for crossing the Rhine into Germany and prolonged the war.

There seems no limit to the ways timing enters into success or failure in military life, for individuals and for operations of all types and sizes.

Three comments are:

- The Bible says there is a time to be born and a time to die. We can add that, in between those two events, there is a right and a wrong time for just about everything we do. Literature abounds with gems like: "Strike while the iron is hot," "Never put off until tomorrow what you can do today," "A stitch in time saves nine," "Too little too late," and "Opportunity knocks but once." Note that all of these deal with a sense of timing, as distinguished from the use of time.

- The most futile of all literary laments is, "Backward, turn backward, O Time in your flight,/Make me a child again just for tonight!" We can rephrase it this way: "Backward, turn backward, O Time in your flight! And make me a lieutenant again—so that I can seize the opportunities missed on my first time around, because I did not recognize the timing involved."

  But, unfortunately, there is no rewind knob on the reel of time that is our life.

- Those who are now lieutenants can do themselves a favor by resolving to make a continuing study of the timing angle in their professional duties and careers. My favorite guideline is Arthur Brisbane's presentment: "Regret for time wasted can become a power for good in the time that remains. And the time that remains is time enough if we will only stop the waste and idle, useless regretting."

With this must go realization that to avoid wasting time is not enough; we must also keep keen and fresh our sense of timing—beginning now. Or, to coin an aphorism: remember the lesson of the sick bear; that proper timing is often the secret of success.

CHAPTER 14
In Command Key Can Be Empathy

Among thousands of words in our English language are a few with well-recognized implications in military service like discipline, morale, courage, loyalty, dedication, responsibility and authority. But there is also a word you seldom hear which has wide application in life in uniform for all ranks. The word is *empathy. Reader's Digest Great Encyclopedic Dictionary* defines it thus: "Intelligent or imaginative appreciation of another's condition or state of mind without actually experiencing the feelings of the other."

That is a fine definition, but further discussion is needed to make clear the part it plays in military service. After assuming command of the 505th Airborne Infantry, 82nd Airborne Division, in 1952, I asked for a report of all men in confinement and those under restriction pending court-martial charges. The reason, of course, was fundamental. Their confinement and restriction could now be removed by my orders and thus their continuing disciplinary state was under my authority. It was my responsibility, therefore, to be sure their continued disciplinary status was justified in my opinion.

In this way I discovered one man under restriction in his company, pending court-martial charges, who had been under restriction for 45 days. This was an inordinate administrative delay, so I called for an explanation—and also sent for the soldier. From him I learned that after return from leave his presence at home had been desired again "to do the right thing" in a delicate situation. So he had requested another leave (without giving the real reason) and his request had been disapproved. As a result he had gone AWOL, and remained absent for an appreciable time.

When asked why he remained away so long the soldier said, "Well, colonel, now I was married. So, *you know,* I just stayed around a while. . . ."

After consulting my empathy, I decided that I did indeed know how it had been for him. Therefore, I relieved my soldier from restriction, told him this terminated disciplinary action in his case—and memory says I gave him a short leave so that he could go home legally to check on how things were there.

Incidentally, you may think giving my soldier that unrequested leave was going overboard on the empathy side, and I do not disagree. But he had been under restriction for more than six weeks and others had made mistakes in handling his case (who were duly so informed). However, looking backward now from the vantage point of an octogenarian, my own compensatory guilt complex was no doubt involved because, as a young company commander, I had mishandled the case of another soldier in a somewhat analogous situation.

One of the best illustrations of empathy in innovative disciplinary action known to me also took place at that time in the 82nd Airborne Division, by our commander, Maj. Gen. Charles D. W. Canham. A former enlisted man himself before entering West Point, Chuck Canham was a tough commander, but with a fine understanding of the problems of young soldiers. He particularly hated to see homesick kids go AWOL and end up in the guardhouse with older and more serious offenders.

His solution was to direct each regimental commander to establish a disciplinary camp for minor offenders, remote from the barracks area—designated in my regiment as Co. Q. There were no guards, and no work details, just an intensified training program under selected instructors. The legal *modus operandi* was simple: when the regimental commander reviewed a court case involving confinement for AWOL or other minor offenses, he could reduce the confinement part of the sentence to time in Co. Q.

Unfortunately, before his idea was firmly established in sustained operation, Chuck moved on to another assignment—and the program was terminated by the next commander. Reason: it was not his bright idea, and the camp he saw lacked the command support of a foot-dragging regimental commander. Some will say this is just another peroration on the importance of the human element in uniform. In some measure, yes. But empathy concerns a special narrow streak within the broad human element—which is above and beyond the good of the service.

It concerns intangible mental and emotional benefit to individuals in specific situations. Consider these two incidents, so inexpressibly far apart in time, place and scope, yet which stem from the same principle, revealing the underlying empathy quotients of an unknown lieutenant colonel and one of the truly great soldiers in our history.

On a night in April, 1933, I was asleep in a pup tent on a field exercise at Ft. Benning, Ga., as a member of the company officer's class at the Infantry School. Well before daylight, I was awakened to receive this message, "Return to the post, and report to the assistant commandant in his office at 8:00 A.M." The messenger could tell me no more.

Obviously, this would hardly be good news, but I was unprepared for the reality when I reported to the office of the assistant commandant. There I faced a tall and graying lieutenant colonel, who said with quiet kindness, "Lieutenant Newman, I deeply regret I must tell you that your mother has passed away." After a pause he added, "How much leave would you like?"

When I was unable to reply immediately, he said in a carefully controlled but sympathetic tone, "It is all right, just take the leave you want. And sign out VOCG."

I never saw him again, and do not know how he managed to short-stop that telegram. But I can never forget his empathy toward me in the greatest loss of my life. He assumed a difficult task himself, honoring my mother and my grief with his thoughtfulness and dignity. He also saved me the ordeal of receiving a telegram in the night in the woods, then left to arrange the administrative details of obtaining permission for me to leave.

Here is another empathy situation about as different from that as you can get, yet which grows from the same precept. It concerns an empathetic footnote to history about a great five-star American, as described in the book, *Allies* (Doubleday & Co.), by Brig. Gen. John S. D. Eisenhower, USAR. He recounts the well-known fact that General of the Army George C. Marshall had been slated for (and hoped to receive) command of 'Overlord,' the tremendous cross-channel amphibious invasion of France in World War II. But it was equally well known he would not ask for it, nor even hint in any way to President Franklin D. Roosevelt that he wanted it.

Finally, on 6 December 1943, in Cairo after the Tehran Conference, the President made his decision and dictated this message, which General Marshall took down in writing on a yellow pad: "From the President to

Marshal Stalin. The immediate appointment of General Eisenhower to command 'Overlord' operation has been decided upon."

General Marshall passed the pad over for the President to sign, and the message was dispatched. But, and this is the point: the next morning General Marshall retrieved that original hand-written draft signed by the President and added his own postscript at the bottom: "Dear Eisenhower: I thought you might like to have this as a memento. . . ."

John Eisenhower's book contains other interesting peeps at how empathy and human nature enter the rarefied air of high-level command in wartime. Also, of course, all officers of long experience have their own memories of such things, good or unfortunate. Some comments are:

- The above happenings range in involvement from a young private to a legendary five-star general of the Army, all relating to intangible benefit to individuals from the empathy of others. The varied situations where empathy enters exceed all counting or imagining. And, as a way of thinking, empathy is a refinement in recognizing the human element in uniform.

- With reference to the special disciplinary Co. Q, established in the 505th Airborne by direction of Maj. Gen. Canham, I selected a top company commander for the job; made sure he received outstanding NCOs to conduct his intensified training program; and gave the idea my command support and personal attention. The result was a "spit and polish" tent camp run as a "tight ship," with an intensive training schedule of fundamental subjects—among other things, stressing discipline.

  In my view, it was a fine idea, returning minor offenders to full duty again as better soldiers, as opposed to somewhat "beaten down" returnees from the guardhouse with their "jail house" tag. The only change I would make—if time could be turned backward and I were a division commander—would be to establish my intensive training camp at division level.

- As to the question of empathy in the military service in general, adding its special streak to the human element in uniform, in my view it is a lot like salt: it takes only a little to go a long way, but that little is beyond value in its hard-to-see but beneficial effect. However, too much preoccupation with empathy can degenerate into coddling, which—like too much salt—becomes destructive, even fatal.

CHAPTER 15
See Yourself as Others See You

I have delved again into my shoe box file of pages from old pocket note-books, clippings and miscellaneous paper fragments with penciled notes on them. Two items come from sources separated by the Atlantic Ocean and more than 150 years in time. The authors were a civilian poet in Scotland and an active-duty American Army lieutenant.

Both of these papers touch on an important intangible of command and leadership, although neither writer realized this. One quote reads:

> *Oh wad some power the giftie gie us,*
> *To see oursels as others see us!*
> *It wad frae monie a blunder free us,*
> *An' foolish notion.*

Scottish poet Robert Burns was not thinking about military leaders when he wrote those lines. But military men in authority should be aware of the image they project by what they do and say.

Even the most beautiful women look into mirrors to see how they appear to others and take measures to improve what they see in the glass. Similarly, military men in positions of responsibility should look into the mirror of their minds with the power of imaginative introspection and empathy to visualize how they look to others—and try to improve what they see. This includes physical appearance, manner and bearing. But far more important, it involves realization in advance of how what they do and the orders they issue will be viewed by others.

The second paper from my shoe box was a typed memorandum, folded to fit in the 3 " x 5 " filing space. When I was a brigadier general, this was handed to me for approval by my senior aide who was preparing to orient a replacement for my junior aide. The memo made me look both good and bad, but I am too old to be coy about kudos or to blush when embarrassed. So it is briefed here, including orchids and warts:

Guide for Aides-de-camp
to Brig. Gen. A. S. Newman

This is written as a guide to what is expected of an aide to Gen. Newman:

- He advocates a professional standard; however, he does not expect you to know everything at once. He does feel that after being told it should be recorded in your mind.
- He likes to see immediate action when a project is given.
- Prior to his attending a review or parade in which he is the reviewing officer, he requires a complete itinerary covering all events and the sequence they fall in (what time he is to arrive, from which direction, by whom he will be met, etc.).
- General Newman is a deep thinker and at times you can go into his office and he will not see you; however, he does not mind being disturbed, so do not hesitate to speak.
- If something is wrong, the general wants to know (once he forgot to put on his star, and another time he left off his U.S. insignia. If noted, tell him).
- When riding in the sedan, the general usually takes advantage of this opportunity to think. Keep your mouth shut until he starts the conversation.
- When attending official functions, if the general is the host, you should keep the party rolling. Greet arriving guests at the door and see that they get a drink. If the general is not the host, it is considerate to see when he needs a drink (he likes his drink with lots of spirits and little water).
- The general likes to keep smooth relations with all staff sections. If you are pursuing some matter for him and hit a "snag," don't push yourself. Go back to him and if he wants you to continue, he will tell you.
- A few eccentricities are: four thumb tacks on all papers on the wall, a border around maps that are posted—the general likes eye appeal and professional appearance.
- Don't have your feelings on your shoulders. If you do you

will get hurt. Remember that Gen. Newman is often under a lot of pressure and may let off a little steam on you. So don't worry about it.
• These are a few of many things you will learn and are offered as an aid to getting acquainted.

It is not often you can get such a candid look at yourself, in a way and to a degree that poet Robert Burns never imagined. (Incidentally, the lieutenant who prepared that memo is now a highly respected general in a key assignment with aides of his own.)

Among the benefits of seeing myself in the eyes of my senior aide was my decision to monitor more carefully any future release of steam. It was also helpful to note that my junior aide would be officially cautioned not to bring me pantywaist drinks.

There are uncounted situations where an officer should consider and act upon his awareness of how he is viewed by those under him—like the time before World War II that a new company commander arrived at Plattsburg Barracks, shortly before we went into the field on maneuvers.

At supper time the first night in the field, the newly arrived captain discovered his company had brought a porcelain coffee cup, china plate and knife, fork and spoon from the mess hall for his use, in lieu of the issue folding aluminum mess kit. So he declined to use that special mess gear, but did not stand in the chow line. After he observed that the company had been properly fed, the company bugler (who was also his runner and orderly in the field) brought the captain's chow in his issue mess kit and coffee in his canteen cup.

Then the company commander discovered they had brought an extra blanket for him because at that time of year the nights were cold. This the captain also refused to use.

The china mess gear and the added blanket were not in TO&Es for infantry company commanders. Thus, he did not want to be in the eyes of his company the kind of soldier who violated regulations by having company supply carry unauthorized impedimenta for his personal use.

Also, with apologies to Robert Burns, it did not require some mystic "power the giftie gie him" to see how he would look to men under one blanket in the chilly nights while he was just yards away, all comfy under two blankets—the second one unauthorized.

There is no catalogue of situations where this principle of "To see oursels as others see us!" comes into play. Often they are controversial. Sometimes decisions will vary with individuals and the *res gestae* of special circumstances.

Three general comments are:

- There is no substitute for constant alertness by military men in authority, from squad leaders up to and including our commander in chief, to consider how they look to others. But, and this must never be forgotten, proper decisions are based on *all* pertinent facts and considerations. Thus, there will be times when commanders make right decisions that they know will make them look bad in the eyes of others who are not familiar with the situation.

- The question of RHIP (rank has its privileges) often raises the question of how others see you. There must be RHIP in some measure and this can lead to abuse, as the above situation on maneuvers illustrates. However, the same situation shows that the company commander should, in addition to other responsibilities, supervise and check all arrangements to insure that good food is well-prepared and served. He cannot do this adequately if he must get his own mess kit and stand in the chow line. The principle involved was stated this way by 1st Sgt. "Big Jim" Redding when he made proper RHIP arrangements for me in Co. G, 26th Infantry: "We take care of you, captain. And you take care of us."

- If you try to impress others with phony grandstand plays, that is the impression you will create. Further, this tends to develop an overly inhibited defensive attitude toward what others may think of you. The key word is *empathy,* an understanding of how others feel. Combine this with commonsense and good judgment; then you can take the advice of my senior aide to my junior aide: "Don't worry about it."

CHAPTER 16
But You Get Only One Chance

When I was in Heidelberg as G1, U.S. Army, Europe, I heard the story about a famous French general who spoke in English to a group of American officers at NATO headquarters in Paris. In his opening remarks he intended to say, "As I look to my past . . ."

What he said was, "As I look to my behind . . ." which drew amused smiles that disconcerted him. But he continued, bringing his hands to chest level and describing semicircular motions as he added, "I see it is divided into two parts . . ."

That brought some subdued laughter, followed by a confused contretemps as the senior American officer present tried to smooth the ruffled feelings of the French general by explaining the language booby trap to which he had fallen victim. Now, as I look to my own past, I find it is divided into many parts, but I will consider here only one category of bygones: some things I would do differently if there were a chance to play the record again (with benefit of hindsight).

To begin with, I would not drift into my military career but would strive to be a real professional, better than par. For example, I tried to be a good cadet at West Point, and did moderately well in my studies but in four years I did not once enter the door of the famous military library there. I just read the lesson assignments in textbooks.

Looking backward now I see the same pattern in my first ten years of active duty: an effort to do well those duties assigned, nothing more. I read the regulations necessary for the job at hand but made no effort to "reach out."

For example, not until my eighth year in the Army (1933) do I recall looking at a company morning report other than to see the first sergeant of whatever company I was in at the time hand it to the company commander for signature.

The first time I saw one up close was when my company commander got sick and, as the senior of two lieutenants in Co. M, 27th Infantry, in Hawaii, I suddenly found myself in command, and the first sergeant handed me the MR to sign.

That seems incredible now; so how did such a dummy get by? Mostly because I did try to do well in my assigned duties. But that is not enough to be a true professional. To accept spoon-fed knowledge can make you a passable soldier, but a "get-by" soldier is not a professional.

If a time machine could send me back to do it again, I would be a self-motivated professional, seeking knowledge of the military past, broadening my understanding of the present and studying the future. It is not work that way but interesting and professional fun.

This was finally clear to me in 1936 at Plattsburg, N.Y., when I had the good fortune of a military lifetime to command Co. G, 26th Infantry, with its wonderful veteran professional sergeants, headed by 1st Sgt. James S. "Big Jim" Redding.

As previously recounted there was a brief interlude from which we both reached a mutual understanding that, although Big Jim would continue to run Co. G pretty much as he had for 11 years, I commanded it. Then, gradually, perhaps without realizing it himself, he began nudging me toward being a better professional in my sphere. He did this indirectly, by asking questions like these:

"Captain, it is getting near rifle-range season. Maybe you could get battalion to get some advance dope about it." (Translation: "Regiment is late getting out a training memorandum on this. If you would goose battalion, we might get a TM sooner—and save a last-minute, hurry-up-and-get-ready.")

Or this one: "Captain, the word is we're going to Camp Drum on maneuvers early this summer. Do you know about that yet?" (Translation: "The last two years Co. G had to run the battalion consolidated mess in the field on short notice. Maybe if you went to see the battalion commander about that now, we would not have to do it a third time.")

Then when we were on extended maneuvers he said, kind of offhand, that the Saratoga Battlefield was not too far away, and he thought I would find it interesting. I did, among other things being fascinated by an empty, unnamed niche in the memorial rotunda, while other niches held life-size busts of named battle heroes.

Then I discovered a marble monument on the battlefield to honor Gen. Benedict Arnold, erected by his comrades in arms—but with no name on it. What kind of man could inspire that, in memory of a traitor?

To find out I read several books about Arnold, beginning with *Renown*, by Frank O. Hough. Also, I studied details of the battle and its strategic implications to understand why at that time (1937) it was considered one of the 15 most decisive battles in history. So I was hooked, innoculated with a gradually acquired desire to know more about my profession, over and above being just "a good soldier."

From Co. G, 26th Infantry, I progressed to the 19th Infantry in Hawaii. There, after a year as a company commander, I became the regimental S2 (and athletic officer). Lucky again, for it was my athletic background that got me up there among true professionals like these (their eventual ranks indicated in parentheses): Col. Charles H. Bonsteel, Regt. Comdr. (Maj. Gen.); Lt. Col. Clarence R. Heubner, Rgt. Exec. (Lt. Gen.); Maj. Alan W. Jones, Regt. S3 (Maj. Gen.); Capt. Clyde D. Eddleman, Regt. Adj. (Gen. and Vice C/S USA); and 1st. Lt. Charles W. G. Rich, Pers. Adj. (Lt. Gen.).

Close contact with such outstanding professionals induced an effort to emulate them. This supplemented the change in my career outlook that began in Co. G, by expanding the scope of knowledge required for that great professional art: command and leadership of military men.

Fortunately, this came in time to prepare me for the challenges World War II would bring. So what's to change in replay?

Next time around I would not waste more than ten years' service as "a good soldier, nothing more," but start in my first year broadening into a professional in attitude and endeavors. In a rerun the war might not wait for me to get ready next time. And the same principle applies for others today.

At a more mundane level, here are some things I would do differently, if given another chance, to reduce the cumulative unorganized mass of papers that cluttered my files. Next time I will report to my first duty station with a high-quality, three-hole looseleaf notebook. In this book I will place a copy of the order commissioning me as an officer, and a copy of the order assigning me to that first post.

The book cover and back spine will carry the label "Official Orders." Then all orders on me, of whatever nature, will be filed chronologically: promotions, changes of station, travel, leave, duty assignments, commendations, admonitions, "replies by indorsement" and the like. When the book is full I'll decide whether to begin a second chronological book, or establish one or more new categories like "Official Papers" and extract from the first book all but official orders.

Of course, these books will not eliminate the use of file folders and large envelopes, but they will simplify matters. Added comments are:

• There are other things I would change if I could come to bat again—and maybe lower instead of raise my batting average. But, higher or lower, I would concentrate from the first day on keeping my eye on the professional ball. There would be time for extracurricular activities, too, for my observations of the best professionals confirmed them as well-balanced men.

They were not without interest in "wine, women and song," thus verifying the Duc de La Rochefoucauld's dictum: "Interest speaks all languages, and acts all parts." But they kept the catholicity of their endeavors within the common-sense limits of the existing situation.

• Recently, I had several old books rebound. That suggested an idea I wish I had thought of 50 years ago: any collection of papers of approximately the same size can be bound in book form. So I am assembling magazine articles (that I've pulled and filed over the years to read again) to be bound into what I'll call a "Browse Book." Some samples are: "What It Takes To Be an Officer" (*The Infantry Journal*, March, 1946); "Strategy and Tactics of World Communism" (*TIJ*, May, 1948); "Battle of the Bulge" (*Combat Forces*, February, 1954); "Unification: How Much and What Kind?" (*ARMY*, July, 1956); "Understanding: Touchstone of Leadership" (*ARMY*, November, 1956); "Our March Toward Weakness" [speech by Rep. Olin E. Teague (D-Tex.), August, 1977]; "The Challenge" (by Sgt. Maj. Lloyd Decker, *ARMY*, May, 1978), among many others.

• And so if only . . . But then, come to think of it, maybe I would boot the ball for more and different errors in the replay. Still, being a professional from the beginning would be a more worthwhile and rewarding career. Also, I would end with a little personal library of three-holed notebooks and bound volumes of "Browse Books" instead of my jungle of bulging file folders guaranteed to conceal anything I want to find.

In this world's life and order of things, I cannot start over. However, just possibly—after the Great Bugler has blown Taps for me—I can be reincarnated as some newly commissioned, eager lieutenant and use my hindsight to help things work out for him.

CHAPTER 17
Paper Handling Should Never be Routine

In ten years as a lieutenant I co-existed with paperwork—neither appreciating its usefulness nor deploring its pitfalls—until the day a document reached the in-basket of my first command: Company G, 26th Infantry. The letter said it had been discovered (on a piece of paper of course) that Private So-and-so had a felony on his record, hence was fraudulently enlisted and would be discharged under existing Army rules.

To everybody along the line—from the paper-checker who found So-and-so's name on the record to the pencil-pusher who wrote that letter—it was routine; just another piece of paper. But to me So-and-so was a quiet 19-year-old in my company who was a fine soldier.

Private So-and-so said that one weekend when in high school he had broken into the gymnasium with two other boys to get some athletic equipment. One boy had taken a typewriter, which resulted in an investigation that sent all three to a camp for delinquent juveniles. He enlisted in good faith, not understanding his high school trouble could make that illegal.

My reply to the letter stated the facts and my intent, under the circumstances, to take no action. Back it came, saying the money value of the typewriter and athletic equipment, combined with breaking and entering constituted a felony in his state—and to discharge Private So-and-so.

Once more I replied (having verified the salient facts by mail) and analyzed the circumstances—including So-and-so's youth and his fine record as a soldier—ending with the conclusion that, while perhaps technically fraudulently enlisted, he was a victim of circumstance. Thus, it was in the best interest of the Army to keep So-and-so in the service.

The reply from corps area headquarters was to the bitter point: I would discharge Private So-and-so forthwith and make no further reply other than report compliance with orders. So, sadly, I accepted defeat—and have regretted it through the years.

Why? With growing experience I realized that just because routine handlers of that letter treated it as a piece of paper—invoking a legal technicality in a vacuum to change the course of a man's life and deprive the Army of a fine soldier—was no reason I should accept it that way. For there were still paper stones unturned.

But I lacked understanding of paper procedures at high headquarters. I even assumed regiment had fully considered the matter before it endorsed the letter, "For compliance." It did not occur to me to go directly to our regimental commander, for Private So-and-so was his soldier too and, almost surely, the colonel had no knowledge of the case. With his broader experience (and rank) he might have called corps area headquarters directly and, among other things, questioned the validity of that "felony."

Further, I overlooked the fact that paperwork was only one way of getting things done. When words on paper fail, a personal visit may succeed. In staff work we call this "foot coordination;" as a commander seeking to change a staff decision it is more of a confrontation.

In Private So-and-so's case I believe my regimental commander would have taken up the cause. With his backing I could have gone to corps area headquarters and, beginning with the action officer, climbed the rank ladder on the staff—possibly even to the corps area commander. For So-and-so was his soldier too.

Twenty years later, I reported to Heidelberg in Germany as G1 of U.S. Army Europe. Once again an out-of-routine paper hit my desk, this time a teletype from Washington about Gyroscope, the new personnel procedure to enable more dependents to accompany their sponsors overseas. So I asked for a briefing.

This was an ambitious and worthwhile project but also a complicated procedure. When each eligible family man was ordered overseas he would request travel with his dependents, stating age and sex of his children, and the information was teletyped to USAREUR. We would decide his assignment, then go through channels to his new unit commander for information about availability of quarters and teletype yes or no in each case. If yes, his port call must be issued to get the man and his family to the right ship or plane at the proper time.

When I asked the eagle colonel for more details, he indicated they had been working on it for months and everything was under control. In effect he said, "You're new to G1 business, General, but we're not. There's nothing to worry about, just keep on smoking those smelly cigars, drink your coffee, relax and leave it to us."

Well, I kept on smoking those smelly cigars, drank my coffee and sent for the file on Gyroscope. That teletype was not just a piece of paper, because I remembered the case of Private So-and-so and many others over the years and knew *people* were involved. In this case many thousands of people, because the teletype denied our protest in which we asked reconsideration of a Pentagon refusal to extend the requisition cycle from six to seven months in order to adequately process Gyroscope applications.

After studying our Gyroscope file, I sent for the eagle colonel again. His reaction to my first question was to seize the file, leaf through it and point to our original letter, the Pentagon disapproval, our protest, and the Pentagon's second refusal.

"You see, General," he said triumphantly, "we're covered!"

I puffed on my smelly cigar, took a sip of coffee, and asked, "Who is going to take this file to Bremerhaven and show it to families getting off the ship, thus proving that while we have no quarters for some of them, it's not our fault because we're covered?"

After obtaining approval of the USAREUR commander I boarded a plane for Washington. G1 welcomed me in the Pentagon and set up a conference. Within an hour the requested seven-month requisition was approved, because the Pentagon was just as anxious to have Gyroscope succeed as we were.

I wish I could report that Gyroscope went off smoothly and no problems ensued. But no; that papers-not-people attitude persisted and produced a snafu.

Once policies and procedures were established and in operation, our adjutant general section took over. Before long a letter from the Pentagon reported trouble. A check of several particular cases revealed that the sending of Gyroscope messages had been progressively bucked down the line in the AG to a low level, where a fuzzy-thinking paper-shover had been sending the wrong form message in one type case. Obviously, a number of such wrong messages had been transmitted.

On directing that corrected messages be dispatched immediately, I discovered Operation Paper Chase in the picture. This was one of those economy operations designed to reduce paperwork and eliminate unnecessary files. A special Paper Chase team had visited staff sections to review procedures and filing systems, and decided the Gyroscope file was a duplication of the general AG file. So it had been tossed out and there was no way of finding who those wrong messages had gone to except by screening the whole AG file which, in time to do any good, was already impossible in most cases.

The blue color of the air in my office when I found this out was not caused by smoke from smelly cigars. Those operating-level people and the Paper Chase outfit looked at that Gyroscope file as just another extra pile of paper—without visualizing what could happen to people if it were destroyed. Nobody will ever know how many families were inconvenienced, how much money it cost them, or how much ill will was created—all because of a "paper attitude" instead of "people attitude" in handling "routine" papers.

Consider these comments:

- Paperwork is indispensable in our modern Army. The heavier the paper load the more vital it is that those who turn the paper wheels be straight thinkers.
- Paperwork is a wonderful way to get things done but it's not infallible nor is it the only way in a special case. Nothing can replace face-to-face discussion.
- Conversely, there is a very definite limit to phone and personal contacts. Papers are and will remain the basic means for handling our vast volume of administration.
- Decisions reached in personal discussion do not eliminate the need for paper; there is no substitute for a piece of paper in the record.
- Finally, when handling any document remember that while it's only a lifeless piece of paper, the actions stemming from it concern living people. Forget to consider this and that paper may come back to haunt you—and probably will.

CHAPTER 18
Use the Personal Touch on Your Personnel

The notice for a luncheon meeting of our local retired officers' club included this item: "Attitude adjustment hour: 11:30 a.m." This proves our language changes with the times, like the shape of heels on women's shoes and length of hair on men's heads. So maybe the censor has mellowed enough to pass this little cocktail-hour story, heard while adjusting my attitude for that luncheon.

It seems two young active-duty officers were visiting their former commander, a grizzled old general whose retirement home fronted on a Florida beach. As they walked along the white sand near foaming surf, a sea gull soaring overhead scored a direct hit on the general's forehead.

"Well," the old soldier said, trying to be nonchalant about the situation, "you two behave yourselves while I get some toilet paper."

As he hurried off one young officer said to the other, "Imagine that—and they say our generation can't think straight! Before he gets back with toilet paper that gull will be long gone."

This highlights the fact that twisted thinking is a form of modern humor. But old-fashioned, sound thinking remains the cornerstone of successful military careers. Nowhere is this more true than in personnel matters, especially when officers need human understanding of the realities for individuals at lower levels.

Before World War II my battalion commander returned an efficiency report to me on a lieutenant in my company. "Newman," the major said, "the regimental commander thinks you have underrated Lieutenant Slaphappy. Look this over again and be sure you have been fair to him."

I reviewed the report but made no changes, because my conscience had been stretched in the lieutenant's favor when I made it out. Several days later, a major on the regimental staff stopped me on the street.

"Newman," he said, "the regimental commander requested that one of his company commanders review an efficiency report he had turned in on his lieutenant, with a view to raising the rating of the lieutenant. But the captain returned the report unchanged."

The major paused, smiled and added, "So the regimental commander remarked that the captain did not appear to have as good judgment as he had thought. He then reduced his indorsed rating on the captain's own efficiency report from superior to excellent."

The major smiled again and said, "Just thought you would be interested to hear about this, as it might be helpful to you in the future."

Two years later I was a company commander again, this time in Hawaii. After several months and some soul-searching, I put in a letter to regiment recommending the reduction of my first sergeant.

The regimental commander sent for me (not a surprise) and said, "Captain Newman, I have your letter recommending 1st Sgt. So-and-so be reduced. But he has nearly twice as much service as you have and has served under several other commanders. While he can be promoted to sergeant immediately, regulations require he must be reduced to private first—and that when he returns to the United States it must be as a private."

He paused to let me assimilate this, then continued.

"Please reconsider this letter (not a surprise). Ask yourself if it would not be better for you to guide and push him to your high standards than ask me to reduce him. In the meantime, tell 1st Sgt. So-and-so he is on probation."

When the first sergeant discovered he really might be reduced (which he had not previously believed), we had no more trouble. I have always been grateful to Col. (later Maj. Gen.) Charles H. Bonesteel for the thoughtful way he handled this case after considering my side, 1st Sgt. So-and-so's side and his own responsibilities to both of us and to the military service.

Ten years later I was a regimental commander myself, of the 511th Airborne Infantry at Fort Campbell, Ky. One personnel action there involved the future of more than one man.

On this day we had a large tactical jump with full field equipment. As I watched hundreds of my troopers loading up, about eight men moved away from the planes. Then an officer hurried over to report these men were "quitters," that is, they were refusing to jump by refusing to enter the planes. He asked if I wanted to talk to them.

It is unusual for qualified troopers to quit. Normally, only one man will surrender to fear, sometimes at the last minute in the plane. But I had seen such a group quit once before, under similar circumstances, and they were transferred out of our regiment before dark that day. You cannot accept quitters in the airborne. In addition to other reasons, paratroopers will not tolerate a quitter among them.

I had not talked to that first group. But the picture of those once-proud troopers marching away in disgrace haunted my memory, because this would sear their hearts and scar their souls for the rest of their lives.

So now I said, "Yes I want to talk to them. Bring them to my office in half an hour."

When they were lined up in front of my desk—young men whose world had suddenly caved in on them—I said to the man on the left of the line, "Do you have a mother?" and he replied, "Yes, sir."

"Does your mother know you are airborne?" and he nodded.

"What are you going to tell her now?" He hung his head.

To the next man I said, "Do you have a father?"

"Yes, sir," he answered, looking at the floor.

"Does he know you are airborne?" He swallowed and nodded.

"What are you going to tell him now?" He looked out of the window in silent misery.

To the next man I asked, "Do you have a sweetheart?" with similar results as for the first two.

To them all I said, "If you are quitters, the regiment is better off without you. But you don't look like quitters to me. Records show you are fresh out of jump school and have never jumped with full field equipment before. Also, I think when you looked in the planes and saw all that heavy equipment hanging on the monorail, one of you backed away on impulse—and others joined him without really thinking."

I paused to let them realize I understood about that equipment mental hazard. After all, there had been a first time for me, too.

"Now, I am going to give you a second chance," I continued, "because I believe in you. I think you were taken by surprise when the cold sweats hit you, and that you really want to jump. If you do want to jump—*today*—when you go out that door report to the adjutant and you *will* jump today, within an hour.

"If you don't jump—*today*—you are quitters. The regiment wants no more to do with you; I never want to see you again and the adjutant has orders to get you out of the 511th Airborne before sundown."

All but one or two jumped and remained airborne.

Of course, I take pleasure in knowing I helped some fine young soldiers avoid making a mistake they would regret as long as they lived. But I also carry with me the memory that I did not talk personally with the first group.

Nothing officers do in official duties is more important than personnel actions they take that affect the lives and careers of others. Loyalty, the good of the service, human understanding, judgment—and when necessary, iron in the soul—are involved. These comments seem in order:

- In dealings with others there will sometimes be differences of attitude that lead to differences of opinions when considering the same facts. Unfortunately, in personnel actions these differences may be with your boss.

  In such cases, it is well to remember that every member of your command is also a member of his command and that, unless an overruling moral or legal issue is involved, in a tie vote, he wins.

- It must never be forgotten that you cannot please everybody all the time, and that there will always be some inequities you cannot avoid or correct. In fact, unless you are more fortunate than I was, there will be times when you are hit from above by what you consider to be sea-gull-type personnel actions.

  In such cases it may help to remember that William Shakespeare said:

  > Sweet are the uses of adversity;
  > Which, like the toad, ugly and venomous,
  > Wears a precious jewel in his head.

  I am not sure what Shakespeare meant by that, but I think of it this way: adversity provides opportunities to practice your self-control and good judgment under stress.

- The difficulty of trying to make right decisions in personnel actions is nothing new. The Bible tells us of the time King Solomon was faced with a personnel decision when two women and a young babe in arms were brought before him and each claimed the child as her own.

After taking thought, King Solomon called for a sword so that the babe might be divided, with a half for each woman. The false mother did not object, but the real mother tearfully gave up her claim—so King Solomon gave the baby to her. He had solved the problem by taking thought.

Most injustices in personnel actions result from failure to do this.

CHAPTER 19
Direct Clearly or Live with the Result

Out-of-routine situations seemed to pursue me during my active-duty years, or perhaps I had a penchant for getting mixed up in them. Anyway, here is a little happening from before World War II which touches on a principle that is as important now as it was then.

I was in my office, as company commander of Company F, 19th Infantry, at Schofield Barracks in Hawaii, when the company clerk placed a mimeographed sheet on the desk in front of me. It was a memorandum from Headquarters, Hawaiian Division and Schofield Barracks, that read:

"The Commanding General directs that all officers read the article, reproduced from the July-August, 1939, issue of *The Infantry Journal,* which follows:

No Mind Readers

Have you noticed how often, when a soldier is bawled out for failure to follow instructions, his first reaction is surprise? And surprise, generally, is followed by a resigned expression, for the real trouble was he did not understand what you wanted in the first place.

But perhaps the case of Maj. Threeput, Lt. Hasty and Sgt. Hashmarks will bring out the point more clearly.

One morning Maj. Threeput, the range officer, decided to prepare the rifle range for the Chief of Infantry's combat squad competition. So he called up Lt. Hasty, the assistant range officer, and put a bug in his ear, explaining exactly what he wanted. Whereupon Lt. Hasty passed the bug along to Sgt. Hashmarks, the range sergeant, like this:

"Get the range ready for the Chief of Infantry combat squad

competition. You know, the usual thing—seven or eight silhouettes in a line, with a surprise target coming up for the automatic rifle."

"How does the lieutenant want the targets fixed this year?"

"Just as I said, sergeant—a line of silhouettes and a surprise target."

So Sgt. Hashmarks arranged an irregular row of silhouettes in front of the butts, and tacked a silhouette on a pole to be raised from the pits as a surprise target. Somewhat of a GI arrangement, but a workable one—in fact the same arrangement the sergeant had seen used before.

But the next morning, Maj. Threeput, who had given his own instructions clearly, promptly pinned back the ears of Lt. Hasty and ordered some changes. When the major's car drove off, the usual chain of command functioned as the lieutenant turned to Sgt. Hashmarks.

"Sergeant, I don't think much of your idea of a surprise target. There should be at least two silhouettes in the surprise target, and some prone silhouettes in the line of targets for the squad."

A look of surprise spread across Sgt. Hashmark's face, replaced by an expression of resignation. How was he to know?

Such things are the result of sloppy thinking, of issuing orders without stopping to think out what you want—and then expect some kind of crystal-gazing act to produce an approved solution.

So, next time, before you call a good soldier to task for failure to carry out your instructions be sure the fault is not your own. Think back first to what orders you issued. American soldiers are the most loyal, willing and intelligent in the world—but they are not gifted with second sight. If, however, they understand what you want it will be done that way.

Company Commander

One glance told me this was my latest "Cerebration" in *The Infantry Journal* (under one of several pen names used before my retirement). So, amused at being directed to read my own pearl of wisdom, I looked up and said, "Why, I wrote that!"

The company clerk seemed a bit nonplussed at this development, and retreated without comment to the orderly room.

That left me a bit nonplussed, too, because the clerk had placed that memorandum right in front of me to read, instead of in my in-basket. Could it be he was trying to tell me something?

In New Guinea during World War II, as chief of staff of the reinforced division-level task force that landed in Tanahmerah Bay, I had issued orders to "corduroy" muddy places on the trail leading through the mountain pass to the Hollandia airdrome complex. The object was to get jeep traffic over the trail quickly, as only hand-carried supplies were getting forward to the spearhead driving toward Hollandia through the pass.

To me, this was a specific directive, meaning that a matting of small tree trunks would be laid close together across the road, thus forming a firm temporary surface to support light-wheeled traffic over those deep, muddy areas.

The next day when jeeps were still not getting through, I went up to see why not. Instead of sturdy small tree trunks making a firm matting across the muddy areas, some finger-size branches had been tossed into the mud. Jeeps had churned these down into the deep mire and were still stymied in efforts to cross.

Fortunately, an organized system of hand-carrying supplies supported the advance elements until the trail could be made passable for jeep traffic. Things were happening, so I did not get around to backchecking on where the chain of command had failed. Now, in retrospect, I wonder if the officer to whom I issued instructions understood my use of the term "corduroy." If he did not, then I shared in the failure to get that trail repaired properly.

Now a word of caution. In applying the maxim, "To get done what you want done, say clearly what you want," we must be careful not to violate another principle: "Give a man the job, but don't tell him how to do it—just leave him alone to do it."

Older officers often irritate younger ones with detailed instructions, because over the years they have been embarrassed when their subordinates came up with unacceptable solutions. One that sticks in my mind is a little housekeeping chore that did not seem to need detailed instructions.

I was chief of staff, 11th Airborne Division at Fort Campbell in 1950, and it was on the maintenance program to repaint the interior hallways of division headquarters. So, before going on a short leave, I left instructions to do it while I was away.

They did. Our nice cream-colored plasterboard walls were converted to a violent, bilious green. You see I had "assumed" the walls would be repainted the same color, but I had not said, ". . . and keep the same color scheme."

Sages say you must live with your mistakes, but after a week I decided it would be in the best interest of the military service to paint over that psychotic green. After all, the mental health of division headquarters seemed important enough to justify the added cost. What the division commander thought about this yo-yo painting procedure I never knew, because he was kind, perceptive and empathetic enough not to say.

Three general comments are:

- To resolve the conflict between giving a man a job and leaving him alone to do it, as opposed to detailed instructions to be sure you get done what you want done in the way you want it done, this guideline may be helpful: if it is a minor project and it does not matter much how it is executed, go easy on detailed instructions; but if it is a major issue, be specific enough to be sure it is done right.

- Do not start giving orders until you formulate in your mind the nature of those orders. The "think out loud" system results in wordy rambling instructions with extraneous details.

- There is a story from the Old Army days in China, about an American officer in Peking who told his houseboy he wanted some crab apple jelly served with meat at dinner. The houseboy, not wanting to "lose face" by asking what crab apple jelly was, produced a plate at dinner with a mold of jello surrounded by cooked crabs and raw sliced apples.

The moral from this is fundamental: how much detail you include in orders is often a factor of your knowledge of your subordinate's ability and his comprehension quotient about the mission you are assigning him. A classic example was Admiral William F. "Bull" Halsey's order to Arleigh "Thirty-One Knot" Burke (later a four-star admiral), then commanding destroyers in the Guadalcanal area during World War II. After telling Burke that a Japanese destroyer force was headed his way, Bull Halsey said, "Proceed. You know what to do." From Halsey to Burke that was a full and complete attack order—as the Japanese found out to their cost.

CHAPTER 20

Don't Trip on Blind Spots

It is not only on battlefields that soldiers come under surprise attack; it happens at cocktail parties, too, even after retirement. I was talking with two gentlemen when the assault came in on my right flank in the person of a dowager type, every pound a-quiver and earrings a-dangle.

Halting, obviously in some kind of dudgeon, she opened fire with, "They say you are a general."

When I tried to blunt the attack by meekly pleading guilty, she pushed on, "And they say you graduated from West Point."

Although beginning to feel a little dudgeon myself I admitted that, too.

"Well," she said, opening fire for effect, "how can you possibly justify spending all that money to educate young men at West Point—then send them to Vietnam to get killed?"

That was a *non sequitur,* but I tried to reduce it to sanity by asking, "Don't you think other thousands of fine young men who enlisted, or were drafted, deserved the best leaders money could buy, thus saving uncounted lives?"

But her blind spot about the interrelation of war and West Point and money and the lives of soldiers on battlefields was complete. "It doesn't make sense," she said, "such a waste!"

And, earrings swinging, she gave up on me and sailed away mumbling, "Such senseless waste. . . "

One of my male cocktail companions chided, "Well, general, that's one battle you didn't win."

In my view I had not lost it either. Now, what professional point warrants citing it here? Just this: all of us have blind spots which we should discover and correct. The way to do this is with careful introspection, remaining alert to avoid them. Also, notice such things in others as reminders that you, too, are vulnerable to "blindspotitis."

The first military blind spot I recall noticing was in one of my first company commanders. As a young lieutenant, I was puzzled to see the captain at Saturday inspections (with his own brass and leather unshined) inspecting neatly uniformed soldiers in ranks—*their* brass shining and leather polished. The contrast was obvious, yet he appeared completely unaware of any fault in himself.

One of my blind spots was pointed out to me in an unforgettable fashion by my battalion commander in the 31st Infantry, circa 1929 in Manila. His method was designed to help him write and indorse efficiency reports on the officers of this battalion, and also to let us see our weaknesses. It worked like this:

- He had mimeographed slips of paper prepared on which were listed (in column) these items from the efficiency report form of that time: Judgment, Intelligence, Loyalty, Force, Tact and so forth.
- Each officer in our battalion then received a batch of these slips, with the names of other battalion officers typed in at the top, one slip for each officer.
- We were then instructed to rate each officer, with numbers from one to five, on each ER listed characteristic and *personally* hand carry the slips to the battalion commander *unsigned.*
- When he collated all the slips on each officer, he considered this unique information in making out ERs. Then he gave each officer all the unsigned slips made out on him by his fellow officers.

When I got my fifteen or so slips back they revealed a glaring blind spot in my professional posture, of which I was completely unaware: my fellow officers rated me very low in *force.* While I knew I would stand up to others for my convictions in matters of substance, if others did not think I would, that was a weakness. However, to erase that blind spot—once I knew it was there—was simple: stop being too polite too often, and grow some rough edges on appropriate occasions. (Thank you, Major Engleman.)

One of the best officers with whom I served was his own worst enemy, because he had a personality blind spot: a penchant for making putdown remarks to others, like, "You don't look so good this morning, how do you feel?" He was just joking, of course, but, when made in a jeering tone and repeated often enough, things like that wear thin.

When he carried that jeering tone into specific criticisms of others—

in their absence—you wondered what he said about you in *your* absence. Also, far more important, critical remarks about others, including superiors and peers, have a way of finding their way back home. It is a serious blind spot, because it violates the fundamental principle of loyalty.

Once the invisible mist of disloyalty shrouds your name, the best *selective* duty assignments are likely to go to others. On one occasion I know it happened to that otherwise outstanding officer.

Another career blind spot is the tendency to seek staff and other special assignments, while avoiding duty with troops. I do not understand this, because troop duty was the greatest pleasure, privilege and pride of my years in uniform. But that in itself became a blind spot for me, because desire for still more troop duty resulted in my avoiding a good Pentagon assignment when it was offered.

This was an offshoot of a common blind spot: the age factor. It was later than I thought, for I was beyond the normal age for division-level duty and had more than my share anyway. This age blind spot is all too prevalent—when you are either too young or too old.

This brings up another kind of blind spot: those who recognize the age angle, but decide they should be an exception—which probably goes beyond being a blind spot into the realm of delusion. Or maybe it can be classified as a malignant blind spot.

Two interrelated blind spots are inherent and congenital in the scheme of things: the staff blind spot in those who lack duty down where the action is with the troops; and troop-duty officers who (usually for good reason) have not been selected for staff assignments.

Without going into detail, the best cure for these two conditions is to recognize they exist, if either applies to you. Recognition is half the battle. That's where introspection comes in: to see your own lacks and make allowances for them. The best way to compensate is to visit the area where you need first-person vision.

The finest illustration known to me of how to cure such absent-from-the-scene blind spots was the way my former classmate, the late Maj. Gen. Joseph P. Cleland, applied that principle when he commanded the 40th Infantry Division during the Korean War.

A former staff officer from Joe's division wrote me about him. Among other things, he said that when Joe moved his division into the line it was heavily committed. Soon thereafter he assigned each headquarters staff officer a front-line company to inspect.

Each officer was also given a list of things to look for that required him to cover every foot of that company's dispositions. Thus, the staff officers—from adjutant types to chaplains and logisticians—learned about life in the front lines. That made them better staff officers. Also, the troops were happy to have the rear echelon see and understand their problems.

Looked at from another angle, this procedure cured what might be classified as a traditional two-way blind spot: not only did the staff officers alleviate their defiladed view of the situation "up front," but troops in the line had the scales removed from their eyes about "incompetent, uncaring staff officers," discovering them to be conscientious soldiers like themselves, doing the best job they could.

On the more prosaic side, there are many and varied blind spots that those so afflicted realize they have but underestimate how much their impaired vision is viewed with disfavor by others. Included are the overweight, who are fatter than they think; drinkers whose alcoholic content is more obvious than they realize; compulsive talkers who would seem smarter if they said less.

Three comments are:
- The basic idea of blind spots was suggested to me by Gen. Bruce C. Clarke in the form of a general principle. But it seemed that such a valid theme should be backlighted with how the principle is applied in military life, with case histories, which I've supplied from my memory bank. Each of you can provide more from your experience.
- Clearly, it is the duty of military superiors to call attention to the blind spots of their juniors, for correction. I recall a day in Hawaii before World War II, when I was a captain on the staff of the 19th Infantry. The occasion was a regimental sunset parade that would soon begin, and 1st Lt. Barfly (we'll call him) was present as a spectator, moving toward the reviewing stand area where our distinguished regimental commander and executive officer were standing.

  It was obvious the lieutenant was happy, content with the world and himself, unaware his alcoholic quotient was showing. So I moved close to him and said, "Barfly, I've got some damn good advice for you." When he looked puzzled I added, "Scram!" and, as his blind spot disappeared, so did he.

- We also have a personal duty to ourselves to discover our own blind spots. How well you do this will surely be a factor in your life in uniform and military career. But there is a caution: do not overdo it, thus losing your self-confidence. In other words, do not let the cure become worse than the malady.

CHAPTER 21
The Fine Art of Listening Pays Off

"Your notebook is your memory's best friend" was penciled on a slip of paper in my shoe-box file. That reminder, on a page from one of my active duty notebooks, was mixed with assorted other *aide-memoires* in that now-disintegrating container. Below that one-liner was this one: "You can't remember what you do not hear." It was that statement of the obvious which sparked this discussion about the importance of listening.

The distinctive place of listening in military life was first dramatized for me by this little happening in the cadet mess hall at the U.S. Military Academy. I was not a witness but heard about it. An upperclassman at one table rapped with a spoon for attention, and plebes at the foot of the table looked his way. He then commanded, "Sound off, Mr. Brown!"

The previously trained plebe began his act in a loud, anguished voice with appropriate stopping, looking and hearing gestures:
Stop! Look! And listen well!
A three-month slug is worse than hell, sir!

Translation: The upperclassman had been caught in some transgression or other—after being warned orally—and ended with a "three-month slug on the area." This meant that for three months (every Wednesday, Saturday and Sunday afternoon) he walked punishment tours in the area of barracks, wearing dress uniform and white gloves.

So the upperclassman's little organized playlet was designed to emphasize and publicize the fact he had been warned of danger and heard the words in a casual sort of way, but had not *listened* closely enough to understand the reality of the warning.

Col. Joseph A. McGovern, U.S. Army Reserve, a Miami reader of "The Forward Edge," wrote me about a little happening he witnessed at the Airborne School. After his jump, he remained in place and observed the parachute of the first man out of the next plane develop into a streamer. The loudspeaker immediately ordered. "Number One! Pull your reserve, pull your reserve!"—which he finally did—just before hitting the ground.

When asked why he delayed pulling his reserve chute, he said that he had followed instructions exactly. After jumping, he counted "one-thousand, two-thousand, three-thousand" and then realized he had a streamer. So he placed his hand back on the reserve chute and counted "one-thousand, two-thousand, three-thousand"—and then realized he had a streamer. So he placed his hand back on the reserve chute and counted "one-thousand, two-thousand, three-thousand" *again* before pulling his reserve.

The moral of this footnote to Airborne history is that if you do not listen closely to instructions, you had better be a fast counter. In this case, the failure to listen carefully nearly cost that man his life. Next time, in a different situation, it could cost the lives of others.

There is no end to the diversity of situations where it is not enough to hear the words. You must also listen to understand the full meaning of what you hear. That is why it is routine procedure after issuing oral orders to ask, "Any questions?"

I encountered another facet to listening soon after reporting as chief of staff, 11th Airborne Division. When I sent for the adjutant general, he arrived with shorthand notebook in hand and said, "Go ahead and talk, Colonel. I will take down your instructions in shorthand."

That gave me pause. So I said, "No, I do not want that. Take notes as may be necessary, but listen and understand what I say. You can then ask questions now, instead of having to come back again later."

What I did not tell him was, "As you take shorthand, you are just hearing words and recording them—but not listening. I want your attention focused on the meaning, so you and I can discuss any points not clear." In other words, I wanted a listening and thinking staff officer, not a tape recorder.

An interesting demonstration of variations in the ability to listen was the way visiting lecturers answered questions at The Armed Forces Information School, the Armed Forces Staff College and The National War College. These speakers were experts in their fields, many of them nationally known.

The most outstanding was Gen. Maxwell D. Taylor who, as the

chief of staff, U.S. Army, was a guest speaker at the Armed Forces Staff College when I was the deputy commandant, Army there. He would stand quietly, looking directly at the questioner, and then pause briefly before beginning his answer. As a result, his answers were brief, clear and to the point. I remember particularly his answer to one long, wordy question; after thinking a while, he just said, "No." This was exactly the right answer.

After another question, however, he paused longer than usual. Then he came up with his own question: "Now, you really do not expect me to try to answer that question, do you?" The class broke into applause because the question had come from a member of another service and was on the curve ball side. General Taylor had listened carefully, noted the curve involved and, smiling, refused to swing.

At all of these interservice schools and colleges, an indispensable part of the curriculum was the variety and competence of guest speakers. There were no written handouts and no tests based on what the speakers had said. What each student gained from the guest speaker program depended on his capacity to listen, assimilate, evaluate and store in his memory selected ideas for future use. Certainly, the ability to listen and remember was crucial to the value of the course.

When I was a student in the 13th General Staff class at Ft. Leavenworth, Kan. (a quickie wartime class in early 1943), one of the first guideline papers issued was a brief study on how to handle the voluminous reading material given to us. Nothing was said, however, about how to remember what we heard in the lecture halls, so I will make a modest suggestion in the final comment below.

I have touched previously on the method involved in how to remember ("Good Memory Is an Asset in Army," *ARMY,* August 1971). Since that was years ago, the following extract will assist in relating memory to the problem of how to listen effectively:

> To paraphrase the famous comment often attributed to Mark Twain about the weather: Many people complain about a bad memory, but they never do anything about it. Since a good memory is a fine professional asset, it is worth investigating to see whether or not there is any way to improve a poor one.
>
> When I was a second lieutenant in Manila in 1929, an item in the local paper reported "one of the seven great memory experts

in the world" had arrived in town and would give classes on how "you, too, can develop a good memory." One class was scheduled for the American-European YMCA gymnasium at 7:30 the following night. I was living in the Y, so decided to get the promised good memory, for a price of five pesos ($2.50 U.S.).

At 7:30 next evening quite a group of us were seated on folding chairs in the Y gym—but no memory expert. After waiting 15 minutes somebody called the expert's hotel, and learned that he had forgotten about the meeting . . . but would be right over.

Of course other residents of the Y gave us a jumbo size hee-haw about our $2.50 donation. But, looking back now over the long gone years, I can say that was the biggest money bargain of my life.

He gave us three principles: (1) You must want to improve your memory, and make a continuing effort to do so. (2) Nobody can remember everything he sees, hears or reads, so be selective: focus your mind on things you want to remember. (3) In focusing your mind, think of how you can relate what you want to remember to other things.

The following example illustrates the "relate principle." My younger daughter's ZIP code is 01944—and 1944 was the year of the Leyte invasion of the Philippines, in which I participated.

Some comments are:

- The three principles listed above for improving your memory also apply to improving listening capacity, especially the requirement to "make a continuing effort." Furthermore, they apply with equal force to routine military conversations, as well as to selecting ideas to remember from guest speaker programs.

- Instead of trying to remember in detail lengthy oral statements by individuals or guest speakers, the effort should be to focus your mind on following the speaker's train of thought and thus isolating ideas of consequence to remember.

- When I assumed command of the 82nd Airborne Division (briefly, in the fall of 1953), the company commanders were young and inexperienced. So I assembled all the officers in the theater for a one-time talk by me on "the technique of command." Before beginning the talk, I said: "Please do not take notes, as a copy of my speaker's notes outline will be given to each of you as you leave. This is to free you to listen closely to what I have to say, following my line of thought for ideas to remember about command."

- If I were starting over again, I would keep a "listen file" for talks and lectures in condensed form. A brief summary of each speaker's *ideas* would go on a single page in a loose-leaf book. In due course, the result would be a fine collection of varied ideas for reference. Such a system would also be a spur to more careful listening during the talks.

     Why not try it?

CHAPTER 22
Punishment: Write it or Say it?

It happened in 1925 at Ft. Benning, Ga., not long after I reported for duty with my first company under (we'll call him) Captain Hardnose. If there were valid excuses or extenuating circumstances, I do not recall them. My offense was being five or ten minutes late that day, so I arrived at the company with some misgivings which turned quickly into realities.

"Mister Newman," Captain Hardnose said in his clipped metallic voice, "you are late. Take reveille for a week."

"Yes, sir," was my automatic reply, following the approved solution for novice second lieutenants of that day: *Just do what the man says.*

Since reveille was at 0600, I set my alarm clock for early the next morning, and walked (no car) approximately a mile from my BOQ room to the company. When reveille sounded the company assembled in ranks, and I moved to position behind the first sergeant as he verified attendance. He then faced about, saluted and reported, "All present or accounted for, sir."

No questions, no smiles, all very military and professional. But this embarrassed young lieutenant—as I trudged back to the BOQ for breakfast, and returned to the company again—decided that not only is "punctuality the soul of courtesy," but that it would be standing operating procedure for the rest of my military career.

This leads to the larger question: what is the best procedure for handling minor disciplinary derelictions? The varied means available include quiet-voiced corrections, harsh-voiced corrections (all right, I mean "bawling out"), and various informal aids to future memory short of formal action, like "reply by indorsement hereon" letters.

Then we have formal actions under the *Manual of Courts-Martial;*

94

these include written admonitions, reprimands, Article-15 punishment and sentences imposed by courts-martial.

Which method to select for any given offense depends on many things, including the personalities of those involved and, especially, perception and judgment. This basic angle of disciplinary responsibility in command and leadership was called to my attention by a recent newspaper item about an inordinate number of "Article-15" actions being doled out in one organization. The result is a permanent adverse entry on an individual's record. This reminds me of the views expressed by an officer we'll call Col. Oldtimer.

In general, he advocated generous use of the Article 15 but objected to review of his actions by his superior, Maj. Gen. Doughty. Curiously enough, however, what he really proved was that our system of command review in formal disciplinary matters is sound. So I replied to him along these lines:

The basic theme, "they don't trust me" is not a new one, but is usually the refrain of younger officers. There always are two sides to such propositions. In this case each member of Col. Old-timer's group *is also a member of Maj. Gen. Doughty's command.* Thus, errors of judgment by Col. Oldtimer in disciplinary matters are of direct concern to Gen. Doughty for the best of reasons: to protect members of his command from injustice.

Col. Oldtimer said, " . . . if he (an officer) gets too rough at an Organization Day party, or fouls up an honor guard, or comes to work in a slept-in uniform, then let's hit him with Article 15."

Are *these* offenses that warrant inclusion in a permanent "crime record?" Not in my book, with the possible exception of that Organization Day peccadillo, if it reached the proportions of "conduct unbecoming an officer and gentleman."

What to do then? A good "chewing job" on the young man is indicated. In our highly developed technical and younger Army this appears on the way to becoming a lost art. The ill-considered use of formal legal punishment for petty derelictions is a pussy-footing policy resorted to by weak commanders, who somehow think this makes them "tough" (soldiers have a better word for it).

In general, the commander who shrinks from "raising hell" is prone to "put it in writing" in minor disciplinary matters. Further, this same type is usually slow to give more than a mediocre efficiency report, and will seldom "put it in writing" on a commendation. Perhaps psychiatrists can explain this apparent contradiction, which I often observed. My opinion is that these gentlemen suffer from a feeling of insecure command personality.

This curious reluctance of some officers to blister your hide verbally deprives them of the most wholesome way to get disapproval off their chests. So they resort to paper disciplinary action, or appear to harbor the memory of little things and withhold full credit in your efficiency record.

Early in my career I received a wonderful object lesson in the exercise of command by my first company commander, the above mentioned Captain Hardnose. He was a tight-lipped, scowling, professional soldier, who demanded everything and everybody be ship-shape at all times.

Any member of our company who failed to meet his standards heard about it right away, often in picturesque language ("Get in step, Snodgrass; you're prancing along like a country whore on Broad St. in her first pair of high-heel shoes.") It was my quickly formed opinion that Captain Hardnose was the most unmitigated SOB in the Army, and that the company hated his guts.

At Saturday inspections some men would actually tremble when he looked them over. Anything Captain Hardnose did not like, he didn't like out loud. But there was seldom an entry in the "company punishment book" or in a soldier's records.

When the day came for Captain Hardnose to leave for a new assignment he had supper in the mess hall, by special request of the company. He arrived as his usual gruff self, but the company was all smiles. Happy to see him go, I figured.

Finally, during dessert, the first sergeant's small seven-year-old son struggled down the aisle lugging a brand new officer's saber—with Captain Hardnose's name etched on the blade. The youngster handed the saber to the captain, a gift from the men (not against regulations then). For the first and only time, the Old Man was stopped cold. He just swallowed a couple of times and sat holding the saber, scowling down at it.

The soldiers widened their grins. You can't fool soldiers—there are too many of them. The captain loved that company and every man in it, and they knew it.

It took a while for me to get that sorted out in my mind. You see, there was *nothing personal* in the way the captain bawled them out. He had no favorites, was strictly fair, so only the incompetents felt the lash of his displeasure, and he had an efficient, happy company.

No, I haven't forgotten about Colonel Oldtimer and his desire to exercise paper punishment. The point here is that there was seldom any paper punishment in that company—because *it was not needed.* The same principles apply in handling officers.

These comments bear on the subject:

- I do not advocate company commanders publicly embarrassing young lieutenants—and I have no knowledge of any other "take reveille" case. But at that time company commanders were veterans of World War I and at least ten years older than newly commissioned lieutenants, often more, and some in that era, like Captain Hardnose, were one of a kind.

   Maybe they would not fit in today's Army of more tender skins, but the direct idea, high standards and toughened hide given me by Captain Hardnose were invaluable for the rest of my service, and there was no Article 15 on my record.

- Situations and personalities and times change, but the value of unequivocal soldier-to-soldier oral correction remains, when used with perception and judgment within the *res gestae* of today. There is a different feeling about being in an outfit where the Old Man (of whatever rank) has a short fuse, blows his top right out in the sunshine, and closes the matter—as opposed to dragging things out, away from public view—and then "putting it in the record."

- While I was not a born SOB like Captain Hardnose, I decided to become a self-made one (with fair success, according to some who claim to know). Anyway, it was seldom indeed that I felt called upon to take disciplinary action that would go in an officer's record.

- Give me the SOB type every time, provided he is a good soldier, too, who has no inhibitions about giving you hell. There is an honest force and command posture involved that can be achieved in no other way. Besides, when you foul up an honor guard formation he'll do an artistic chewing job on your stern perhaps—but nobody will read that on your record 20 years later.

PART TWO

Field Grade Officers

Majors, Lt. Colonels, and Colonels

The big difference when you progress from company grade officer to field grade is that you deal directly with enlisted ranks at company level, but as a field grade officer your direct contacts are primarily with officers—with greatly increased time, space and numbers. In addition there are two basic complications for the field grades (1) Greater need for visualization and anticipation in operating through others, and (2) The necessity for more detailed coordination and cooperation in developing plans and orders.

At company level the action takes place in your vicinity, and amendments or corrections to orders can be made quickly. But at field grade levels a radically different time factor requires the ability to see into the future, and organize operations taking place remote from you. In other words a more complex mind and broader experience is needed to control actions directed by you but supervised by others out of your presence or ready contact.

CHAPTER 23
Integrate the Work of Others

Years ago I saw what was reputed to be a copy of Ben Franklin's letter of advice to a young man. One line read, "There is no skill but can be improved with practice."

Old Ben did not have command of troops in mind, but it applies there, too—only then we call it experience.

That recalls his warning, "Experience keeps a dear school, but fools will learn in no other." Also, one of the notes in my aide-memoire cites Prince Otto von Bismarck, the Iron Chancellor, as saying, "I prefer to learn from the experience of others."

So now we come to the question: how can we learn from others' experience?

One way is to avoid mistakes you see them make. A more selective way is to seek out those who have had the type of experience in which you are interested and whose judgment you trust. Then listen to what they say, or read what they write. Next you have to place their ideas on the scales of your own judgment to be sure they fit your own command situation.

I served over fifteen years as a company grade officer. So if experience, like good bourbon, is improved with the aging process, then my company-level experience has been aged in the bone for 37 years. With that as justification, let me pontificate a little about the technique of company at company and battery level.

On my first day of duty, I was instructed in the most basic element in exercising command. My assignment was platoon leader, so platoon Sergeant Fugate arrived at the orderly tent (yes the 29th Infantry at Ft. Benning, Ga., in 1925 was housed in pyramidal tents), to escort me for inspection of our platoon.

When that was over Sergeant Fugate, a decorated combat veteran of long service, came to attention and said, "Lieutenant, I'm supposed to get things done for you. Any time you want me, pass the word and I'll come a-running."

It is hard to express how that took the mystery out of things for me, yet it did. I did not realize then, however, why he said that, or think to analyze its significance. But that aged-in-the-bone process has developed these answers:

- He had seen pristine second lieutenants arrive for duty before, so he was just extending a helping hand.
- He was also instructing me in the most basic element in the technique of command: when you want something done, tell the right man to do it—in this case, Sergeant Fugate.

Years passed and the challenge of command and leadership was a never-ending fascination. So I tried to pass on my experience and fan the interest of subordinates in the art of leadership and the techniques of command.

After assuming command of the 511th Airborne Infantry at Ft. Campbell, Ky., in 1950 (my first peacetime regimental command), one of my first acts was to establish an officer's school in an old mess hall building. There was a school hour at the end of each drill day but no "faculty." There was only a published schedule of subjects, with every officer in the regiment taking his turn as instructor. There were also a few outside experts like the division ordnance officer. Barring earthquake, flood or some division-assigned duty I was always present and thus able to comment when it seemed desirable—*but not too often.*

The grapevine reported this school to Ft. Benning which brought a request to me for an article for the *Infantry School Quarterly* (now *Infantry* magazine) on details of how the school worked (it appeared in the April, 1951, issue). The school's primary objective was training company-level officers (keyed to our regimental training schedule) because it had been proved to me that the foundation of an officer's career was a thorough grounding in and understanding of command at company level.

Later, as commander of the 505th Airborne Infantry and as assistant division commander of the 82nd Airborne Division at Ft. Bragg, N.C., and (briefly) as interim division commander, this training of officers remained one of my main interests.

Upon assuming command of the 82nd Airborne, there was a continuing need for training relatively inexperienced company-battery grade officers. So I decided on a quickie, one-time talk (not a lecture) on the technique of command at company and battery level. I made this talk to all officers in our division theater, and included my personal experience and observations. To prepare for this, I drafted an opening followed by readable "speaker's notes." These were typed and mimeographed and copies given to each officer after my talk.

Since the principles seem to me to be as valid today as when I made the talk on 5 October, 1953, here are several selected brief items extracted from it:

- It is difficult to train a soldier in our complex modern Army but far more difficult to train officers because it is not easy to condense time and experience. All circumstances considered, our young company- and battery-grade officers are doing an outstanding job; in fact, I wonder whether at their age I could have done as well. But one of our continuing problems remains: to train commanders, particularly platoon and company-battery commanders.

- Naturally senior officers should train subordinates, passing on their experience. Our military schools, textbooks and manuals are excellent, but they cannot take the place of senior officer leadership of junior officers—especially with reference to that intangible we call "technique of command."

- The weapons of today are different; the tactics in the field are modernized, but a company-battery still consists of men with tasks to do. The commander's job thus remains to control, organize and train his men to get their tasks done up to the highest standards— and the basic technique of doing this has not changed.

- Lieutenants and men look to their company or battery commander for organization of their work, not for him to do it for them. They want to do their jobs but cannot until he does his job first.

- Example: drill instructors need subjects assigned early for time to prepare lesson plans; time to prepare training aids; time for rehearsals, if necessary; time for thought and study. Commanders themselves should do less instructing but give careful thought to selecting and supervising instructors, who become better with experience—and save you time.

- Example: tell platoon leader to have platoon sergeant plan a platoon problem; two squad leaders plan a patrolling exercise, for review by lieutenant, okay by you; three selected sergeants to plan company-battery squad problems—ways of doing this are limited only by the imagination of the commander. One man keeps others busy, organization happier, better trained, many working, contributing ideas; you are the hub of the wheel. Things revolve around you, not you around them.

- The company-battery commander is a combination coach and quarterback; he plans plays and calls signals but cannot carry the ball on every play. The best quarterbacks seldom carry the ball, but when they do, carry it well. Their jobs: carry the mental ball, integrate the work of others, which is technique of command.
- Give careful thought to how you look to your men: Are you fair, firm, just? Do you think of men as soldiers, not privates? Do you do your job as well as you expect them to do theirs? Do you have enough but not too much iron in your soul? Do you have enough but not too much milk of human kindness in your heart? Do you have in your brain knowledge of your job, good judgment and human understanding? If so, by working very hard you can be a good company or battery commander.
- Command techniques apply not only to officers but with equal force to NCOs. It is not a case of "let Joe do it"; *you tell Joe to do it,* in garrison or in battle. I once saw it expressed this way: "A trip through your plant with an observing eye will do more good than a trip to Washington."

On a recent visit to a large Army post I came in contact with officers and men. Never in our history have we had young men who faced such complicated problems so early in their careers. Further, an officer's time at company-battery level today is comparatively short yet remains the foundation for all that comes later.

One of my contemporaries whom I admired greatly as a young officer was later relieved in combat as a regimental commander in World War II. He was again a regimental commander in Korea, and again relieved in combat; it was not for lack of courage in either case. He had been a "one-man Army" as a company commander, where you can get away with that in some degree, but not at higher levels. So it is important at company-battery level to understand that you are not only responsible for the efficiency of your unit but also for learning *the* technique of command today that will prepare you to meet your greater responsibilities tomorrow: *integrate the work of others.*

CHAPTER 24
Of Semantics, Discipline and Dogs

In the late 1930s, Capt. Ichiji Sugita of the Japanese Imperial General Staff (later chief of staff, Japanese Ground Self-Defense Force after World War II) was attached to Company G, 26th Infantry, which I commanded. One day he was at the head of a marching column with me when a soldier said, "Boy, my dogs sure are growling!"

"Dogs?" the captain asked, looking around, puzzled. My explanation that the soldier meant his feet hurt, left the captain more puzzled than ever.

Soon thereafter, on payday, the first sergeant walked into our orderly room and said to me, "This is a great day for the dog-faces, captain."

"Dogfaces?" Sugita asked, looking up from his desk. I explained the sergeant meant "soldiers"—but that no one except another soldier should ever use that word. Obviously, this did not make sense to him.

Then we had a full field inspection on the parade ground, with pitched tents and displays of individual equipment. Prior to my walk-by inspection, 1st Sgt. "Big Jim" Redding blew a whistle and ordered, "All dog tags out!"

"Dog tags?" Capt. Sugita echoed. He understood each soldier wore an identification tag on a cord around his neck, and that the sergeant meant pull it outside where it could be seen and checked. But why "dog" again?

As I prepared to explain that one, Sugita looked at me and smilingly shook his head to indicate he knew he was never going to understand— because he had just learned that soldiers lived in "pup tents." So I decided not to tell him that, as company commander, I had a "dog robber."

This exercise in semantics simply points out that such references to dogs and men in uniform were soldier slang in my day, with no derogatory implications when used among the troops themselves.

Similarly, no adverse inferences are involved when I connect a world-famous experiment, using a live dog, with discipline in the military service. Further, I am sure that the great Russian physiologist, Ivan Petrovich Pavlov, was not thinking of discipline in military service when he discovered the principle of conditioned reflexes.

His experiment was simple: every time he fed his dog, he first rang a bell, until the dog expected food when the bell rang. As a result, the dog would salivate when he heard the bell, even when no food appeared. The dog was Pavlov's instrument to demonstrate the principle of conditioned reflex, whereby an animal which has been exposed repeatedly to certain visible, audible or other stimuli, followed always by the same result, develops a conditioned reflex that causes the animal to automatically react every time in the same way it did in previous, similar situations.

The accepted definition of discipline includes "the instant and willing obedience to all orders. . ." Thus, military training that produces a "well-disciplined outfit" has, among other things, established a conditioned reflex that impels obedience to orders as the habitual result of receiving orders.

There are many illustrations of reflex actions in battle situations. One is that a trained soldier will automatically aim his weapon in battle—without thinking—in the same way he was trained to do. This is nothing more or less than a type of trained reflex.

When we speak of how "disciplined troops" perform in battle, as opposed to "green" or relatively untrained troops, we are in some measure comparing the relative degree to which their conditioned reflexes have developed. The best and most striking illustration of this is the way troops move forward under fire when ordered to attack, or how firmly they stand and fight when attacked. Good training conditions them to act bravely.

Our training is often criticized as dull because it is repetitious. But repetition is the very feature of training that enhances "discipline." In other words training stores up in the unconscious a supply of conditioned reflexes designed to help men in combat. One of the strongest of these reflexes is obedience to orders, even in the face of imminent death.

There are exceptional cases, where an order can and should be ignored, such as one issued by a commander remote from the scene who patently did not know the actual situation. Of course anyone who disobeys an order assumes the responsibility of having to justify his failure to obey, and, if things go wrong, the justification had better be good.

A vivid battle memory for me illustrates several kinds of conditioned reflexes in action. In the ground battle for Leyte during World War II, my regiment was driving west on the road from Palo to Jaro. As a calculated risk in that particular flat and intermittently wooded area, our flank protection came primarily from speed of movement, maintaining proper intervals on the road, and alertness in returning any fire. As we approached Jaro, one sharp-eyed soldier gave a shout and pointed toward a native shack on our right flank. The first floor was on raised poles, so that the doorway could be seen above the intervening four- or five-foot high *kunai* grass, about 300 yards away.

I saw what others saw at the same instant—several Japanese were setting up a machine gun in the elevated doorway of the native shack. This sparked a complex series of conditioned reflexes stampeding into action among us.

Since I was the senior officer present, the conditioned reflex seized me to take active command and issue orders. To do this, the conditioned reflex to first assess the situation went into action as I automatically looked from that native shack to others responding to conditioned reflexes around me. In the forward element where I was, a 37-mm gun crew, in practiced trained motions, was swinging its gun to fire on the enemy.

At the same time, the crew of a nearby 85-mm armored support gun was swinging its short, stubby muzzle toward the same target. As I noted this, the conditioned reflex to analyze and reach a decision took over in my mind. All of this happened virtually automatically, and in seconds. It looked to me that the 37-mm was going to get off the first shot. But that might not knock out the gun and its crew, so if a couple of them survived that first 37-mm round (which seemed likely) then the surviving Japanese could grab the gun, jump down from the raised doorway—thus being out of sight instantly—and we would have a live enemy machine gun on our flank.

So I ordered the 37-mm not to fire until the 85-mm got in the first shot. The crew looked at me in amazement but, fighting against their conditioned reflex to fire on this definitely located and imminent enemy threat, they automatically obeyed my order. As seconds ticked on, I really sweated because if my estimate was wrong, and that Japanese machine gun fired on us before our 85-mm could fire, I would be second-guessed from then to eternity.

But the boom of the 85-mm came first. Bull's eye! No more Japanese or machine gun. The point here is not whether I made the right decision, but that all of us reacted instantly under the conditioned reflexes of our training—each one in the groove of his own reflexes.

Let me add, however, that it is not only in split-second situations that conditioned reflexes come into play. Nothing I saw in combat impressed me more than the lead scouts who, at the command, "Scouts out!" automatically moved toward the enemy as living targets; quiet, unhesitating, knowing they might not hear the first shot fired, because you do not hear the one that hits you.

Some will say habits and reactions that stem from repetitious military training are not properly classified as conditioned reflexes. Others will ask what is the dividing line between mental conditioned reflexes and calculated thinking. To this I can give no precise answer. There are many types of related human reactions but for our purpose here—in connecting them to the value of the repetitious element in military training—we can group them generally under the tent of conditioned reflexes. Further comments are:

- Once this principle of conditioned reflex (broadly interpreted) is understood, then the repetitious element that permeates military training can be seen as an important factor in producing disciplined, trained soldiers.
- Further, in the light of the requirement for fast action in battle, it is clear why military training emphasizes "instant and willing obedience to all orders." When civilians criticize this aspect of military life they fail to understand the fundamental principle upon which it is based.
- Conditioned reflexes are not confined to individuals. In wartime, a major factor is the will of the people of a nation to fight. That is one reason I believe the national preoccupation with a no-draft, all-volunteer Army is a fundamentally unsound concept in the present world situation. In my opinion, it is creating a national conditioned reflex in men of fighting age to believe that they will never have to fight: "Let the volunteer do it—we will pay him for it."
- Finally, it is vitally important that, as individuals, we do not become slaves to our conditioned reflexes as a substitute for thinking. The requirement is to recognize the multi-angled sides of conditioned reflexes in military life, and use this aspect of human behavior to advantage, remaining on guard to avoid the booby traps it can lead to. Nowhere is this more important than in building that great military asset we call discipline.

CHAPTER 25
Command Posture is Nebulous but Vital Quality

In Gen. Douglas MacArthur's autobiography, *Reminiscences,* he tells about the first baseball game ever played by West Point cadets against midshipmen of the Naval Academy at Annapolis, on 18 May 1901. He was in left field for the cadets, which placed him next to the Navy stands.

At that time his father, Gen. Arthur MacArthur, was much in the news as governor general of the Philippines. So when Cadet MacArthur took the field, Navy fans began to razz him, chanting this little ditty:

Are you the governor general
Or a hobo?
Who is the boss of this show?
Is it you or Emilio Aguinaldo?

Late in the game, with the score tied at three to three, Cadet MacArthur came to bat and worked the Navy pitcher for a walk. Then, on the first pitch to the next batter, MacArthur broke for second base. The resulting hasty peg to second was wild, so he took off for third and forced another hurried bad throw. Taking advantage of this, MacArthur continued on to score what proved to be the winning run of a four to three game.

Thus, his clear eye and cool judgment at the plate, followed by daring base running, answered the chanted question, "Who is the boss of this show?"

That question is another way of saying, "Who is in command around here?" Throughout MacArthur's long and brilliant career his distinctive "command posture" never left the answer to that question in doubt.

In the exercise of command there are many intangibles, separate and distinct from strategy, tactics, logistics, administration and other military procedures involving concrete things. These intangibles have to do with what we call "command posture." There is no limit to the number and variety of ways this nebulous yet vital intangible quality affects command and leadership.

Soon after taking command of my first company—it was my great privilege to command Company G, 26th Infantry at Plattsburg, N.Y., for three years—the matter of command posture faced me squarely. It happened this way.

We had a vacancy for private first class, so I asked 1st Sgt. James S. Redding for his recommendation. In reply he submitted a written company order for my signature, promoting Pvt. John Doe to private first class. Although I did not say so, I had Pvt. Joe Blow in mind for reasons that do not matter here. So I placed Big Jim's recommendation in my HOLD basket.

The next day Big Jim said, "Captain, you have not signed the promotion order for Pvt. John Doe. He cannot be paid in that grade until the order is published."

My reply was to ask for recommendations from the platoon sergeants, three names from each, listed in order of preference. Not surprisingly, they listed John Doe first choice. Also, I was interested to note they listed Joe Blow as their second choice. So I left the order unsigned in my HOLD basket.

The next morning I noticed, posted on the company bulletin board, a carbon copy of the order promoting Pvt. John Doe to private first class. So I sent for Big Jim and said, "Have an order prepared for my signature, promoting Pvt. Joe Blow to private first class."

"But, Captain," he protested, "the order has already been published making John Doe PFC!"

"No," I replied, "I have signed no such order. So please have the order prepared promoting Pvt. Joe Blow."

When the order arrived in my IN basket for signature it read, "Pvt. First Class John Doe is disrated to private, and Pvt. Joe Blow is promoted to private first class."

So I called for Big Jim, handed him the order and said, "John Doe has never been a PFC, because I did not sign that order. So please have this retyped for my signature, promoting Joe Blow. And post the signed copy on the bulletin board."

That was a bitter pill for Big Jim, who had been first sergeant of that company on that post for eleven years. Those two notices told their own story for the company about "who is the boss and who is in command around here."

I have never had a more valued friend than Big Jim Redding. No soldier of any rank, including four-star generals, taught me as much as Big Jim did about what makes the wheels go around in the Army. But I believe those three wonderful years in command of Company G could not have been so pleasant and rewarding if I had failed to establish my command posture with the first sergeant.

One of my earliest memories of military service on my first post concerns the command posture of an older colonel. His habitual stance was to draw a little apart from any group, usually with hands clasped behind his back. One of my fellow lieutenants said, "Col. So-and-so looks like he is practicing to be a general." Maybe so and maybe not, but he did end up wearing stars.

An important angle about command posture is that you should always be aware of how others feel about their own. Years ago, when I was a senior colonel, I entered a room where my boss, a temporary brigadier general, was seated at one end of a long sofa. When he invited me to have a seat, I chose the opposite end of the sofa on which he was seated.

Apparently he considered this a violation of his dignity, because he bounced to his feet as though he had sat on a tack. Our business was then conducted as he paced the rug, while I looked upward at him in some mental discomfort. That little scene involved "command posture" for him—and let it be entered in the record that he eventually retired as a four-star general.

On my last duty assignment as chief of staff, U.S. Continental Army Command, I encountered an intangible in command posture that was not new to me. In fact it had been present in some measure in every headquarters of the eleven generals for whom I served as chief of staff. The only difference was that, in this case, the staff officer was a major general and should have known better.

Sometimes when a staff officer came in to brief me on a subject I would have him brief the commanding general and I would listen in. On other occasions, a formal briefing would be set up for the CG in his office, and I would listen in.

Some briefing officers, including the major general at USCONARC, would start the briefing and look at the CG as they talked. If the CG looked down, or out of the window while he was listening, and the briefing officers thus lost eye contact with him, they continued the briefing— looking at me. This does violence to the command posture of any commander who suddenly realizes the briefing is being directed toward his chief of staff. So I would turn my head and look at the CG. And so would the briefer.

If the briefer did not get this straight after a few such occurrences I would tell him, "When you are in the CG's office, talk to him—and look at him, not at me." For younger officers I would explain the vagaries and intangibles of command posture. The commander should be stage front, center.

Some general comments are:

- "Who is the boss of this show?" must always be clear in any organization. That is the primary reason for variations in rank and maintaining "date of rank" within each grade. Visual indications of command posture include such things as green shoulder tabs to indicate commanders, star automobile plates and star flags for general officers and the fact that no member of an organization stands abreast of its commander at formal parades and reviews. All of these, and many more, are factors in command posture.

- Junior commanders should recognize and respect the command posture of their seniors—like not sitting on the sofa with him when other chairs are available. I have seen commanders relieved when their exaggerated command postures brought them into conflict with the command posture of their bosses. In fact, I believe this was the underlying reason that Gen. Dwight Eisenhower relieved Gen. George Patton in Germany after World War II.

- The senior also has the responsibility to respect the command posture of his subordinates. One of the ways this principle is often violated is for a senior to bypass the next lower commander by issuing orders directly to lower unit commanders. This also applies in staff channels when some commanders bypass the chief of staff too much, dealing directly with staff section chiefs on matters that require general staff coordination.

- The overall command posture principle is not confined to military organizations. When our headquarters staff was having a steak cookout one night in Australia during World War II, our division commander said to me, "Red, I understand your wife (who was then an Army nurse back in the States) has been promoted to captain. How long will it be at her present rate of promotion before she ranks you?"

"General," I replied, "the number and frequency of her promotions will not change the chain of command in our house."

CHAPTER 26
Seniors, too, Must Show Courtesy

For some perverse reason of inverted thinking, the words, "military courtesy" have the connotation of courtesy by juniors toward seniors. But courtesy is a two-way street. The difference is that seniors can correct lack of courtesy by juniors, while the reverse is not true. As a result, some seniors seem unaware of their discourtesy toward juniors.

Thirty-five years ago I wrote an "open letter" to Emily Post, at that time a widely published authority on good manners. My letter (under a pen name) appeared as a Cerebration in the April, 1950, *Infantry Journal,* predecessor of *ARMY.* As a start toward examining more deeply the courtesy obligations of senior officers, let's take a brief look at that letter:

Subject: Inspection Manners
To: Emily Post
Your book on etiquette needs a new chapter, so that the manners of some senior officers inspecting troop areas can be more adequately covered. It may be they do not know their bad manners are showing. Here are some types who need enlightening:
• *The Morose Scowler.* Characteristics are:
  (1) Belligerent stare on arrival.
  (2) Returns salute in grudging silence.
  (3) Has nothing much to say as he inspects, but by faint smiles and slight sneering expressions gives idea he thinks things stink.
  (4) When he leaves, silent unhappiness lingers in those places he has been. This type may be unsure of himself, and his manners probably spring from an inferiority complex.
• *The Aggressive Charger.* Characteristics are:
  (1) Walks at high rate of speed—to no purpose.

(2) Generally sticks chin out and asks questions in loud, accusing voice.

(3) Barks telegraphic corrective orders on the run—which often show he was in too big a hurry to see the true picture.

(4) Leaves a unit feeling he has just finished an unpleasant chore by inspecting it. This type is generally a show-off at heart, thinking mostly of putting on an act.

• *The Bombastic Haranguer.* Characteristics are:

(1) Points out a defect, then launches into long discourse on the heinousness of such a dereliction.

(2) Apt to find what he says reminds him of what is wrong with the Army and the world in general—so expounds in general.

(3) Eventually departs, in retreat from his own garrulousness as much as anything else, and leaves everybody trying to remember if he said anything worth remembering. This type may have a talkative wife who does not let him have much to say at home.

Of course, there are other types, too, Emily. But these are enough to show the need for that added chapter in the next edition of your book on etiquette.

Sincerely,
Stone Borealis

New ideas about courtesy are where you find them. On one post where I was stationed my wife saw a seven-year-old boy chopping on a tree with a hatchet. "You should not do that," she said to him. "If other little boys did that, too, all our trees would die. Then we would have no shade and we would get very hot."

"No," he replied. "All the others have to do is for everybody to cut on this tree and only one tree will die."

"But," my wife said, "the others will not know to come and cut on just this tree."

"Well," the small boy reasoned philosophically, "if it gets too hot around here, we can just take a bath."

It is hard for a seven-year-old to understand the principle that no one is a law unto himself, and that what he does must be measured in the light of how it affects others. Military leaders know this, like sharing supplies and other tangibles of the give-and-take in military life. But it is also important that the principle be applied in the niceties of daily living with others.

While I was stationed at the Armed Forces Staff College in Norfolk, Va., we were invited to a lawn reception at the home of the Supreme Allied Commander, Atlantic, a four-star admiral. The reception was to honor a famous World War II hero, a marshal in the Army of one of our European Allies, who was a house guest in the admiral's home. The reception was scheduled for 1700 hours but the marshal did not deign to put in an appearance until 1815.

Invited guests arrived punctually, so, although the bar was opened, there was quite a bit of standing around before meeting the distinguished visitor. Some with other commitments, including a four-star Air Force general, had to leave before meeting the marshal. Also, my wife and I were embarrassed, as we were late returning home to greet our own dinner guests that evening.

While seven-year-old boys may be forgiven when they behave as a law unto themselves, senior military men have no such license. Failing to be on time, no matter what the occasion or situation, violates one of the most basic rules of military courtesy: *never keep the troops waiting.*

Admittedly, the above is an extreme example of an infrequent type of discourtesy. But the reverse is a more common type: the guest of honor or senior officer present who does not know when to go home. Since others do not usually leave before the guest of honor, the senior should depart before his presence becomes a roadblock. Memory brings back a cocktail party many years ago where a visiting older colonel was the guest of honor and ended up in the chorus around the piano singing "Show me the way to go home."

On hearing this, the acidulous wife of a middle-aged captain said, "What the old goat needs to know first is that it is long past time he was on his way."

Do not let me give the impression most senior officers, especially those of high rank, are prone to discourtesy. Few of them are. It may be apocryphal, but the grapevine reports the time a colonel was walking his dog on one of the Army's large posts. As he passed a major general's house, the general invited the colonel in for a drink, saying, "Bring your dog in, too."

In the house the colonel found another guest, a lieutenant general. As the colonel took a sip from his drink, his dog lifted a leg and wet the trouser leg of the host major general. In the resulting embarrassed silence the colonel said, "I'm very sorry, but Bowser has never done that before. Maybe all these stars around make him nervous."

Whereupon Bowser waddled over, lifted a leg and gave the lieutenant general's trouser leg a couple of squirts, too. Before the mortified colonel could think of what to say, the lieutenant general said:

"Colonel, your pooch needs instruction in military courtesy because he treats me just like he does major generals. Tie him outside and we'll have one for the road when you get back."

That was a special situation, which was met with special understanding courtesy by the lieutenant general.

In 1955, the G1 of U.S. Army, Europe, in Heidelberg, Germany, established a policy that no one who came to his office door to see him could be turned away without his personal permission. One day a young female school teacher arrived at 1700 hours, the end of the office day. So the general's civilian secretary told him of the teacher's presence, saying she would tell the young lady to come back another time during office hours. However, the G1 directed the teacher be brought to see him.

One of his G1 responsibilities was general staff supervision of the school system in Europe for military dependents. It so happened that a couple of rabble-rousing teachers were causing unfavorable publicity about the vagaries of the civil service system under which they were paid. So the young teacher had come to see the general to find out about this. She remained well over an hour, while he answered her questions, to include explaining details of the law passed by Congress under which she was paid.

Several weeks later, a letter was endorsed down to the G1, through channels from Washington, D.C., to go in his official personnel file. It was a letter of appreciation to the President of the United States, written by that young teacher. She thanked the President for sending a general to supervise the school system in Europe who not only understood the problems involved, but who had showed her the courtesy of receiving her at the end of the day, without an appointment. Also that he had listened to her after office hours, with interest and patience, for as long as she wanted to talk.

Crime (discourtesy) does not pay, but courtesy does—sometimes in totally unexpected ways, and often in ways that you may never learn about.

This final comment seems pertinent:

- The hand salutes, standing at attention, use of the word "sir" and other set requirements of military courtesy, are the outward form of courtesy in a limited number of situations that can be categorized. But there is no substitute for awareness and alertness to recognize the countless situations of courtesy vs. discourtesy not covered by regulations.

In such cases good judgment, common sense, a sound understanding of military service and, above all, an instinctive respect for and consideration of your fellow man are the best guides.

CHAPTER 27
Of Notebooks, Careers and Character

Many years ago I mentioned to a four-star general that a newly promoted brigadier general we both knew seemed destined to reach multi-star rank.

"No, Red," he said, "he will not go any higher because you have to keep him away from feathers."

This puzzled me, so I asked what he meant.

"Well," the four-star general replied, "he has a tendency to go off on wild tangents. If he ever gets a feather in each hand he will try to fly."

That made his point clear. After thinking it over I had to agree that he was probably right—and time proved him to be. One characteristic of multi-star generals is that they are basically conservative, so it is hard to get them out on a limb. I had forgotten about this fact until last week when I saw my file memorandum stating it on a 3 " x 5 " slip of paper.

This note from long ago came to light sometime after it occurred to me that, to quote Satchel Paige, "Somethin' might be gaining on me." So as a first step, in case that "somethin" is Father Time, I bought a large letter-size looseleaf notebook, and pasted this label on the cover: TAPS.

Then I began the laborious task of sifting through the mass of papers which have accumulated in my files over the years. Selected papers I would put into the indexed TAPS book; some I would refile, but most I would destroy ruthlessly. One musty file box contained a thousand or more 3 " x 5 " paper slips with jottings on them.

For 25 years before my retirement I always carried a small notebook as a work tool. Sometimes the random notes (as opposed to action notes) in these books were simply thoughts, quotes, or interesting fragments of information. When a notebook was used up, I pulled out the random-note pages and put them in what I called my "Memory Idea File," which also contained small clippings and other notes on odd scraps of paper.

As I riffled through these old aide-memoires under the heading CAREER, I found that some were undecipherable and others were out of date. There were still others that an editorial censor would not allow to get into print, but many—like that feathers idea—are just as valid today as they were then. Here are several which, when reflected upon, underline a basic principle of professional success as a soldier:

- You can overwork a willing horse and he will try to pull the load. My observation is, however, that the commander who overloads a good staff horse will ridicule or whip him to more frantic efforts, but nobody seems to reward the man who struggles to carry a load beyond his capacity.
- I once served with the officers that one of my notes reports had this conversation: "Colonel," the captain said, "I do the best I can for you, I give you all I've got and I tell you the truth. I didn't ask for this job; you asked for me. I am tired and need sleep, and owe it to my men to go to sleep now. If I stay here I'll continue to do my best, but if that is not enough you will have to get another man."

  "All right, I understand," the colonel replied. "Go and get the sleep you need."

  I do not remember who told me this, or what the circumstances were. But that conversation reveals an intangible something about each of them—and both became outstanding general officers in later years.
- An ambitious wife will do her husband no harm if, with quiet and conservative good judgment, she banana-oils her husband's superiors. And she can lose nothing by buttering up their wives, too. But if her man is not a good officer, nothing she can say will make him one.
- President Calvin Coolidge said, "I never heard of a man listening himself out of a job." To mix some metaphors, it is folly to speak unwisely when silence is golden. That is why many people, like cats, lick themselves with their tongues.
- Brevity in speech and writing is a time-saver and the mark of an efficient officer. To speak clearly and well is a valuable asset in command and leadership. But you cannot talk and think at the same time, which is why the "cool, calm and collected" officer is admired. He never flaps his trap without thinking first.
- A British liaison officer said to me over a cup of coffee, "In command, all of an officer's finest traits blossom; he looks good if he is

good. But staff work is the slow consumption that destroys the hearts and nervous systems of keen and conscientious officers who, because of their ability, are often mercilessly sacrificed on the altar of the selfish ambitions of others."

- Every officer should have troop duty commensurate with his grade at some time while serving in that grade. This is not only to acquire technical knowledge in the intricacies of command but, even more important, to build a viewpoint and mental attitude that is troop oriented toward living men, not staff oriented toward words on paper.

- When Admiral Arleigh A. Burke was Chief of Naval Operations in Washington, D.C., he said, "The future is limited only by our imagination and zeal."

- Rear Admiral Harold Briggs told me that he had known Admiral Burke well, and said, "At negotiations with the communists in Korea I saw Arleigh Burke writing and working; even when others were off duty, he was always working. So I asked him good-naturedly 'What are you doing writing a book?'

   "Admiral Burke replied seriously, 'No, this is for my use. I always work at trying to expand my knowledge, to gain the most from my experience as a naval officer.' "

   Admiral Briggs then said to me, "You can see why it was not strange that Arleigh Burke was suddenly promoted over some 90 senior admirals to be Chief of Naval Operations."

- Why do so many generals pay so much attention to details? That they paid attention to important small matters is one reason they were made generals.

- Note to me from the executive officer in the engineer division of USAREUR at Heidelberg, Germany, dated 16 August, 1956: "This correspondence was signed by General McNutt on the 9th as dated, but was delayed due to an error of mine. I hope the delay will not inconvenience you unduly." (signed) Bruce D. Rindlaub, Col. C.E. (I am happy to say this fine conscientious soldier became a general officer, but am sorry to report his career was cut short by an untimely death.)

- There will always be those you do not like, and those who do not like you, and there does not have to be a reason for this. But to succeed in the Army you have to live and work with everyone successfully.

- If you take time to allow the light of objectivity and logic to illuminate a problem, the solution will usually come clear. That is why to "sleep on" something that is troubling you is a wise procedure.
- "Men best show their character by trifles, when they are not on guard. It is in insignificant matters, and in the simplest habits, that we often see the boundless egotism which pays no regard to the feelings of others, and denies nothing to itself."—*Arthur Schopenhauer.*
- "Character is higher than the intellect,"—*Ralph Waldo Emerson.*

After listing these memoranda the questions now emerge: what have they in common? What basic principle do they support?

They, and others in that musty file of paper slips, point up in more specific detail the conclusions, reached in Chapters 54 and 55, that character, with its countless facets, is the controlling factor in the development of officers selected for star rank. These comments are pertinent:

- Without a broad, many-sided character no specialized excellence can lift a man to starry heights.
- Keeping a notebook is a basic tool for an officer efficient in daily operations. But as illustrated, it can be used also to focus your attention on facets of character that, in the aggregate, lead to the top.
- The physical act of writing helps to fix your attention on the ideas involved. Maximum benefit, however, comes from periodically reviewing the notes. Yours will differ from mine in detail, but not in principle. They will increase awareness of your own personality and character, and act as a spur to correct any faults you may thus see in yourself.

CHAPTER 28
32 Years Later: Leavenworth Revisited

In February 1975 it was my privilege to return as a guest speaker to the U.S. Army Command and General Staff College at Fort Leavenworth, Kan.—thirty-two years after I graduated in one of the World War II "quickie" general staff classes. As I faced the challenge of my talk to modern students there, memory turned back to how it had been yesterday.

There was magic then in the word, "Leavenworth." The Command and General Staff College was justly famous as a tough and demanding school of the highest professionalism. And General A. was an uncompromising taskmaster.

For those who did not know General A., he was the ubiquitous (and mythical) commander of troops in "marked" map problems and exercises. Some idea of his character and personality was revealed when one student, turning in the last "marked problem" of the course, appended this message at the bottom of his paper:

"Goodbye, General A., you vacillating old SOB."

After all these years, I still smoldered when remembering the "U" (unsatisfactory) I received on one "trick" problem involving a motorized movement directed by General A. This included the limitation, "Do not use trucks of the 424th Transportation Co."

Without those forty-eight transportation company trucks it was nec essary (and permissible) to use kitchen trucks from division trains, since the tactical situation was static. But I fell for the adroitly planted booby trap and failed to exempt the kitchen truck of the 424th Transportation Co. This was ruled that unforgivable sin: "Violation of General A.'s directive." Thus, it was an automatic *unsatisfactory.*

So, after arriving at Fort Leavenworth for my lecture, I inquired about the health and status of General A. He is unknown there now. That he is extinct is just one of many improvements the changing times have made in the U.S. Army Command and General Staff College.

The C&GSC plays an even more important role today than in the past. The program is attuned to the challenging world situation of our atomic fusion and electronic era. An obvious indication of this is the younger and more dynamic leadership of the command, staff and faculty.

My mission at the lectern was to discuss the assigned subject: "Under the elective course titled Advanced Staff Direction, examine staff operations from the perspective of the commander, the chief of staff and the staff section chief." It was further stated that to do this I should, "Relate your experiences in the variety of staffs on which you have served."

My talk presumed to be no more than that, along with what I thought were implications of my experiences. It was then up to the student officers to decide how many of the principles I espoused in the past were applicable today.

One of these is the requirement in command and staff relations to work in harmony and cooperation with others—without the power to command obedience or concurrence.

The wide application of this principle was made clear at the Armed Forces Staff College when I was Army deputy commandant there. We sent letters to high-level commanders around the world asking for their recommendations to improve our course, based on observations of how our graduates had functioned in their headquarters.

Only one meaningful answer came back: *teach them how to get along with people.* This led to two case histories in my talk.

In mid-1942, I pinned on the quick eagles of a spot promotion to division chief of staff, just fifteen months after leaving my happy home as a company commander. Several days later I went to see the division commander and said, "Sir, I have to know the answer to this question: do you want me to operate as your chief of staff, or in the way my predecessor operated?"

The general threw back his head and laughed because he knew exactly what I was talking about. He replied, "You are my chief of staff, Newman. If you need slowing down, I'll tell you."

My predecessor was a colonel fifteen years older than I, the same age level as the division commander. When a chief of staff is the same age as the commanding general it is harder for the chief to operate, because the CG is alert to be sure nobody thinks the chief is running things and restricts the authority of the chief. Age does make a difference in command and staff relations, especially when the senior is the same age or younger than the junior.

Another experience was my year as chief of staff of the Iceland Defense Force. This was a hastily assembled task force air-landed in Iceland under our NATO commitments to prevent a possible communist takeover there. It was a unified command and thus included members of all the armed services.

Soon after our arrival in Iceland, I noticed some foot-dragging by one of my J-staff section chiefs, a fine looking Navy officer. So I asked him who was his boss and he replied, "The commander." Then I asked who made out his efficiency report and again he replied, "The commander."

When I disagreed, he informed me with great dignity that he was a Navy officer and under Navy regulations the commander—and no one else—must sign his fitness report.

"Come with me," I said, and led the way into the commander's office. There I explained the situation to our commander (an Army general officer), who promptly told the J-staff section chief he would indeed sign his fitness report, if that was the way the Navy wanted it. He then added, "But my chief of staff will make out your report—and I will sign it just the way Colonel Newman makes it out."

It is preferable to have others do willingly what you ask, but there are times when some persuasive action is needed. This also illustrates another idea: when you have trouble "getting along" with an individual it is usually possible to figure out why—and act accordingly.

Here are two footnotes to my visit at Fort Leavenworth:
• My talk was at 1900 hours, thus some student officers were in civilian clothes and a few brought their wives. The second hour was devoted to questions and the last question was from one of the wives: "Where does the Army stop and husband and father begin?"

My reply summarized three cases. The first concerned an outstanding major, then my battalion commander. When the major was away on detached service, the regimental adjutant suggested I escort the major's wife to an official social affair.

During the evening I mentioned the hardship she faced with her husband away. She replied, "When Alan asked me to marry him, he said that before I answered he wanted me to consider these things: that he was a soldier and he was going to remain a soldier;

also that questions about where we were stationed, including absences from home for duty requirements, were professional matters. Therefore, decisions in such situations would always be his."

She agreed to that and they had a fine marriage. And let the record show he commanded a division in battle during World War II.

In another case an outstanding colonel was offered a command assignment in a rather remote area where there was little social activity. His wife did not like this, so he obtained a nice staff assignment in a more social area—and did not receive another chance to command in the grade of colonel.

Although a superior officer, he never reached star rank. In my opinion, his wife's intervention in professional matters was a factor in his failure to be promoted.

The third incident happened six years ago when I received a letter from the wife of a young lieutenant. Her husband enlisted, she said, and received his commission through Officers' Candidate School. He loved the Army, had just received his regular Army commission and was very happy about that.

But he was now ordered to a special six-week school course. The Army would not pay his wife's way to go with him and he could not afford to pay her way either. She could not accept this lack of concern for her, so he would just have to get out of the Army. She just had to confide in somebody, she said—and knew I would understand.

I did understand. Unfortunately, she did not sign her name so I could not write and tell her the basic answer to this conflict between wife, duty, husband, and father: If a woman is not willing to be a soldier's wife, she should not marry an Army officer.

- For this old soldier of yesterday it was an inspiration to visit today's U.S. Army Command and General Staff College. And it was a proud privilege to express some thoughts there, including this Confucian-type guideline (source not remembered):

"Men do not stumble over mountains, but over molehills"—especially when it comes to getting along with people in command and staff relations.

CHAPTER 29
To Command You Must Control

As a young lieutenant I went to a stage play in New York City: Aristophanes' famous Greek comedy *Lysistrata*. The story line was that Athens and Thebes were at war, which left the able-bodied and lusty wives of the warriors at home with the old men and children. Thus a vital element of a full life for the wives was missing. Since Athens and Thebes were periodically going to war, the women decided something had to be done to stop the wars.

So the wives of the two cities agreed on a deterrent. When the men came home, all fired up for a little romance after their long absence, in both Thebes and Athens they were met with this ultimatum: nothing doing, until they signed a permanent treaty of peace.

This principle of deterrence has incalculable variations in the control of human beings and nowhere is this more important than in the military service—which leads us to a specific case.

From the coffee-call grapevine I heard about a letter written by the father of a young soldier to the Army chief of staff. The father took the Army to task for not having instilled discipline in his son, who had been in trouble twice in his first six months in uniform.

In reply the chief of staff said, "It seems hardly fair to blame the Army for failing to do in six months what you were unable to do in eighteen years."

The control of young soldiers, like the one above, encompasses a wide blanket of interrelated intangibles known as "command and leadership." No element of command is more important than control, which is divided into many threads. Each must be understood separately if the whole is to be comprehended.

The essential thread of coercion is based on the principle of deterrence—the same one used so effectively by the ladies of Thebes and Athens—that enables a commander to enforce his orders. At best, this is an unpleasant aspect of control and should be avoided unless circumstances make it necessary. An extreme example of iron control was used in the great English Navy that halted Napoleon's expansion by destroying his fleet in the Battle of Trafalgar.

To begin with, consider Article 19 of the British Naval Articles of War of that time: "If any person, in or belonging to the Fleet, shall make, or endeavor to make, any mutinous assembly, upon any pretext what so ever, every person offending herein, being convicted thereof by the sentence of a court martial, shall suffer death."

There was no room for clemency. If convicted, death was not only certain but was carried out publicly, the mutineers being hauled at the end of a rope to the yardarm of a ship of war as a warning for all to see.

Nor was this the ultimate deterrent punishment. Being publicly flogged aboard ship with a cat-o'-nine-tails is generally known as a severe punishment of that time. But it is not so generally known that this could result in being flogged to death for certain serious offenses. There is a vivid description of one such case in *Mutiny on the Bounty* by Charles Nordhoff and James Norman Hall: a sailor was "flogged through the fleet" for striking an officer. The procedure followed was designed to gain the maximum deterrent effect.

The offender was stripped to the waist and tied down in a small boat, with his bare back exposed. When a signal gun was fired, men aboard all war ships in the harbor were paraded on deck "to witness punishment." The boat was then rowed through the harbor to pass all ships of the fleet anchored there. As it passed each ship, the boat stopped, an officer read the charges and sentence and the boatswain's mate of that ship—in full view of the entire crew—climbed down to the boat, removed his cat-o'-nine-tails from its red baize bag so that its cruel, knotted thongs dangled free. He then delivered two dozen lashes with his full strength, laid on the offender's bare back.

By the time the boat had progressed halfway through the fleet much of the flesh had been beaten off the victim's back and he was dead. But the grisly parade, to the sound of the drummer's mournful tattoo of the "Rogue's March," continued on until the boat-swain's mate of each ship of the fleet had delivered his allotted blows on the mangled back of what was once a man.

This is a barbaric example out of the past of control by deterrence. Still, it must be viewed in the context of that era.

Now skip forward to the time I was the new captain of Company G, 26th Infantry, at Plattsburg Barracks. Soon after my arrival, I instructed the platoon sergeants during inspection of quarters to stop men from throwing cigarette butts on the latrine floors. When this produced no noticeable results, I directed 1st Sgt. "Big Jim" Redding to announce to the company that if we could not keep cigarette butts off latrine floors the easy way, we would have to do it the hard way.

Sure enough, at my barracks inspection the next morning there were defiantly thrown butts on the latrine floors. So an order was published on the company bulletin board establishing—for as long as necessary—a 24-hour guard in the latrines. This was mounted in Class A uniform, with sidearms, to prevent the throwing of cigarette butts on the latrine floors.

In the next two days there were no butts on the floors, so the guard was discontinued. The problem did not come up again. Just another illustration of control established by using the principle of deterrence.

In between these two cases of control by deterrence—so radically different in the facts and situations yet so similar in principle—we have the whole spectrum of "crime and punishment" as contemplated in and controlled by the Uniform Code of Military Justice. Yet there will always be problems of control which the UCMJ does not cover, like those cigarette butts in the latrines long years ago.

There are also variations based on the UCMJ, yet not covered in its legal provisions. When I joined the 82nd Airborne Division as regimental commander of the 505th Airborne Infantry, the division commander, my former classmate and friend, Maj. Gen. Charles D. W. Canham, ordered each regiment to establish a special training camp as a supplementary means of disciplinary control. Men were housed in tents near good training areas.

These camps were highly organized training units, somewhat like recruit camps. Young first-time offenders, sentenced by court-martial to confinement at hard labor, were, at the option of the reviewing authority, placed in and restricted to these camps (their confinement at hard labor suspended) under carefully selected instructors for intensified individual and small unit training.

Several advantages accrued from the special training camps: soldiers who went AWOL missed training not only while away, but also while in the guardhouse on their return; and young soldiers (especially those who had never been in trouble before and often were just AWOL homesick kids) were kept out of the guardhouse, thus away from hardened offenders.

Of course, there are other forms of control, too. These include proper organization for tactical control in combat, administrative control of paper work, preservation and control of supplies, traffic control and others. But it is important to note that coercive control, or control by deterrence, must be available when needed for "command action" to enforce all other types of control required to insure military effectiveness.

These comments are pertinent:

- The more control can be achieved without deterrent action, the better. But, when necessary, the deterrence must be adequate and appropriate to accomplish its purpose.
- Abhorrent as the cruel cat-o'-nine-tails was in the British Navy of the Napoleonic era, it should be viewed in the light of that time. It was used to control restive crews, many of whom had been kidnapped by "press gangs" from the streets and pubs of London. Others had been "recruited" by stopping British merchant ships at sea and forcibly removing some of the crew to serve as British sailors. Under such conditions only extreme deterrent measures could control men so "enlisted."
- In our day such reprehensible measures are unthinkable. Our Uniform Code of Military Justice is designed as much to protect military men as it is to control them. Men in uniform today, ashore, afloat or in the air, respond more to leadership, as opposed to the deterrence of disciplinary measures.

  But even the finest leaders, to be effective, must have behind them the availability of command action for deterrence when necessary.
- All Americans can take pride in the fact that our armed forces operate less by deterrence and more by leadership than do those of any other nation. But this does not change the fact of life that deterrence to insure control will always be with us.

CHAPTER 30
Ask Questions, Make Wiser Decisions

In July, 1970, an unfortunate decision by a U.S. Coast Guard ordered the captain of the *Vigilant* to return an iron curtain defector to his Russian ship. In fact, the Russians were allowed to board the *Vigilant* and take a Lithuanian national back by force. There were reasons for the decision. There are always reasons for and against any unwise decision, or a decision would not be necessary.

This poses a question: are there guidelines for decision-making which, if recognized, might have prevented this error in judgment? In my opinion, yes.

Little incidents illustrate basic principles—like the decision that faced me in 1949 as chief of staff of the 11th Airborne Division at Ft. Campbell, Ky. The day before Thanksgiving a messenger arrived at my office, carrying a large and beautifully roasted turkey on a tray. This was a present from the head of a commercial firm in a nearby town who did business with the post. The decision to accept or reject the turkey posed no problem.

"Take the turkey back to Mr. So-and-so, with my thanks. And tell him Army regulations prohibit my accepting gifts from business firms."

Then, turning to my chief clerk I said, "Take him out the way he came in, so everybody who saw that turkey come in sees it go out."

That was a "policy decision," because regulations were explicit that no gifts be accepted from anyone doing business with the military anywhere. The fine old gentleman intended that turkey as a personal, friendly gesture, and sending it back hurt his feelings. But that could not be helped.

The *Vigilant* case violated this "policy principle," because the United States has a long-established policy of granting political asylum to defectors from iron curtain countries. Two of the most famous are ballet star Rudolph Nureyev, and Josef Stalin's daughter, Svetlana.

Now for another key principle violated in the *Vigilant* affair: it not only was against established policy, and a decision that could have been delayed until instructions were received from Washington, but once made, *it could not be reversed by higher authority.* This angle alone, if considered at the time, should have prevented that unfortunate error in judgment.

One of my most valuable lessons in decision-making came as an infantry lieutenant at the old Cavalry School. We averaged half of each day in the saddle, and were assigned three horses: a jumper, a schooled horse, and a remount to train. The trained jumpers and schooled horses were rotated periodically, but you kept the remount for the full nine-month course. So choosing that remount was an important decision.

I picked a big gelding named Pegasus, who had one walleye that had a tendency to roll wildly. But he seemed placid, had the nice sloping pasterns of an easy-gaited mount—with marks on his back that indicated he had been ridden before. That turned out to be true. But it soon developed that he was scared of everything that moved suddenly, like a piece of paper or windblown leaf. Also, he was jumpy about noises.

We will skip over my troubles riding that kooky horse for eight months to my last ride on Pegasus. On this day the class rode the pistol and saber course on their remounts. As expected, when I fired my first shot Pegasus took off cross-country—with the reins in my left hand, the loaded and cocked automatic at "raise pistol" in my right.

To drop it or holster it was to risk being shot, so I just went along for the ride until he pooped out. Then I put the safety on, holstered the pistol and galloped my charger back to the range, both of us lathered and sweated up.

The instructor ruled no more firing off Pegasus, so we started on the saber course. The saber in my hand scared the oats out of him, too. As I speared the first dummy near a shallow ditch obstacle, he ran blindly into the ditch, making no effort to jump. So down we went. After nearly rolling on me, Pegasus got up lame, while I just had the wind knocked out of me.

That ended eight months of riding a psycho horse that took frequent frantic counsel of his fears, so only luck saved me from injury—and all because I did not follow two basic principles of decision-making:

• Failure to ask for expert advice. Any cavalryman in the class would have warned me away from that walleyed gelding.

- Basing my decision on the wrong reason: trying to make it easy on myself instead of picking the best horse available. Any time you let a personal factor distort your thinking you risk riding for a fall.

Another angle to decision-making comes up when you need a decision from somebody else. I was chief of staff, U.S. Continental Army Command, in 1959 when the World Championships in the modern pentathlon (riding, fencing, pistol-shooting, swimming and running) were held at Hershey, Pa. The civilian chairman of the organizing committee there called me one day to request that the Army provide motor transportation for the athletes.

He had called Second Army at Ft. Meade, Md., and the chief of staff there had turned him down because they had no money to provide gasoline for that purpose. He then called the Office of the Secretary of Defense and, after the request was staffed, received the answer that it was illegal to provide transportation because Congress had not appropriated gasoline money for such use.

To me this decision was vacuumized thinking, for athletes from many nations would be there, most of them young army officers. Not only that, but experience over 47 years showed that many of these men would rise to influential positions in their countries. Thus, it was a wonderful public relations opportunity at the international level—and the money required was peanuts. So I took the matter to my four-star commanding general.

He called the Army vice chief of staff in the Pentagon. After checking, the vice chief's answer was that because a decision had been made on a legal basis, at secretary of defense level, the Army could do nothing about it.

This brings out an interesting angle: when the organizing committee chairman got turned down by Second Army, if he had called CONARC next, I would have taken it to my CG and we would have found the gasoline some way. But by jumping to the top, and getting a refusal in a legal vacuum, it was not possible for lower headquarters to reverse the decision.

The principle involved is obvious: it is not only proper procedure in requesting a decision to start at the lowest level of authority, it also increases your chances of getting the decision you want as you go up the ladder of authority.

From these case histories we see three general types of decisions:
- Those that the time element requires be made at once.
- Those that can be delayed, thus providing the opportunity to get more facts—or consult higher headquarters.

- Those where, when all the facts are properly researched and evaluated, the proper decision is obvious.

Of course, nothing can replace judgment in decision-making, but an organized way of thinking will help. One method is revealed by the smart little dog who met a porcupine for the first time. Since he was a smart little dog, he did not decide to finish off the 'pine right away but circled around it, barking questions:

"What's that queer-looking thing doing here? Should I attack it now, or watch it for a while?"

"Is any regulation involved?"

"Should I ask somebody for advice who knows more about such spiky-looking animals?"

"Or maybe go get my master to see if he wants to sic me on it?"

"Will any harm result if I just do nothing?"

So, being a smart little dog, he decided the 'pine was not his problem—and opted to walk away and do nothing about it.

Applying this smart-little-dog method to making decisions is effective in clarifying and evaluating factors involved. Here are some useful questions:

"Is this my decision to make? If in doubt, who else might consider it his problem?"

"Is a regulation, policy or precedent involved? If not, will the decision set a policy-making precedent?"

"Will my decision be irreversible? If so, what steps can be taken to double-check its correctness?"

"Is a time element involved? If so, what is it, and why?"

"Who should be consulted, if anybody? Should I ask for expert advice?" (Not the same thing.)

"If I just hold off and do nothing, will the problem go away?"

"Who is going to be mad if I make decision A? Who will it make happy?" Same for other possible decisions.

"Are there any political aspects? Is money a factor?"

Some comments are:

- There will be a different set of questions for each problem.
- If you have the relevant facts, and ask yourself enough of the right questions, the proper decision will nearly always come clear and sure in your mind.
- Where judgment really counts is in the "toss-up" decisions that

might go either way. For them you need a special quality of perception and prescience. And when results prove your lack of omniscience, it is helpful to have a tough hide, impervious to the arrows from second-guessers.

CHAPTER 31

How is Your Skin? Too Thick or Too Thin?

Shortly before I became deputy commandant, Army, at the Armed Forces Staff College, they asked major military headquarters around the world how our AFSC graduates were doing. The query included this question: "What changes should be made in the college curriculum to help future graduates do better jobs?"

Several replies included this meaningful recommendation: "Teach them how to get along with people."

The higher you go the more complicated is this requirement to get along with others as a catalyst in getting your job done. Among the array of facets, characteristics, personality angles, quirks and mental attributes that go into this is the thickness of your skin. It is widely known that a thick hide, insensitive to criticism and the rights and feelings of others, is a professional handicap; but so is an unduly thin skin, with tender feelings stuck out in all directions to be hurt. Since we are talking about mental skin, each thinking man should control how thick his skin gets or how thin it remains.

"Thinskinitis" involves witless nursing of hurt feelings, sometimes called "sulking in the service"—a self-inflicted wound of the psyche. When I was a company commander, 1st Sgt. Big Jim Redding gave it a simpler name. We were having a quickie stand-up coffee in Sgt. Honest John Smith's kitchen when I noticed a young soldier on KP who had been in the company several months. Pvt. Crusty (we'll call him) looked a bit unhappy.

"What's the matter with Crusty?" I asked Big Jim, who always knew everything that went on in the company. "He's been looking down in the mouth lately."

"Sure he has, captain," and Big Jim chuckled. "He thinks he's leading a hard life because he's got a bad case of 'rabbit ears'—always getting his feelings hurt over nothing. So Stinson (one of our sergeants) has been giving him the needle to work him out of it.

"Yesterday I heard Stinson say, 'Listen, Crusty, instead of thinking about the trouble you're having with me, think of the trouble I'm having with you.' Then Stinson walks off and leaves him to figure that out."

Big Jim took a sip of his coffee, looked over to where Crusty scowled at the spuds he was peeling, and added, "Leave him to Stinson, captain. He's got a gift for curing the rabbit ears of recruits."

As usual, Big Jim was right, for Sgt. Stinson could kid the devil out of his pitchfork and make him like it.

As men grow older they may become more vulnerable to the malady of an overly sensitive epidermis. Sometimes when two of them "don't get along" one has taken offense at some trivial unintended slight, then makes himself "difficult" to work with as a way of "getting even."

Consider this incident from the Pentagon during my tour there after World War II. Perhaps readjusting to peacetime service and learning to wear reading glasses addled my perceptivity. Anyway, I was slow to realize that one senior colonel had developed a distant attitude that made our official dealings more difficult. Finally, I identified the booby trap in our formerly pleasant relations as my new reading glasses, which I usually left on in the hallways and at the stand-up snack bar we patronized. This made me very nearsighted, which suggested the explanation that I had appeared to snub him in the hall or snack bar. Thus it was he who thought *me* distant and unfriendly.

The next time I entered the snack bar the colonel was there, so I took my lunch to the vacant place near him. After putting my sandwich and coffee on the shelf I took off my glasses, held them up and said, "These things are a nuisance, and I keep forgetting to take them off when leaving my office. They make me so nearsighted I can't get a good look at the secretaries in here, much less recognize my friends in the halls. Bifocals make you look middle-aged, but I'll break down and get a pair."

He smiled and said, "What's the matter with looking middle-aged? That's what we are. I've been putting off getting glasses, but guess I'll join you in a pair of bifocals." We were back on friendly terms, and stayed that way.

One reason this facet of human friction seems important to me is that in spite of plebe year at West Point, and long exposure to the tanning effect of life in the Old Army, I was troubled with residual "thinskinitis." Then, while serving as director of instruction at the Armed Forces Information School in 1948, I was permanently cured (well, almost cured).

Anyway, on this day we had a cocktail hour and dinner at the officers' club for our local military-civilian liaison committee. This group of key officers on the post and leading citizens from the town of Carlisle worked together in solving problems between the military and civilian communities.

Early in the liquid refreshment phase of the function I noticed a civilian, some forty years old, standing alone. Since we had never met, I walked over to introduce myself, smiling and extending my hand. But he stared coldly at me, ignoring my out-stretched palm; so at the last second I retrieved my ostracized hand and passed on without saying anything.

With my feelings badly bruised, wondering how I could have offended this man, I went over to the bar. Several old-fashioneds helped me reach the logical conclusion: "Who wants to shake hands with that fellow anyway? Next chance that comes along I'll give him the cold shoulder!" So, feeling better, I had another dose of anti-sulk medicine.

Then dinner was served, and I found my name card directly across from the man who had refused my hand. By this time that anti-sulk elixir was working pretty good. So I now decided, "To hell with you, old buddy, but I'll turn the other cheek anyway."

With that I sat down, looking straight across into his blue eyes, nodded my head and smiled brightly in preparation for announcing my name—and was stopped cold again by his expressionless, unresponsive stare. As I sat silent and confused, racking my memory for some hint to how I had offended him, the man on his right reached over and began cutting his meat for him. Because the gentleman was blind!

That lesson produced this resolve: Never to let any apparent slight make me take needless offense again; anybody who hurts my feelings in the future will have to make a real effort.

Of course, every man has his own memory record of little things that made getting along with others more difficult. Varied personalities will not always follow the same methods in overcoming such obstacles. But the important thing is to be aware of the booby traps, and be alert to avoid them. These comments may be relevant:

- Others coin words, so why can't I? Therefore, I suggest lexicographers include in future dictionaries the word *snope,* along with this definition: *A dope who snubs you because he imagines you've snubbed him.* With that word at our disposal we can then accost any snubber in this way, "Who is the snope—you or me?"

When you hear a soldier or officer criticizing his immediate superior there is a good chance he is a snope—taking offense from orders he has received, when none was intended. Maybe the CO's sharp voice is a personal mannerism, or perhaps he was not feeling well, or maybe he was in a hurry, or nursing hurt feelings over orders from his boss, or maybe he had a fight with the little woman at breakfast, or any number of other things. Sounds silly, but it is serious, too, because I have seen it happen countless times. As Rudyard Kipling said, "be warned by my lot." So take it from a former snope: you're just spitting against the wind.

- In my opinion, many of those who leave military service saying, "I just don't like the Army," are really leaving because they suffer from the hidden malady of "thinskinitis," which can cause them just as much trouble in civilian life as in uniform.

- As proved in the answer from high headquarters around the world to the query from the Armed Forces Staff College, your ability to work in harmony and concert with others is a major factor in professional success. Many things go into this, not the least of which is to periodically look inward and ask yourself, "How is my skin—too thick or too thin?"

CHAPTER 32
No Substitute for Planned Thinking

It was an education to be around my fellow lieutenant, Raymond R. (Robbie) Robbins. Consider this valuable lesson from his Saturday afternoon "home brew" party in Hawaii (circa 1934), at the beach cottage where he and Ruth lived. After handing me a stein of their brew (Prohibition was still alive), Robbie said, "Now watch closely, Redhead, because you are next."

He then invited a young lady to have a seat on the floor for an intelligence test, produced a black block of wood about $10'' \times 10'' \times 15''$ and placed it on the floor near her. Next he took the block apart into nine pieces, which was possible because it had been cut through lengthwise with a band saw in two wavy vertical lines, and also with two similar wavy horizontal saw cuts. After jumbling the pieces in a pile in front of her, he looked at his watch to time her reassembly of the pieces back into a block.

Actually, it turned into a fascinating demonstration of her lack of an organized thought process. She grabbed two of the irregularly shaped pieces of wood, tried to fit them together and failed, tossed them back on the pile; grabbed others in a hit-or-miss manner and continued to get nowhere. So she gave up in confusion.

The woman flunked the test because she had not looked at the problem as a whole, then followed a planned procedure. Yet the solution was simple, once you gave the problem (the block) an analytical look.

There were four corner pieces; four middle pieces with one flat side, and one center piece. Logical thinking called for selecting a place to start, say a corner piece, and placing it on the floor.

Next take a one-flat-side piece, try it against the floor side of the corner piece; if no fit, swap ends, try again: if still no fit, place it aside—*not* back on the pile. And you can continue from there.

140

For the rest of my service I never forgot the lesson: thinking should be an organized planned procedure. Or, stated another way, we should have a mental *standing operating procedure* (SOP). Most people will say, "An SOP for thinking? That is ridiculous." But, in fact, we have specialized mental SOPs for some situations, although not identified that way. Two are the standard paragraphed form for a field order, and the prescribed form for an "estimate of the situation." There are also others.

The specialized mental SOPs—for that is what they are—insure orders and estimates are complete, by *thinking them through* in the same logical sequence each time. Further, this facilitates reading and understanding them. The basic mental SOP principle can be stated like this: for each problem select a place to start, and examine the problem systematically by proceeding through it in a consciously organized and logical sequence.

From my files here is an illustrative hypothetical problem, with a solution by Major Spasmodic, S3 of an infantry regiment in division reserve:

Lieutenant Colonel O'Donnell, division G3, phoned Major Spasmodic this warning order: "Division attacks at 0700 tomorrow, 20 October. Your regiment moves to assembly area vicinity of Foxhole after dark tonight, closing prior to 2400. Officer messenger will bring division field order by 1600 today."

"Yes, sir," Major Spasmodic said, and hung up.

Random thoughts flashed through his mind. Then he glanced briefly at his map and noted the regiment must move approximately two miles to reach Foxhole.

Again Major Spasmodic allowed the problem to come to him mentally in route-step order. "Lieutenant Compere," he called to his assistant S3, "have the draftsman and typist ready for a regimental FO."

"About what time, sir?"

"I don't know yet—tell you later."

Suddenly another thought arrived unbidden. Major Spasmodic seized it, walked over to Major Henry, the S4 and said: "We move to an assembly area near Foxhole tonight, closing before 2400. You better have trucks ready."

"We have trucks for only one battalion. Where and when do you want them?"

"I don't know yet—tell you later."

On a sudden thought Spasmodic reported to the regimental commander, Colonel Hightower. "Well," the colonel said, "what are you going to do?"

"I thought the colonel would issue a field order."

"Hell, yes, I'll issue a field order, but what are you going to do in the meantime? Make notes of what you are going to do, the order in which you are going to do them, and report back to me."

In due time Colonel Hightower got himself another S3. When Lieutenant Colonel O'Donnell phoned a similar warning order to Major Ross, the new S3, there was a difference in how Ross went about things—although he probably did not realize he was using a mental SOP.

After hanging up he reached for pencil and paper, looked at his map closely, then leaned back in his chair to think. First, he ran quickly through the problem mentally to be sure he understood just what he was getting ready to do. His summary ran like this:

It's now 1430—Div FO via Ln O by 1600

Regt O required—CO could dictate by 1700

Trs move after dark—probably by marching, as distance short and we have few Trks

Send someone to check route and assembly areas, and notify all staff Os

Tell CO of situation, request decisions on which to base plans

Next, after writing down a few more notes, Major Ross reported to Colonel Hightower: "Colonel, division telephoned this warning order," and he repeated it. He then asked, "Shall I prepare for a Regt. FO about 1700?"

"Yes, I'll dictate the order and you confirm it in writing. Have battalion commanders come in person."

"I recommend, sir, we move by marching, starting at 2000; dark will be at 1925. I can have an oral plan for the move in about 20 minutes."

"All right, Ross. Have warning orders issued."

Back in his office, Ross called in Lieutenant Compere, assistant S3, and Master Sergeant Wheeler, operations sergeant.

"Wheeler," he said, "have your draftsman and stenographer ready at 1630 to put out a field order."

"Compere, telephone the following warning order; write it down: Rgt moves by marching to Foxhole tonight, beginning at 2000; division attacks at 0700 tomorrow. Details later. A Regt FO will be issued orally at Regt command post at 1700 today.

"Have all units send representatives to receive it; battalion commanders come in person. Also notify the staff."

Major Ross then picked up pencil and paper again. He now had his basic decisions and was ready to think the thing out in detail. So he selected as a starting point the time he received the order, and thought through the problem chronologically until the regiment closed in Foxhole, like this:

Received Div warning O at 1430—informed CO
Div FO due at 1600
Decision is move by marching—CO dictates FO at 1700
Wheeler directed to get ready—Compere issuing warning order to units and staff

(These he checked off, as they had been taken care of. Now he started on notes of things to do):

Determine the order of march—select initial point. . . . And he continued to work through the problem in his mind, and make notes of actions to take.

From these notes Major Ross outlined his plans to Colonel Hightower, received his okays, decisions and additional instructions, and added to his checklist to carry out the CO's directives.

When I drafted the above little mental training exercise involving Major Spasmodic and Colonel Hightower (for peace time training), I had already been a division chief of staff and a regimental commander in war, and was just fixing in my mind what I had learned from experience. No matter what scoffers may say about "planned thinking," I believe a mental standing operating procedure (SOP) is practicable, and in those of logical minds is unconsciously followed by them.

There are, of course, a few whose brains resemble "an avocado without a pit," and nothing can be done about them. Then there are those who do not want to be bothered to think—like the overstuffed female figure in the cartoon, looking down at and addressing a similarly overstuffed male figure sprawled in an overstuffed chair. The caption reads: "You never want to do anything we can do together—all you ever do is sit and think!"

Funny—sure, in that context. But there is nothing funny about the results from an absence of good organized thinking in the military service. Two comments are:

- For those of us above the avocado brain level and below the brilliant computer-type mind, I believe experience teaches certain methods of thinking. But anyone who will give deliberate thought to organizing his thinking can facilitate this learning process and evolve an orderly mental procedure to be consciously followed.

- There is not, nor can there ever be, a mechanical substitute for the magic processes of our brain which we call thinking; nor can any system increase the brain capacity of a given individual for the solution of problems. But there very definitely is a mental procedure through which an individual can insure getting the maximum thought results from the brain capacity with which he is endowed.

CHAPTER 33
Little Slips Can Result in Big Troubles

Everybody knows the military parable: "For want of a nail the shoe was lost; for want of a shoe the horse was lost; for want of a horse the rider was lost; for want of a rider the battle was lost—all for the want of a horseshoe nail." We know, too, that the Army no longer uses horses in battle, but the Horseshoe Nail Principle is more important now than ever because there are many more places for weak links, bottlenecks and minor oversights.

In a company a common horseshoe nail situation can result from little things that cause equipment to break down. Soon after I took command of Company D, 19th Infantry, we began firing our old water-cooled Browning machine guns for record on the 1,000-inch range, and one of the guns had a series of stoppages. Our experts checked the little things that might cause this, without success.

"Get Corporal Hardbitten," the first sergeant said.

A medium-size corporal, weather-beaten from long service, walked up to the gun and stared at it a moment. Then in morose silence and with a long-suffering look he sat behind the gun, slapped down the cover, yanked on the belt-feed tab, pulled the bolt handle back a couple of times, and pulled the trigger. The gun fired one round, and stopped.

Whereupon Hardbitten stood up, stepped back a pace and addressed a few carefully chosen exotic words to the gun. Then he stepped forward, gave it a vicious kick—and that fixed whatever was wrong. Whether it was knowing the right words, or the right place to kick, I'm not sure, because when I tried it on another gun the only result was a bruised big toe on my right foot.

Most horseshoe nails are not so nebulous. We had one gun that was scattering its shot groups, which meant lower scores unless we corrected the trouble. Our armorer diagnosed the horseshoe nail, and drove in a metal shim. This thin piece of tin, in just the right place, made a big difference in the scores of all who fired that gun.

The number and diversity of horseshoe nails vary with the area of responsibility. The key idea is to discover the little things and correct them before they cause big troubles. In this case a kick in time (along with the right words) and a tin shim made a lot of difference in our company's qualification record. And your company's weapons qualification record is no small matter when you are a company commander.

Several years later I faced a whole raft of new little things that caused big troubles, for World War II was in full swing and I was a division chief of staff, training in the Australian countryside. Some of our horseshoe-nail emergencies were in the paper war. Like the day our adjutant general reported we were out of stencils for the mimeograph machine, so he could not issue the daily bulletin—not to mention the rest of the river of paper that flows from a division headquarters.

Now *there* is an emergency for you: A general staff in the wilds of Australia, with nothing to do but write poop sheets, yet unable to fire the mimeograph machine. All for want of a few sheets of greenish-blue stencils, because nobody checked on that horseshoe nail ahead of time.

Later, when we staged on Goodenough Island for the Hollandia invasion in New Guinea, the final draft of the amphibious order for our task force hit my desk. By this time experience had transmuted me from an average nice guy into the established head administrative SOB and chief nitpicker. So I didn't just give the draft a quick once-over-lightly, but looked for embryo problems, and noticed that the rear echelon strength to be left back from our force of about 33,000 was listed as 159. Recheck revealed the typist had left off the last digit: the figure should have been 1,590.

That was a real small thing, just a typographical error. But our rear echelon would not have thought it such a small thing if, later, their chow resupply was based on a strength of 159. Another interesting point came out of this. When the final mimeographed order was ready for field distribution it was discovered that that last digit was still missing. So the page had to be run over.

This brings out a command and staff lesson. When mistakes are found it is not enough to order corrective action; it is doubly important to recheck the correction, because the cussedness inherent in paperwork endows mistakes with a mystic capacity for survival.

Four years after World War II, I was back in the chief of staff business, with the 11th Airborne Division at Fort Campbell, Ky. We were preparing for a large airborne maneuver (Exercise Swarmer) when an alert staff officer spotted a horseshoe nail of embarrassing potential: the requisitioned tiedown chains to anchor heavy drop equipment in the airplanes had not arrived. A telephone call revealed the chains were still in a depot in Chicago. But the depot's offer to ship them by the next train was declined, because time was too short to risk another administrative misadventure.

The division commander was informed, and we dispatched a truck with two selected drivers to get the chains, accompanied by a back-up truck also with two drivers. We did not leave it to somebody else to fix a horseshoe nail which could produce major complications for us. The time factor is often critical in horseshoe nail situations, thus my call for out-of-routine expediting measures.

Not only in paperwork, field exercise and combat operations do little things create big results. Perhaps most frustrating is the personal kind that you have taken action to avoid—and it happens anyway; like the time, as deputy commandant (Army) at the Armed Forces Staff College, when I was invited to a Rotary Club luncheon in Norfolk. This was a civilian-military liaison occasion to foster mutual goodwill.

It was official business so I went in an official car, but stopped a block and a half from the congested traffic area of the downtown hotel where the luncheon was held. I gave the driver money for lunch and to feed the meter in the nearby parking area, and told him I would meet him back at the car in about an hour and a half.

When luncheon was over, there was quite a traffic jam at the hotel entrance, as anticipated. Then, while still congratulating myself on avoiding this, I saw that much of the trouble stemmed from an official car parked right smack in front of the hotel entrance—my car. The driver, standing alertly by, saw me and promptly uncovered the star plates and opened the door for me.

There was no escape, so I crossed the sidewalk under the hostile stare of the harassed policeman in the street, the exasperated glare of the hotel doorman, and what can only be described as taxpayers' displeasure in the expressions of those on the crowded sidewalk and in the backed-up cars impeded by my parked vehicle. Thus, whatever civilian-military goodwill my presence may have engendered at the luncheon was largely negated, for many of those at the luncheon were among disapproving witnesses to the manner of my departure.

I couldn't fault the driver, who was showing initiative in doing what he thought was right. My own minor oversight caused my big red face because I had failed to tell him, explicitly, not to try to pick me up at the hotel door in the noon hour traffic rush.

It is impossible to imagine, much less categorize, all horseshoe nail situations. But these comments seem relevant:

- Major issues and large obstacles seldom if ever take you by surprise. The pestiferous, unanticipated, little things are what often cut you down from ambush.
- There is no way to avoid every small booby trap, but advance thinking as a matter of calculated habit helps. The rider would have found that loose nail had he regularly inspected his horse's feet—standard preventive maintenance procedure in all good horse outfits.
- The basic idea was expressed this way by Roman author Publius (or Publilius) Syrus, more than 2,000 years ago: "He is free from danger who, even when he is safe, is on his guard." In other words, we are not likely to discover horseshoe nail situations in advance unless we look for them.
- If some perverse little thing gums up the works under Murphy's Law ("When anything can go wrong, it will"), then it is well to remember what my hippie philosopher friend, Hairy Harry, says: "Cool it, man. All us cats get a flea now and then."

CHAPTER 34
Stop, Think Before You Answer

I was given an old lesson in a new way on a recent visit to Chicago for a weekend with some World War II friends. Among those present was my boon bottle dialectician from past reunions, Spike O'Donnell. But it was Ken Ross who reinstructed me in a basic fact of life.

"Red," he said, "have you been reading all this newspaper publicity about birth control?"

When I nodded he continued, "There is nothing new about it because the Carthaginians solved that problem more than 2,000 years ago. They just ground up the roots of banyan trees and compressed the grindings into pills for one-a-day use."

As Spike handed me another refill, I asked, "Did that really work?"

"Well," Ken said, "you haven't seen many Carthaginians around lately, have you?"

So there it was again, that old fact of life that has been made clear in so many varied situations over the years: when asked a question or when asking one, "take time to think."

As a company commander, I wrote a little treatise in *The Infantry Journal*, (Nov.-Dec. 1939) on this subject:

The Pause That Clarifies

There is no doubt that a question instantly answered conveys a favorable impression of alertness and efficiency—sometimes. But all too often the opposite is true when a snap reply must be corrected, amended or amplified.

Seconds seem to drag when we are asked a question and we feel that to pause is to appear vacillating, ignorant or both. But there is no need for such reactions. A pause to think before answering or asking a question adds the force of better phrasing, as well as insuring more well-considered thought.

A good illustration of this principle often occurs when the officer of the day inspects sentries on guard. "What is the seventh general order?" he asks the sentry, and receives a snap answer like this:

"To give the alarm—er—no sir, that is the eighth. To talk to no one except in line of duty." (General orders may be modernized now, but that is the way they were then.)

A momentary pause enables the sentry to begin the correct order with assurance and finality far more impressive than the nervous tension of a reflex answer, even when the reflex is correct.

The pause for thought is normally barely perceptible, but sometimes may be prolonged. In such cases you lose no stature by saying, "I have not thought about that, sir, and would like to consider it a moment."

Or maybe you will be in your orderly room and a soldier comes in with a problem which requires a decision. It is a temptation to settle the issue with quick finality—which may later cause trouble. Your soldier thinks none the less of you if you say:

"Well, Jones, you come back in an hour after I've had time to think about that for a while."

If the situation affects him personally he will appreciate your giving the problem full consideration. If it affects the company as a whole, rest assured your men respect their "old man" more when he pauses to figure out all the angles. They have had to countermarch and to reset tent pins, they have been late and ahead of time and undergone many petty annoyances because a decision was made quickly with much military promptness—but with little thought.

So take time to think, not too much and not too little. Use the pause that clarifies.

(signed) Company Commander.

Many and varied experiences over the years since I wrote the above have proved this "pause principle" is by no means limited to company level matters. And not just in replying to or asking questions, but in solving problems posed by circumstances. The wide-ranging value of consulting the computer with which each of us is equipped was demonstrated in the solution of an esoteric dilemma that faced me in 1951.

A situation developed in Iceland that resulted in the decision to fly in a U.S. task force of Army, Navy and Air Force elements to prevent a communist takeover there. I was chief of staff of this emergency force which remained at Keflavik as a unified command.

It takes some doing to get a new unified staff to pull together in harness and harmony. The technical complexities are made no simpler by the necessity of getting officers—strangers to each other and from different training backgrounds—to compromise and cooperate.

Of course, interspersed with weighty problems there were little personality bumps in the unified road. One of these for me was a personal relations problem with the deputy commander, Navy. His job did not require much effort, but mine needed "overtime" at night.

So when he wanted to play chess and pass the evenings with a little bottled balm, I gave some thought to avoiding this without giving him the brush-off. When we played at his place I had more liquids than I wanted, which sabotaged my staff homework. It was the same way when he came to see me—until I figured out my curveball martini gambit.

As host in my place one night I encouraged his consumption of martinis, but made my own with water and a teaspoon of sherry to give it a martini color. This brought the evening chess game to an early close and he ended up with a definite hangover the next day. But I was bright-eyed and bushy-tailed, with my staff homework done and Army-Navy relations intact. And from that day on he left me, chess and martinis, pretty much alone.

Whether he suspected my finesse or just decided I was too fast company for him, I'm not sure. But either way, if he reads this I hope he will forgive my duplicity since it was done only after due thought that the means was justified by the end: to foster better interservice relations and still maintain a high level of unified staff work.

One of many and diverse situations where it is wise to pause and give your built-in computer a chance to function is during phone conversations. Phone talks are uniquely vulnerable to a special type of booby trap: misunderstandings.

That is why it is good operating procedure to pause after hanging up the phone and review what has been said to be sure you have got the word. Unfortunately, I sometimes failed to do that; consider this occasion when I was chief of staff in headquarters, U.S. Continental Army Command at Fort Monroe, Va.

As usual I was embroiled in the distracting minutiae that so often bedevil chiefs of staff. Perhaps this was the day we had a special parking area reserved for some visiting congressmen, but one of our conscientious MPs ticketed their cars. Anyway, I answered a phone call from the Pentagon, took the message, hung up, and failed to pause and consider the implications.

There was nothing complicated about that message. A lieutenant colonel just told me that the next time I was in Washington the secretary of the Army wanted to see me. So about ten days later when I was in the Pentagon I called the secretary's office and, after a brief delay, was informed the secretary no longer wanted to see me.

I did see the secretary once later, but not close enough to speak to him. However, his cold, flat look said plainer than words, "Just who do you think you are to wait ten days before deigning to comply with my request to see you?"

Of course, I had complied literally with the secretary's request (if it was relayed to me correctly). But that must remain one of my most, if not the most unenlightened performance of my career. If I had stopped to think after hanging up the phone, my next consideration would have been to figure out what business I could have that required me to be in the Pentagon the following day.

Why did he want to see me? St. Peter will have to ask him because I do not know.

Three comments are:

- By their very nature, personnel actions deal with the lives of others. In my view, there is no more important place to pause and think out personnel problems than at company level, where you deal directly with the individuals involved.
- Nothing can replace the calculated pause to think in the out-of-routine situations of military life, at all levels. Often, only a few seconds are required, but sometimes hours or even days may be needed.
- The greatest enemy to clear thinking is to surrender to the monomania of chasing too many inconsequential details. What may begin as "dedicated devotion to duty" can degenerate into the stupidity of failing to pause long enough to distinguish between what needs to be done without delay and what can be put off for ten days.

CHAPTER 35
Loneliness Is Part of the Job

When the mail was delivered one day to the newly created Iceland Defense Force (circa 1951; no dependents), there was no letter for the chief of staff. But the chief's lonely disappointment was not evident (he hoped) to the fine young captain who now appeared—smiling, because he had received a letter from his wife. After completing his business with me, for I was the chief of staff, the young captain said:

"Colonel, I've just read a letter from my wife, and I have got to share it with somebody." Then he told me.

When he received emergency orders for overseas (destination unknown, without family), he signed papers to have most of his pay delivered to his wife. Then stationed in Iceland he had found himself a little short, so wrote her, "Need a little money, honey . . . please send $25 for cigars, liquor and stuff."

Her reply was to the effect, "Here is $15 for cigars and liquor; I don't think you need any stuff while you're up there."

We shared a laugh over that one, but lonely months ahead remained for us. Such separations are an inherent hazard of military life, always have been, and always will be.

By chance recently, I received a unique document, from more than 100 years ago, that limns this problem in a special period of American history: during the Indian Wars, on our Western plains in the buffalo era. This was the diary-letter of S. B. M. Young during a two-week scout in September and October, 1873. A distinguished veteran of the Civil War, he was destined thirty years later to become Lt. Gen. Samuel Baldwin Marks Young, first chief of staff, U.S. Army. Here are pertinent condensed extracts:

Sept. 29, 1873: We arrived at Camp Supply the 21st . . . making the march across the Staked Plain, striking the head of White River, which is the north fork of the Brazos River, thence north, crossing the tributaries of the Red River, then across the Canadian River on the 100th parallel of latitude, next north by east to Camp Supply, having marched a measured distance of 532 miles. . . .

We marched out of Camp Supply this A.M., west on the south side of Bear Creek, camping after 17 miles . . . grass good, wood and water abundant.

Sept. 30: Marched 18 miles today; camped on the Beaver at the mouth of Kiowa Medicine Lodge Creek. Mr. Pullman killed a buffalo, another killed by myself . . . plenty of fresh meat and all comparatively happy . . . It seems very long since I heard from my own sweetheart and lovely little darlings. God bless and keep them.

Oct. 1: I have been constantly thinking of my dear good wife all day . . . how lonely she must be. Poor darling, the paths of her life are not strewn with flowers. May the good Lord bless and comfort her and give her strength in the great work of training our dear little ones in the way they should go.

We are camped again on the Beaver; plenty of water and wood, grass poor, duck, geese, antelope, and buffalo plenty. Distance marched nine miles, road sandy in places . . . crossed the Beaver three times, heavy work with axes, picks, spades and shovels. Quicksand bad, mules tired, drivers vexed . . . and I not as pleasant as my wont. . . .

Oct. 2: The guide knows nothing of the country . . . of no use to me, except to butcher buffalo and antelope and spin me old and uncertain yarns. Have been suffering from rheumatism all day . . . would give anything to be with my darling wife and children tonight.

Oct. 3: I think a mean mule is the most provoking animal that wears a harness. . . .

My health improved . . . killed one buffalo, two prairie chickens and six ducks today—the chickens broiled for supper. Moon almost full . . . I pray God bless and comfort my wife and children. To be separated from them so much seems my destiny; perhaps it will change. I love them dearer than life. . . .

Oct. 4: Look at the map of Indian Territory on the 101st parallel west of Greenwich, 37 minutes north of the 36th latitude and see the spot where your absent husband is camped . . . I shot a buffalo, 22 ducks, a plover and four snipe; we will have a nice Sunday dinner tomorrow.

Old Frank DeLisle, my guide (who knows nothing about the country), is spinning me one of his invincible yarns. Accordingly, I commence to go to sleep . . . Goodnight, my love, Maggie dear. . . .

Oct. 5: We must find wood today. Perhaps you ask, "How do you cook without wood?"

Nature makes good provision for such emergencies. The buffalo provide fuel; we find their dried droppings in abundance (called "buffalo chips"), though not good in rainy weather. One morning we had to march 16 miles for breakfast.

We have eaten buffalo meat cooked with fuel furnished by buffalo, been warmed by fire from fuel provided by buffalo, slept on robes from skin that encloses the meat that is cooked by the fuel that is furnished by the buffalo. In addition, I have enjoyed dangerous and exciting sport in the chase after a wounded bull . . . saw between seven and ten thousand buffalo today. . . .

We have a beautiful camp on the Pala-dura; plenty of driftwood, but grass is shorn off by bison, and our animals fare poorly. Unless we find great improvement in grass soon we may possibly arrive at Bascom on foot. . . .

Oct. 6: My dear one, marched 20 miles . . . good roads for wagons, except two deep gulches. Many buffalo in sight; hundreds of carcasses merely stripped of hides. It is a gross outrage that ought to be prevented. . . .

My heart yearns for my darling wife. Sometimes I feel I must fly to meet you, then a still small voice whispers, "Patience," and I think, surely, if she can have patience to endure I must do the same. I know 'tis not your wish that I resign, and I do not take it into contemplation. . . .

Oct. 8: More buffalo in sight than I've ever seen; many say we passed at least a million today. I *do say* with confidence that I saw, with the naked eye from a slight eminence, over a level plain, *50,000* buffalo . . . in looking with my field glass I could see nothing but buffalo, and the sight was the same during 20 miles of march. The country could not be shorn so clean of grass with the best lawn mower made. . . .

Not a shot fired today. I have made it a rule, strictly observed, not to kill game except when we need it . . . God bless and protect my beloved wife and children. . . .

Oct. 10: In sight of "Canon Bonito" I saw many animals of different colors, deployment made of the entire force at the trot. It was a large party of Mexicans (50) from Las Vegas down jerking buffalo meat. We succeeded in giving them fight. . . .

Very tired tonight . . . pleasant evening, plenty wood, large fire, tobac smokem, heap talkem, soon sleepem. . . .

Oct. 12: Ten years ago today I received a bullet through the right elbow joint when in command of two squadrons of my regiment in the Battle of Sulphur Springs. Many friends have gone since. . . .

I always send you the most beautiful of everything within my power to obtain. The most beautiful of all things is pure unselfish love, and that I send every day. . . .

We are camped at Red River Springs, 35 miles from Bascom.

Oct. 14: Last night the boyish wish came to me to be in Cleveland . . . wondering what you and the little darlings would say to see Papa walking in just as you were having evening prayers. How you would all run to greet me and climb on me and kiss and overwhelm me with love. . . .

I intend to lay abed for at *least* 48 hours after arriving at Bascom tomorrow. As mail will leave there following my arrival, I shall send this in lieu of a letter. After reading such portions as you find interesting, amusing and entertaining, you might give it to Edith and Burton to manufacture lamplighters. . . .

Now I must close, and may our Heavenly Father's blessing be with you always.

Your fond husband,
S. B. M. Young

If the above words of a great soldier fail to make the problem clear, nothing I can add will. These comments seem pertinent:

- It takes a mix of qualities to make a good soldier, but high on the list is toughness of character with the emotional strength to endure separation from loved ones. This is over and above military skills, training and battle courage.
- When some young soldiers face this test for the first time they are

taken unawares by the intensity of the problem—and leave the service (often to their later regret). As the diary entry of 6 October 1873 by Gen. Young reveals, he faced this problem, and was sustained by the knowledge that his wife could meet the challenge and shared it with him.

• The obvious sequel to the preceding comment is this: before you make military service your career, you must first decide you can meet the challenges involved. Similarly, in all fairness, you should face the issue squarely with the young lady you ask to enlist with you for the duration.

You both can meet the loneliness of separation better (when the time comes) if you have anticipated the test from the beginning. The right Army wife will provide the same intangible support for you that our first chief of staff received in his day.

CHAPTER 36
Many Athletes Make Fine Soldiers

In 1921, as a new plebe at West Point, I walked into the foyer of the cadet gymnasium and looked around. In front of me was a stone archway leading to the main gym floor, with bronze letters set into the gray brick wall over the arch:

> Upon the fields of friendly strife
> Are sown the seeds
> That, upon other fields, on other days
> Will bear the fruits of victory.

Those words were composed by our superintendent, Brig. Gen. Douglas MacArthur, and have become nationally known. With his extensive and spectacular combat service in World War I he had observed that, other things being equal, athletes were the best soldiers. That is why as superintendent he initiated the intramural athletics in which all cadets are required to participate in a broadly organized program. If General of the Army MacArthur were alive today I am sure he would be interested in the following case histories.

Not long ago it was my privilege to talk with one of the Army's great combat commanders, retired Maj. Gen. Ernest N. ("Old Gravel Voice") Harmon, (DSC-3 DSM-2 SS-3 LM-BSM-PH). A veteran of World War I, he was a famous division commander in World War II, promoted in combat to corps commander.

I commented on the fact that he, like Gen. George S. Patton Jr., had been a member of the U.S. Olympic team in the modern pentathlon (cross-country run, free-style swim, dueling-sword fencing, steeplechase ride, pistol shoot). He was also a member of the West Point football team, and middle-weight boxing champion. So I observed that his career reinforced in my mind the validity of those words over the archway in the cadet gymnasium.

"You know, Newman," he said, "here is an interesting fact. When I was a student in the 1934 class of the Army War College in Washington, I played in a softball game there. I do not remember the outfielders of my team, but I do other members and their final military rank in the service, besides myself . . ." and he gave me this line-up and their eventual grades:

Catcher: Ernest N. Harmon (Maj. Gen., division and corps commander); first base: Vernon E. Prichard (Maj. Gen., armored division commander); second base: J. Lawton Collins (Gen., Army chief of staff); shortstop: William F. Halsey Jr. (Fleet Adm., five stars); third base: Dawson Olmstead (Maj. Gen., chief signal officer); pitcher: Omar N. Bradley (Gen. of the Army, Army chief of staff and chairman of the Joint Chiefs of Staff); umpire: Jonathan M. Wainwright (Gen., Medal of Honor).

This flashback to more than 40 years ago is an amazing confirmation of Gen. MacArthur's thesis, as stated in those bronze letters on the gymnasium wall. My own experience and observations have time and again proved its validity. From many possible empirical illustrations, here are two of particular interest.

In another area of the cadet gymnasium, after I walked under that stone arch, pictures of past Army football teams hung on the wall. This included the undefeated team of 1914 (Gen. of the Army Dwight D. Eisenhower's class), and some of those in that picture are now world-famous.

To verify my memory, and to complete the record, I wrote to West Point and requested the names of those on that team. It has thus been possible to check those names with their later military careers, as recorded in the 1974 *Register of Graduates of the U.S. Military Academy.* Of the 28 names listed, 10 did not complete a full military career. Of those 10, one was killed in an air crash, one retired disabled, and the remaining 8 left the Army in the early 1920s for civilian life in the eclipse of the military that followed "the war to end all wars."

It is not possible to go into details of special cases, but here is the box score, with the highest grade reached by those remaining 18 members of that great team who went all the way with the Army:

- *Class of 1915:* Omar N. Bradley, Gen. of the Army; Dwight D. Eisenhower, Gen. of the Army; Hubert R. Harmon, Lt. Gen.; Walter W. Hess, Brig. Gen.; Leland S. Hobbs, Maj. Gen.; Thomas

B. Larkin, Lt. Gen.; Vernon E. Prichard, Maj. Gen.; James A. Van Fleet, Gen.; Roscoe B. Woodruff, Maj.Gen.
- *Class of 1916:* John F. Goodman, Brig. Gen.; William M. Hoge, Gen.; Hugh Mitchell, Col.; Robert R. Neyland, Brig. Gen.; Joseph J. O'Hare, Brig. Gen.; Alexander M. Weyand, Col.
- *April Class of 1917:* William O. Butler, Maj. Gen.; Elbert L. Ford, Maj. Gen.
- *August Class of 1917:* Edward W. Timberlake, Brig. Gen.

As the mathematics books used to say: QED (which was to be demonstrated).

Sidelights to the above include the fact that Gen. of the Army Eisenhower was not a player on that great 1914 team. However, he made his "A" in his second year, before a serious knee injury ended his playing career. But he continued as an assistant coach for what was then called the "Cullum Hall Squad." So in my view, for the purposes of this inquiry, his name belongs here with his class.

General Hoge is another special case. He played in four games in 1914, starting two of them. One of those he started was the Notre Dame game, in which he played all periods—there were no offensive and defensive teams at that time. Injury then cut short his playing, but he won his "A" the following year.

Brig. Gen. Neyland had it both ways. He left the Army in 1936 to coach the University of Tennessee football team, then came back during World War II and won his star in the China-Burma-India Theater.

One more sidelight to the military careers of that championship 1914 team is the remarkable battle records of the two four-star generals. This is reflected in their decorations, as listed in the *Register of Graduates,* covering combat service in three wars (World War I, World War II, Korea). They are Gen. James A. Van Fleet (DSC-3 DSM-3 SS-3 LM-3 BSM-3 PH), and Gen. William M. Hoge (DSC-3 DSM-3 SS-LM-BSM-PH). Those Purple Hearts are what the legal eagles call incontrovertible evidence.

At Schofield Barracks in Hawaii, in early 1941, some young lieutenants decided to organize a basketball team to play in the civilian league in Honolulu. They called themselves the Mainland Collegians, soon decided they needed a coach, and recruited me (then a captain) for the job.

We had a fine team. I still have and prize the cup they won, but that is not the point. So, once again, we will look at the military careers which followed:

Forward: Charles R. (Monk) Meyer (DSC-2 SS-2 LM-2 BSM-2 PH); forward: Jesse Meachem (DSC posthumous-PH); center: Howard D. Balliet (BSM); guard: Thomas E. (Jock) Clifford (2 DSC, second posthumous-SS-LM-BSM-PH); guard: name not remembered; Hawaii National Guard on active duty, career unknown.

Another lieutenant with great drive and energy came out for but did not make that playing five. He later had brilliant combat service in World War II, Korea and Vietnam, and climaxed his career as Army chief of staff: Gen. William C. Westmoreland.

Only one officer from Schofield Barracks came down to see our games in Honolulu. He was Lt. Henry A. Mucci, later selected to command the task force that liberated the POWs at Cabanatuan. His World War II record reads: DSC-SS-LM-2 BSM-PH.

Finally, here are two footnotes to history. The first is that Gen. of the Army George C. Marshall was an athlete at Virginia Military Institute, an outstanding member of the football team. As Army chief of staff during World War II he once said: "I want an officer for a secret and dangerous mission. I want a West Point football player." A bronze plaque on a large granite rock now memorializes this at the U.S. Military Academy. It is located just north of the northeast corner of Michie Stadium, where cadets of the Corps can see it on the way to games.

Three comments are:

- The incidents recounted above are not mere isolated oddities. For example, the "Big Five" basketball team on my first post (Fort Benning, Ga., 1926) consisted of two enlisted soldiers and three officers. The three officers are now retired generals. Jimmy the Greek, the Las Vegas betting analyst, will tell you that does not square with the unassisted law of averages.

- Of course, being an athlete does not insure military success, as some athletes make poor soldiers. Conversely, it is not necessary to be an athlete to excel as a soldier, but it helps—especially in combat.

- An athlete (whether or not he goes to college anywhere) is a self-starter with a sound mind in a healthy body. He copes with the necessity to make quick decisions in physical action, with the stamina to endure and the self-confidence to make the most of his abilities. These are among the key qualities required for success as a soldier and leader—especially in battle.

CHAPTER 37
Responsibility Cannot be Delegated

In the "Letters" department of *ARMY* (October, 1975) Ralph H. Routier suggested I discuss the question of how authority can be delegated—but not responsibility. As the saying goes, "That is a good question, and I'm glad you asked."

The words "authority" and "responsibility," in this context cannot be defined as easily as the old country preacher explained the difference between "knowledge" and "faith" when he said, "Sister Johnson here in the front pew *knows* that is her son—that's knowledge. Brother Johnson *thinks* that is his son—that's faith."

No such simple parable or simile can delineate the functional difference in how authority and responsibility are integrated into command and leadership. One of the best capsule comments on this was made to me by Gen. Henry I. Hodes, then a major general commanding V Corps in Germany when I was assistant division commander, 5th Infantry Division, under him. He said, "When things go right, I pat the lower ranks on the back. When things go wrong, I chew on the top."

It takes a little meditation to relate that to the delegation of authority in contrast to nondelegation of responsibility, but the idea is there. To consider the matter in the light of how the cookie crumbles, not just a recitation of the recipe to bake it, here are several case histories.

In a biography of Gen. George S. Patton Jr., by Maj. Gen. H. Essame of the British Army, he records that when Gen. Dwight Eisenhower relieved Maj. Gen. Lloyd Fredendall from command of II Corps in Africa during World War II, he gave that command to Gen. Patton. Gen. Essame quotes Gen. Eisenhower as giving these instructions to Gen. Patton:

> You must not retain for one instant any man in a responsible posi-

tion when you have become doubtful of his ability to do the job. . . . I will give you the best available replacement or stand by any arrangement you want to make.

He was announcing as a policy the principle stated by Gen. Hodes: "When things go wrong, I chew on the top." The ultimate method of "chewing on the top" is to relieve the commander when things go wrong. He is responsible. But relief should never be a mechanical, automatic procedure, because command and leadership are an art above and beyond set rules.

Authority can and must be delegated, but responsibility in large measure remains above. To exercise this responsibility wisely when things go haywire may take varied forms, such as:

- Issue new and more detailed orders.
- Provide reinforcements.
- Recognize it as the strong enemy situation, not command failure that resulted in the snafu.
- Decide command failure is involved, and relieve the ineffectual commander.
- Decide there was command failure, but adequate corrective measures have been initiated. Further, that drastic action from above would be "Monday morning quarterbacking"—which is in itself a command failure.
- Sometimes the best decision is to accept responsibility for failure of one of your subordinates, thus shielding a fine and able soldier from distorted blame for an understandable misstep. In so doing you may win his loyalty—and the respect of those under him—to a degree you can achieve in no other way. When and under what circumstances? That is where the art comes in.

Most of our service is during peacetime, but this delegation dilemma is omnipresent then, too, in matters large and small.

In May, 1952, when I arrived at Fort Bragg, N.C., as a colonel slated for promotion to assistant division commander of the 82nd Airborne Division, fate was kind. Congress had limited military funds so that all military promotions were frozen, thus I had the good fortune to assume command of the 505th Airborne Infantry temporarily—my third regimental command.

We soon went on the rifle range to fire for record, one battalion at a time. Although I knew little about the battalion commander, I let him get started on the range a couple of hours without breathing down his neck—thus delegating authority and some measure of responsibility, too.

As I prepared to go out to the range, word came for me to report to the division commander. He informed me that things were not going well with my regiment on the range. My reply was that I was giving the battalion commander a chance to get started on his own, and was about to go out there.

His reply was simple and to the point, "You are the regimental commander, colonel."

Both of us were professionals and the only adequate reply was, "Yes, sir." Things had gone wrong so he was "chewing on the top," because it would not have been good command procedure for him to take over on the range. He was exercising his responsibility, and I accepted mine.

On the other hand, if he had found everything fine on the range he could have "patted the lower ranks on the back." One way to do this would be to say to the battalion commander within hearing of others, preferably including one or more enlisted ranks, "Things look well-organized here, and I like what I see. Tell your regimental commander I said so."

This would be saying indirectly, "You are part of my division and I am responsible for what you do, and so is your regimental commander. I delegated authority (but not responsibility) to him to get the job done. He redelegated that authority (but not responsibility) to you, and I like the way you have exercised the authority passed on to you."

That way, command and responsibility channels remain clear and everybody feels good about the whole thing.

There is no better way to get command and leadership principles straight than at company level. Young lieutenants sometimes fail to understand when they say, "Give me a job and leave me alone to do it," that it is not that simple. Their commanders remain responsible. Also, there are certain specialized areas in which authority cannot be delegated. Consider this hypothetical case:

An infantry soldier, after a night on the town, comes back to his room in one of the new modern barracks we now have. He is in an alcoholically pugnacious mood, picks a fight with his roommate and, in the process, smashes the glass out of the window in their room. This wakes up others of his platoon in nearby rooms and he has to be taken to the hospital for several stitches in a gashed hand.

When the first sergeant reports this to the company commander the next morning, what should the captain do? Handle it himself? Or tell the lieutenant-platoon leader to handle it? Or is the proper solution more complex than just "either-or"?

Here are some factors which may influence his decision on what procedure to follow:

- How long has the captain been in command?
- How much service does the lieutenant have and how long has he been in the company?
- Is there any special consideration that might operate to prevent the captain saying to his lieutenant, "He is in your platoon, so you handle it"?

The answer to this last prevents that unlimited "you handle it" delegation, because the captain cannot delegate his power to take formal disciplinary action. The lieutenant is a platoon leader, not platoon commander. A basic legal question is involved, just as a division commander cannot delegate his authority to convene a general court.

One good course of action is for the company commander to direct the lieutenant to investigate and report the facts, along with his recommendation for formal disciplinary action, if any.

There is no simple answer to how and when and to what degree you can and should delegate authority, but not responsibility. Three comments seem pertinent:

- When you give a man a job you delegate reasonable authority to do it—unless you put him on a leash for some reason, limiting his authority. Circumstances and personalities are involved. Another facet to delegation of authority is for the senior to instruct his junior in some angle he considers important. General Eisenhower did this in cautioning General Patton that he expected him to face up to the onerous task of relieving an ineffective subordinate.
- In the company-level situation there is no cast-iron delegation procedure that fits all cases. If the company commander has been in command for a year, thus having prior knowledge of the culprit as a trouble-making soldier, but the lieutenant reported last week with a brand new commission for his first active-duty assignment, we have a special situation. This includes the possibility of permanent injury to the soldier's hand, which may require a "line of duty" decision.

The captain might well have the pristine lieutenant kibitz his handling of the case, as a means of instructing him in how to manage military discipline.

- To develop and nurture the art of controlling and directing others requires study of our profession, including learning from experience, to arrive at an understanding of how to apply basic principles to specific cases.

No angle of command and leadership is more far-reaching in its implications than an understanding of how, when and to what degree authority (but not responsibility) can and should be delegated.

CHAPTER 38
The Battle of Schofield Barracks

Many of the wars in the past hundred years have started with a surprise attack, so there's no reason to suppose the next won't begin in the same way. My experience, limited to one such attack, was less than heroic. But there are lessons to be learned from my worm's-eye view in a ringside seat on that unhappy occasion.

When the Japanese attacked ships in Pearl Harbor and planes on the airfields of Hawaii, on 7 December 1941, things happened elsewhere too which have been overlooked by history. For example, until you read this, you probably have not heard of the Battle of Schofield Barracks. This is my previously unrecorded after-action report as G2 of the Army division at Schofield.

On that historic Sunday morning I was reading the newspaper in bed, my black cat asleep at my feet. At around five minutes before 0800 there was an explosion, with the feel of a real concussion.

Another explosion. Then a sharp staccato sound, unlike any other in the world. This snarl of sound—unmistakable to the professional ear— was a burst of machine-gun fire as the plane which dropped the first bomb strafed the off-post town of Wahiawa where I lived.

I jumped from bed, scattering cat and bedclothes, and headed for the porch. From there I could see nearby Wheeler Field, and the flaming destruction of the surprise attack.

One of the first bombs hit the oil storage at Wheeler, and a mushrooming cloud of black smoke boiled upward, leaping red flames at its base. An airplane dived toward the hangar line, pulled upward, and another bomb exploded on target. How could it miss? The range was about that a hen uses when she lays an egg. On each wing of the airplane, sharp and clear in the morning sunlight, was a red disk—the Rising Sun of Japan.

Defense plans went into automatic operation, troops dispersing to planned positions. In any battle, especially a first battle, there are curious incidents that stem from psychological shock and chance circumstance.

As a Japanese plane flew low over the barracks area, after laying its eggs on Wheeler, the G3 of our division held a Garand rifle he had just drawn from the supply room. He saw the plane coming, and attempted to push a clip of ammunition into his rifle. But the Garand had recently replaced the bolt-action Springfield, and he had never had one in his hands before.

"Holy cow, Red!" he said later, "here I was an expert rifleman, a semiautomatic rifle in my hands. That guy drifted along, almost dragging his wheels on the barracks roof, just asking for it. My chance to be a hero—and I didn't know how to load that damned rifle!"

There were some irrational reactions too. Like the supply sergeant, with the concussion of exploding bombs quivering in the air, who wanted receipts before he would issue arms and ammunition. Or the young lieutenant who shouted to soldiers setting up a machine gun in the barracks quadrangle, "Don't shoot—or they'll shoot back!"

These minor aberrations live as "war stories." Who wants to hear about men who met the shock of violent surprise with quiet courage and efficiency?

After that first savage blow at Wheeler Field and machine-gunning of Schofield Barracks and Wahiawa, no more air strikes hit us. However, the battle continued to rage at Pearl Harbor, Hickam and other airfields— outside my view and knowledge. These have been duly chronicled.

Concurrently with violent action elsewhere in the battle known as "Pearl Harbor," our division headquarters moved into a concrete barracks at Schofield. In peacetime maneuvers G2 was, at best, tolerated. Now my status changed. What did I know? What was the situation?

There were reports of troops landing by parachutes and gliders. This did not make sense. From what base could they have come? It's still a puzzle to me why half a dozen such messages were received; one of them ended, "This is a confirmed report." But all proved unfounded when checked.

One artillery OP reported a submarine offshore, and called in data to bring fire down on it. The fire was reported "on target;" next, that the submarine had fired back at the shore; finally, that it must have been sunk, because swimmers were in the water.

As nearly as I could determine, what happened was this: The OP
sighted the black back of a large porpoise offshore, erroneously identified it as one of the Japanese midget submarines—but gave correct fire
data. When the sub "fired back," it was one of our artillery shorts landing on shore. "Swimmers in the water" were porpoises, understandably
excited about artillery shells falling around them.

By 2200 that night I didn't believe what nobody said about nuthin'—
when the blacked-out door to headquarters was yanked open by the
middle-aged chief of a technical service staff section. He was fat, white-
faced, out of breath, and gasped, "Gas! Gas!" as he staggered across the
room and scrambled into his gas mask.

Others went for their masks too, but not me. I was immune. Until I
called the post S2 on the phone, but could not hear him clearly.

"Make a noise," I said. "Speak up! I can't hear you."

"I've got my gas mask on," the S2 said.

At this I looked to see if my gas mask was handy, then back-checked
the gas alarm. Without realizing it, I was following correct procedure:
chase every phony report or rumor back to its source and, along the way,
make everyone eat it who passed it forward unchallenged or unchecked.

The gas alarm started at the post dump, still burning as night increased tensions. Because of the black-out, a water hose was turned on it.
Water on the burning refuse generated a peculiar smell, so an officer and
a sergeant went out to investigate. As they walked in the dark the smell
got stronger, and the officer said to the sergeant: "This may be gas, and
we might both be overcome. You stay here. If I don't come back in fifteen
minutes, give the alarm."

So he set out bravely, bending over near the ground now and then in a
sniffing "test for gas." A sentry saw the stooped, sneaky looking figure,
and snapped off a shot at it. The officer dived into a convenient ditch,
stuck his head up, got shot at again—and went back into the ditch to stay.

The sergeant, not knowing this, gave the alarm: "Gas!"—and in
minutes, thousands of men were wearing gas masks.

Many other things could be reported. I doubt if there was ever a night
of so much sweat and so little danger. The Navy had taken the brunt of
the losses, in lives and ships. The Air Force (then Army Air Corps) had
been hit hard too, mostly in planes destroyed on the ground and men
killed in bombed barracks. But Army losses were light.

While the "Battle of Schofield Barracks" sounds like comic opera, remember this: Thousands of fine soldiers who lived through it would never see their homes again—for they had their date with eternity on the bloody battlefields of the Pacific yet to come.

Now, as to lessons learned.

The mental and emotional shock resulting from a sudden and unexpected attack is often far more devastating in effect than the physical damage justifies. That's why one of the principles of war is Surprise.

It's this psychic shock, many times magnified, that we must guard against at national levels in a sudden nuclear attack—if it comes. A grave miscalculation could result from tremendously exaggerated estimates of damage, thus setting the stage for possible premature decision to end the war. One anonymous pundit said it this way: "The side with the poorest communications will win, because the other side's surrender message will arrive first."

For another lesson from Pearl Harbor and the Battle of Schofield, consider this little parable.

Suppose you put a small boy in a room with a cat and a canary, with orders for the boy to watch and be sure the cat doesn't get the canary. Sooner or later the cat—who can wait for the right unwary moment—will get the canary. You can't depend on human vigilance alone, but must give the canary some passive protection. Like a cage.

In Hawaii parked airplanes and ships massed in Pearl Harbor were the canary, while the great Japanese carrier fleet was the cat in the Pacific. In addition to fallible human vigilance we needed adequate passive defense, like underground hangars for our strike-back planes and dispersion for the fleet. Then there would have been no Pearl Harbor, thus no Battle of Schofield Barracks either—because successful surprise attacks fall only on the vulnerable and unprepared.

This raises the multi-billion-dollar question for today's missile and nuclear era: What kinds of passive protection for our strike-back capabilities do we need—how much and where? And do we have them?

CHAPTER 39

Experience: the Best Teacher

Experience has many meanings, but its significance as a way of learning is undisputed. Consider the lessons I learned from the following convoluted experience during World War II.

After our corps-level task force, under Sixth Army, captured the Hollandia airfield complex in New Guinea in 1944, the 24th Infantry Division settled down to prepare for our next operation. As division chief of staff, I received reports on the subsequent amphibious attack on Biak Island, about 300 miles farther west. The word was they were having problems.

When a courier returned from Biak in one of the Marine amphibious planes based in nearby Humbolt Bay, it seemed I might wangle a trip there, too, and learn things of value for our next operation. My division commander said, "Okay—if you can get permission from higher headquarters and the plane ride."

So I called the corps chief of staff who said, "Okay, Red, arrange your own transportation." It was about 8:00 P.M. when I contacted the headquarters of those amphibious planes by phone. Yes, a plane was leaving for Biak that night and there was a seat for me.

Twelve hours after I got that bright idea, my plane landed offshore from Biak and taxied to the beach. There the chief of staff, 41st Infantry Division, was Col. Kenneth S. Sweany, whom I remembered most pleasantly from our days in the same company at the U.S. Military Academy, West Point.

Ken took me in to meet the division commander, Maj. Gen. Horace H. Fuller, who said I could go anywhere and look at anything of interest to me. I also met the assistant division commander, Brig. Gen. Jens Doe.

Then, after a briefing on the combat situation, Colonel Sweany equipped me with a jeep and a driver, said, "You are now on your own," and returned to his pressing duties.

Maybe I had permission from proper authority to be there but, obviously, my presence was on the pushy and brassy side. However, I was never treated anywhere with more professional and personal courtesy.

Biak was densely wooded with tropical forests, virtually uninhabited, but was far more heavily garrisoned and strongly defended than anticipated.

What gave it military significance was its strategic location and Mokmer airfield, constructed near the sea by the Japanese. The battle problem stemmed from the way Mokmer was guarded by the sea on one side (no landing beaches), and on the land side by a crescent of wooded hills of limestone formations, honeycombed with caves, which the Japanese had developed into a fortified area.

American forces landed on Biak's beach nearest Mokmer airfield, and attacked toward Mokmer from two directions. One regiment advanced along a narrow dirt road, with the sea on one side and steep cliffs on the other. The second regimental attack was inland, through the jungle toward those protecting hills.

As my first combat "kibitzing" effort, the jeep driver headed down that narrow seaside road, where I soon saw the stark realities of what was referred to vaguely from hundreds of miles away as a "problem." It sure was.

The primitive road bordered the sea on one side and was hemmed in by wooded limestone cliffs on the other. The principle of fire and movement in a coordinated conventional attack was impossible. It required laborious digging out of dug-in defenders with patience, determination . . . and casualties.

The next day I visited the regiment taking the inland route, over the cliffs from the beachhead and through the jungle toward the hills guarding Mokmer airfield. There was no road, not even a native trail, but this was a "military first"—the drive was led by a bulldozer, traveling on a magnetic azimuth to those cave-studded hills around Mokmer. Also, because of the unique geologic formation of Biak, there was no water source available. Water had to be transported from the beachhead—an unforgettable example of a universal, mandatory combat logistic requirement: drinking water. And, again, the problem was the agonizing slowness of the advance. Our 24th Infantry Division had not faced such frustrating situations in the Hollandia operation.

The third day involved a radically different experience. In anticipation of a possible breakthrough to Mokmer by that bulldozer-led drive, Gen. Doe decided to make a waterborne flanking movement offshore from the cliff-blocked road and approach Mokmer from the sea in a single alligator, that hybrid combination of a hollowed-out tank and a landing craft. The alligator's steel tracks were designed to function like little paddle wheels, which would also provide forward motion in swamps and on land. Its top speed on water was $2^1/_2$ miles an hour.

That looked like a pretty chancy maneuver to me. But I was a new kid on the block who had come to Biak for all the kibitzing experience available, so I asked if there was room aboard for another proponent of Russian roulette (although I did not phrase it that way). There was, and we put to sea at $2^1/_2$ miles an hour.

Once our alligator was offshore, bypassing that regimental attack along the seaside road, we began to feel like a floating bull's-eye; but the Japanese had no heavy weapons on those cliffs sited out to sea, so we rounded the headland to a position offshore from the airfield and turned toward land.

Suddenly, there was a loud detonation overhead where a puff of smoke gradually dissipated. Then another shell burst overhead and our alligator began a slow sleepwalking turn toward where we had come from. Although the Japanese had no heavy guns sited seaward (since there was no landing beach on shore), they might find a way to depress that antiaircraft gun enough to get a direct bead on our alligator, so we eased along in retreat at $2^1/_2$ miles an hour.

Eventually we made it back before dark, and found another amphibious plane had arrived with the chief of staff, Sixth Army, Col. (soon to be Brig. Gen.) George Decker. While I was surprised to see him, judging by the look he gave me he was even more surprised to see me. I realized then that corps had not told Sixth Army my information-gathering staff reconnaissance had been approved. Anyway, there seemed nothing more for me to gain at Biak, and the plane was returning to Hollandia—so I was soon on my way back to the 24th Infantry Division.

Some comments:
- My esoteric Biak venture was a once-in-a-lifetime kibitzing opportunity. However, there are varied peacetime kibitzing opportunities. On your post, or within any major unit, experience need not be limited to normal duties. Any professional activity is an oppor-

tunity to broaden your experience. Illustration: if you are an infantry company commander, contact another branch unit commander in your area and offer to swap instructional visits within your respective units and areas of expertise.

- Biak emphasized the basic principle that when there is trouble up front where the fighting is, do not condemn it *in absentia*—go see. Further, I gained experience of incalculable value to me. To my brief observation at Hollandia of one infantry regiment in combat, Biak added observations of two more regiments in radically different battle situations. This experience was of great help when I commanded the 34th Infantry in the Leyte invasion of the Philippines months later.

- I also obtained some very different experience. Before taking off for Biak, I should have made sure (not just assumed) that both Sixth Army and 41st Infantry Division headquarters were informed—thus giving them the chance to nix the idea. Apparently, corps did not pass on the okay they had given me, and I was too recently removed from company level to understand that protocol is cumulatively more formal and necessary as you advance up the ladder to star and multistar headquarters. Gone were those unfettered days when I could walk from my company over to another, unannounced, and say on arrival, "Is it possible to get a good cup of coffee in this outfit?"

- Some may think the preceding comment overemphasizes the protocol angle, but consider this: nearly fourteen years later, when I was the new chief of staff, U.S. Continental Army Command at Ft. Monroe, Va., word was received from the Pentagon of a periodic General Staff meeting. In accordance with past policy it was expected that I would be present to listen in. Present at that meeting also was the former chief of staff, Sixth Army, who was the new chief of staff, U.S. Army. Immediately following the meeting, he came up to me and said, "What are you doing here?" (His question was a reverberation from Biak.)

- Live and learn: that is how you get experience. Samuel Taylor Coleridge said it best: "This is one of the sad conditions of life, that experience is not transmissible." So I suggest this principle: do not wait placidly for experience to come to you, seek it—but with careful and well-considered judgment.

CHAPTER 40
Assuming Command Means Assuming Leadership

In 1948, under the pseudonym of "Colonel Riposte," I recounted in considerable detail my experience while in command of the 34th Infantry in the World War II invasion of Leyte: what I did and why ("Command Performance," *The Infantry Journal,* July and August 1948).* Looking back to those days again, certain topics invite discussion, like "Assume Command," "Before Combat," and "Command in Combat."

This article considers the requirement to reach out for the minds and hearts of soldiers: to "Assume Leadership."

Much has been said and written about leadership, yet it is still nebulous and intangible. To review my experience may be presumptuous, but I consider it no more than one man's solution to special leadership problems, told in day-to-day incidents and actions.

The initial leadership problem was time, for in three weeks we would jump off from New Guinea for the amphibious assault on Leyte. Thus I had to become acquainted quickly with officers and men—and they with me. Two ideas were the foundation of my thinking:

- First and foremost, a regimental commander needs the respect of his regiment, based on his men's belief that he knows his job and is a competent commander.
- For the regimental commander to gain this respect, it is necessary for officers and men to feel they know him. He must not be an abstraction to them.

Therefore, definite measures were required to bridge the lack of past

---

* Republished in detail in my first book, FOLLOW ME, *The Human Element in Leadership,* Presidio Press, Novato, CA, 1981. Chapters 49 & 50.

contact between me and my regiment. There were three possible ways: writing messages, perhaps addressed to "Soldiers of the 34th Infantry;" assembling battalion-size units and speaking to them (sometimes called "haranguing the troops"); or providing opportunities for officers and men to learn what their new CO was like from their own observations of him.

This last seemed best for me, besides talking to three small selected groups in the chain of command.

My first step was a conference of regimental staff officers and commanders of battalions and separate units.

Next, all officers of the regiment were assembled. After a brief talk, I held a receiving line formation to shake hands with each of them, stopping to exchange a few words now and then.

On the second day all first, technical and master sergeants (not nearly as many then as now!) were called to regimental headquarters. To these fine soldiers—the backbone of enlisted strength in the regiment—I said a few things: That I did not get canned as division chief of staff, but asked for the regiment as the highest honor an officer of my grade could hope for; that I had been a lieutenant for ten years, mostly with troops; as a captain I had been a company commander for five years; to my regret, I had never commanded a battalion, and this was my first regimental command; that I knew and understood the place they held in the regiment and that I was depending on them.

Finally, any one of them could come to headquarters to see me at any time, because I felt a special relation existed between the highest commissioned officer in the regiment and the highest noncommissioned officers of the regiment.

The adjutant was directed to make the following special arrangements:

- A daily commanding officer's orderly to be within call of my office tent from first light in the morning until dismissed by me at night.
- So that duty hours would not be too long, have four orderlies each day—one from each battalion, one from the separate companies.
- Each orderly to come from a different company of the battalion each day.
- These would be picked men, and from them I would select my bodyguard for combat.

This arrangement placed one man from every company in the regiment adjacent to my office tent every four days. They would see me dealing with my staff, checking planning and otherwise getting ready for the operation. And, human nature being what it is, I knew they would tell their companies what the new regimental commander was like. Since I felt I knew my job, I would carry on "business as usual"—there would be no "act." (You can't fool soldiers, anyway.)

This also gave me opportunities to show consideration for the orderlies, like asking the man on duty if he had eaten or knew the arrangements for his meals. My interest was sincere, and I wasn't kidding anybody. In this and other small ways my regiment would learn before we went into combat that the Old Man was interested in the welfare of each soldier.

The executive officer was instructed to organize a refresher school for me—and make no bones about it: a school. As chief of staff I had been out of touch with changes in unit equipment, weapons and organization. Instructors would be staff section chiefs and unit commanders, to review things within their spheres that I as regimental commander should know, according to this schedule:

- Each staff section chief would have one evening after supper to brief me on his job, including status of personnel, equipment and training.
- On six consecutive afternoons unit commanders would set up demonstrations and instruction as follows:

1st Battalion. Parade all weapons (including grenades and small arms) of an infantry battalion. Be prepared to explain their characteristics and capabilities, and let me fire each type.

2nd Battalion. Set up a battalion field command post, complete with signal installations, and explain how it operated.

3rd Battalion. Parade all transportation of the battalion; explain each piece, its uses and limitations.

Headquarters Company. Set up a field regimental CP and show its operation; describe plans for moving—all details necessary for me to understand how my CP functioned.

Cannon Company. Parade weapons and equipment and brief me on what they could do.

Service Company. Parade and explain their stuff.

This refresher training proved invaluable. In addition to bringing me up to date on equipment and operational techniques, the school gave me a chance to size up my regiment and gave them a chance to size me up.

At all hours, including early mornings before breakfast, the new CO spot-checked food being prepared and served. Wherever I went, for whatever purpose, chow lines and kitchens could be looked over in minutes. Always I stopped for a word here and there, and liked the feeling of personal contact with officers and men. Further, they would sense this, thus maybe decide the Old Man knew what was going on.

My jeep driver had orders never to pass a soldier on foot when we had an empty seat. This provided many chances to talk with individual men.

With an amphibious field order to prepare, how was there time for all this moving around? Well, my executive, Lt. Col. Chester A. Dahlen, was a fine soldier who headed an efficient staff. They had my planning directives, so it was easy to check each evening what they had accomplished during the day.

This left my days free to do things my staff could not do for me.

In planning small boat formations I reserved space to land with the leading assault battalion, and told the battalion commander not to announce this—but it was no secret. The news would, I knew, spread by the grapevine.

My uniform and equipment were those of an enlisted man, including a stripped pack containing packaged field rations. It also seemed wise for me and my bodyguard to test-fire our carbines, so word would get around that the regimental commander was not preparing for battle by sharpening colored pencils.

There were other things, too, but these are enough to show the method one man used to influence his impact on his regiment in a rather brief period. When time came to supervise ship loading for the Leyte operation I believed we were ready to enter combat together, because wherever I went there seemed to be a greeting in the eyes of officers and men. Not that flat, expressionless look soldiers have for officers they don't know or whom they dislike.

I don't mean to imply, however, that leadership involves a popularity contest. Nothing could be more wrong! It is vital in "assuming leadership" that at the same time you also "assume command"—establish respect for your authority by demonstrating a capacity to become a revolving SOB when necessary. Which I had managed to do, too.

It was and is my opinion soldiers want a professionally qualified SOB for a combat commander, the kind who has enough iron in his soul to lead them to hell and back—because that's where they're going. But however harsh and steely orders must sometimes be, American soldiers also want to believe their commander feels a continuing personal interest in their welfare. Then, and then only, will men face eternity and capture objectives in a way command orders alone will never motivate them.

Few officers are that rarity, "a born leader." But leadership, like command techniques, can be studied, analyzed and planned. It should not be left to chance or unthinking impulse. Any commander, from squad to army, can raise his command potential by developing carefully considered measures to "assume leadership." This will vary with individuals and with the situation—even for the same man on occasions. There is only one set rule:

Never try to kid the troops with phony acts or empty gestures. They won't work.

CHAPTER 41

The Purple Heart Should Rank Higher Up

It is only fair to say at the outset that I am carrying a torch because the opinions at the end of this discussion are not dispassionate. To put things in perspective we will start with the 2nd Battalion, 34th Infantry, on the second day of the invasion of Leyte in the Philippines during World War II. To be more specific, we'll take an up-front look at the Purple Heart. This is a continuation of the action on the second day ashore, as recounted in "A Reunion: Red Beach Plus 30" (Chap. 58 in my book, *Follow Me*). That account ended with my orders for the immediate transportation to the rear of twenty to twenty-five silent, immobile forms, casualties from the early morning Japanese counterattack against our sector of the beachhead.

My primary focus then was on one casualty: Pvt. Harold Moon, who would receive the (posthumous) Medal of Honor, although I did not know this then. I said nothing about recognition of the others.

Now we'll focus on the regimental D-Day-plus-one objective, a hilly ridge-line parallel to and overlooking our beachhead—and Purple Hearts.

Our rapid advance attack was on a one-battalion front, Co. E on the right, Co. F on the left. Since the higher part of the ridge was on the right, I followed Co. E, pushing up a steep trail through head-high *kunai* grass. The terrain was such, however, that I could look across and see Co. F reach its objective—then see it driven off in a violent counterattack.

I sent the battalion commander over to stabilize the situation, pushed on up the trail and met two casualties coming down, each stumbling along semiconscious, arms draped over the shoulders of two buddies. One man had been hit in the abdomen, his front widely bloodstained, head lolling and eyes nearly closed; the other had a bullet crease along his skull above his right ear, eyes staring wildly and unfocused.

As they continued their tortuous way down, I continued up to ensure the high ground now occupied was held, in spite of the fallback on the left. But enough about the tactical situation and more about those two wounded men, and the twenty to twenty-five silent forms transported to the rear. All had one thing in common: *each would receive the Purple Heart.*

That thought did not occur to me then, but I've carried memories of that day and those men with me. One thing is vivid: Pvt. Harold Moon received the nation's highest honor, but, unless there were citations for one or two others, none received any recognition except his Purple Heart. This gives that distinctive ribbon and uniquely shaped pendant a special luster and mystique.

On our third day ashore, Co. F attacked to recapture its section of the ridge-line, preceded by an artillery preparation and with close air support. Since the 1st Battalion was in division reserve and the 3rd Battalion was occupying our beachhead, I decided to go with the attack and educate myself on what it is like to be with a platoon in attack. The only way up the ridge through the high *kunai* grass was to pick a trail, and go—which I did, on the right flank.

In due course I came out on top of the ridge, the first to reach it in that area that day. But there lay the body of one of my soldiers, who had reached that spot before me in the attack the preceding day—and remained there. It was quiet along the ridge now; air bombing and .50-caliber strafing of the reverse slope of the ridge had broken up that defense tactic. We had our objective, so I looked around.

I looked first at my soldier, who lay on his back; he had been killed instantly by a machine-gun burst as he reached the top. The fire had been so concentrated that it shattered the hardwood stock of his Garand rifle just back of the trigger guard, which now dangled from its leather sling at the butt point of attachment.

On looking around for the source of fire, I found it in a cleverly placed, open-pit machine-gun position on the reverse slope, sited down the ridge line. It was now occupied by two dead Japanese, casualties of the .50-caliber strafing from our close air support, one of whom had completed the job with a grenade held close to his throat.

The machine gun was gone, but several long brass strips were lying around, strips in which the Japanese set machine-gun ammunition instead of our type of belting. So I picked up two of the strips, and walked back to my dead soldier. As I looked at him, then at the brass strips that had held the ammunition that killed him, an idea formed in my mind. So I reached down and cut the leather sling on his Garand rifle and the butt end of the rifle stock came loose in my hands.

As a career professional soldier I had iron enough in my soul to order what must be done. But in situations like this one, inside and unseen, my heart bled. The idea that had formed in my mind was this: this soldier at my feet was a symbol, for in carrying out my orders he reached our objective—because here he was. In my heart he would be my Unknown Soldier. After the war I would use these brass strips and the broken stock of his rifle to fashion a special monument to him.

So I handed them for safekeeping to the soldier who always accompanied me (orderly or bodyguard, take your choice) and turned down the ridge-line to check the rest of the situation.

This thinking happened in a very brief time, but I never fashioned my special monument. Eight days later I fell in getting my Purple Heart, and all my personal effects (brass strips and rifle stock included) were lost when I was evacuated. But I've carried the thought in memory.

I did not think of Purple Hearts that day, but have since. Also I've given thought to the problem of awarding decorations, but until now have not considered the relative rank of various decorations. It takes special performance, with a written citation recording the facts, to produce a decoration—except for the Purple Heart. That is awarded on *prima facie* evidence: a combat wound, including fatalities. Further, it can only be awarded under the one situation that justifies the very existence of military forces: in hostile action against an enemy.

It seemed odd to me after World War II for the Purple Heart to remain "Tail-end Charlie" in rank among decorations. Now I discover that Defense and other decorations have been added since my retirement—all above the Purple Heart in rank, which now stands 17th among decorations available to members of the U.S. Army:

Medal of Honor
Distinguished Service Cross
Defense Distinguished Service Medal
Distinguished Service Medal
Silver Star
Defense Superior Service Medal

Legion of Merit
Distinguished Flying Cross
Soldier's Medal
Bronze Star Medal
Defense Meritorious Service Medal
Meritorious Service Medal
Air Medal
Joint Service Commendation Medal
Army Commendation Medal
Army Achievement Medal
Purple Heart
Good Conduct Medal

Somehow, remembering those Purple Heart cases I've just re-counted, and others—including the suffering and wrecked lives I've seen in hospitals and elsewhere—the location of the Purple Heart on the above list seems out of balance. Uncounted thousands have died of wounds, paid the ultimate price, whose only decoration from their government was the Purple Heart. In deference to them, as well as in recognition of the living, it would seem that those who have never endured the feel of maiming steel or other violence to their bodies could not in reason object to a higher recognition to those who have.

Some comments are:

• There is nothing new about a change in regulations for the relative rank of decorations. When the Legion of Merit was established during World War II, it ranked above the Silver Star. The reaction to that was so strong that the Silver Star was moved above the Legion of Merit, where it remains.

• There was also a change in regulations after the Bronze Star was established. It soon developed that a high proportion of them were awarded on staffs and in rear areas, away from the cutting edge of combat. Result: relatively few combat infantrymen were so recognized—and thus found themselves ribbonless among staff and rear area personnel with the Bronze Star. Later, regulations were changed to award Bronze Stars to all who qualified for the Combat Infantry Badge—but that was rescinded after World War II.

• The appearance of added medals in the above list (six since my retirement) emphasizes the lowly position of the Purple Heart. Sure, sometimes there are freak "cheap" ones that get talked about, but that is true for all decorations. The difference: only the Purple Heart is awarded on a hard, cold fact—all the others are matters of opinion and paper work.

- I am a long way removed from the active scene, but sometimes distance sharpens perspective. Anyway, in my view the Purple Heart belongs just below the Soldier's Medal. Of course, some winners of other medals win it, too, concurrently in the only way possible.

- Finally, the basic reason for my preceding comment is that medals are awarded for their effect on those eligible to receive them. When you place such a low valuation on the lives and limbs of your soldiers, you downgrade the value of that beautiful and highly respected medal—and thus reduce the effect it was established to produce.*

*After publication of this article, Senator John Warner (R-Va) initiated legislation in the Senate that upgraded the Purple Heart 6 places, to just below the Bronze Star.

CHAPTER 42
Unique Battle Power of Cold Steel

History reveals that with the advent of gunpowder and the rifle, the basic concept of the hand-held spear was not lost. My favorite footnote about that is a verse that comes from our Revolutionary War song, "Yankee Doodle."

> Cap'n David had a gun.
> He kind o' clapt his hand on't
> and stuck a crooked stabbing iron
> Upon the little en on't.

Today, however, some military pundits claim modern weapons make the bayonet a useless anachronism that should be eliminated—but I am not one of them. As a regimental commander in World War II on Leyte in the Philippines (1944) I was near, but not a participant in, two bayonet charges. As a result, I have a clear understanding that the value of the bayonet cannot be determined by counting bayonet wounds.

Since 1944 I have wondered about certain details of those charges, with particular reference to the second one. Both involved Co. F of my 34th Infantry. Thirty-nine years later, the former gallant company commander of Co. F—Paul Austin of Fort Worth, Tex.—attended our annual reunion of the 24th Infantry Division in August, 1983, at Savannah, Ga. So we shared memories and information.

As recorded in the preceding chapter ("Purple Heart Should Rank Higher Up"), while following Co. E to its portion of our D-Day-plus-one ridge-line objective on 21 October 1944, I heard shouts and noise from the Co. F sector to our left, and looked across to see that company driven from its part of the ridge in a violent counterattack.

From my observations when we recaptured the Co. F objective the next day and from talking with Paul Austin in August, 1983, that charge worked like this: the Japanese commander set a clever trap, using a reverse slope defense. This avoided exposure to our artillery fire, and set the stage for his bayonet charge.

His plan included a well-concealed open-pit machine-gun position on the reverse slope of the high end of the ridge, sighted down the ridgeline—covering exits from several trails through head-high *kunai* grass that led to the top of the ridge from our side.

His scenario permitted our scouts to come up out of the trails on top of the ridge and find it apparently undefended. Then as more men debouched from the trails, that hidden machine gun opened fire—which was the signal for the Japanese to leap from their reverse slope concealed positions in a shouting *(banzai!)* bayonet attack.

There was a confused melee as those who had reached the top were overwhelmed by numbers and surprise, and others still on the trails leading up were caught at a hopeless disadvantage, with grenades rolling down the trails into them. There was nothing for it but to pull back.

The significance of this company-level action lies in these points:
• The Japanese plan was based on a surprise bayonet attack.
• There were no bayonet wounds, but that naked cold steel in the rapid-moving, shouting attack was fundamental to its success. Otherwise, there would have been time for those on the trails to join the action.
• From that shattering experience, how would Co. F react in the future?

Our division mission was to reach the other side of Leyte before reinforcements could be landed there from Luzon. So the 34th Infantry was soon headed down the road toward Jaro and the far side of Leyte, leapfrogging battalions. The Japanese were fighting delaying actions, and on 28 October our 1st Battalion was stopped cold at the steel bridge over the Mainit River.

It was clear that a flanking action was needed. The 2nd Battalion was ordered to cross the river on the right, well away from the bridge, where a Filipino scout said it could be forded. I went along and watched the lead company wade over at knee and thigh depth—and it was Co. F, Capt. Paul Austin in command.

When the company had crossed without opposition, I went back to ensure the 1st Battalion put on the pressure again at the bridge—which we promptly captured when Co. F evened up the bayonet-charge score. At Savannah in 1983, Paul Austin summarized it this way:

On the far side of the Mainit River there was a gravel road running parallel to the river toward the bridge. I placed Sgt. Roy Floyd with his platoon across the road facing the bridge, and another platoon between the road and the river.

Then I ordered the 60-mm mortar section to fire into the wooded area beyond the open field that lay in front of us. I also directed a light machine gun section to leapfrog their two guns down the road with our advance, firing to our front and into the trees to our right.

At that moment a Japanese soldier came running toward us, unaware of our presence. Several men fired, he clutched his middle and went down—so now the enemy knew we were there. Quick action was needed.

I ran to the middle of the road where I could see and be seen by our company, as the road was raised a foot or so. On my right, Sgt. Floyd stood in front of his line of riflemen, and the sun shone on their fixed bayonets. Floyd had come to fight.

On my left, more bayonets were ready to go. I shouted to both platoons, "Don't stop until you get to the bridge!"

I waved my arm forward and, holding my carbine at port arms, began trotting down the road. Then a puff of blue smoke came out of the ground ahead and to the right, from a Jap mortar trench, the shell and smoke angling up and toward our 1st Battalion and the bridge. To my right, Sgt. Ernest Reckman charged it, tossed a grenade in the trench, crouched for the explosion, then jumped in the trench to make sure.

Everybody was trotting—another puff of smoke. I had a foot race with Reckman, and we got the two men while they were still in the mortar pit. Another nearby puff, and Reckman and one of his men took out the third mortar.

When I returned to the road, trotting, there were yells and shouts. To the right there was a deep draw ahead, and Floyd and his men raced to it and fired down. Dana Wallace said several Japs down there were eliminated.

More running, much yelling, dashing into and out of bushy areas to my right and left—then a Jap mortar shell exploded in the road ahead of me. When I turned from the concussion and flying gravel and took a couple of steps in the wrong direction, a voice from my right said, "Uh, Cap'n, uh, we're going this way."

What a guy, gigging his company commander in a bayonet charge!

We were all running now. I saw the bridge behind some trees to the left, and shouted, "There's the bridge—don't stop!"

Men yelled back and ran for the bridge as our mortar shells were blasting the wooded area across the Jaro Highway.

On the right, two of Floyd's men were on the ground. Homer McClure fired his M1 in a duel with a machine gun, but lost—the gun was too much.

Clinton Short bayoneted a Jap who had tossed a grenade at him. A bullet then knocked the helmet from his head, but he charged on—and was killed near the bridge.

In the center of the bridge there was a large stack of boxed Japanese heavy ammunition. A wire led from those boxes to a grove of trees, and near the end of the wire were three dead Japanese soldiers. Two were killed in our surprise charge, and one wounded man had killed himself with a grenade.

As I said, Sgt. Roy Floyd had come to fight—and so had others. Nobody shouted, "Remember the Alamo!" But if they had, I would have understood.

Thank you, Paul Austin, for your delayed after-action battle report. And now these comments:

- Large-scale bayonet attacks, like cavalry saber charges, have been relegated to the pages of history by modern weapons. But not so the bayonet. Consider the battle of Gettysburg, where Confederate Maj. Gen. George E. Pickett's famous charge failed on 3 July, 1863 with 15,000 men. However, Col. Joshua Chamberlain's 60th Maine Regiment's great and successful bayonet charge the preceding day, 2 July, was the real turning point at Gettysburg.
- A regiment of that era had nine companies of 30 to 40 men, thus a strength of about 350. Therefore, the regimental commander had roughly the same leadership responsibilities as a modern company

commander. That was the size force that faced the critical situation at Little Round Top, as described in *FM 22-100*, "Military Leadership" (Coordinating Draft, January, 1983):

" . . . He (Colonel Chamberlain) knew his unit, out of ammunition, would be enveloped by the superior numbers and firepower of another Confederate assault. He could not withdraw—to do so would cause the defeat of the Union Army. . . . Then it came to him. He would fix bayonets and charge—not for heroism, but because that was his best chance for success . . . attacking downhill, the surprise and violence might provide the necessary power to win. . . ."

And it did. This may have been the turning point of the war: a company-plus size bayonet charge, seizing an opportunity that would not have existed without the bayonet.

- As to the overall value of the bayonet today, let the veteran company commander of Co. F, Paul Austin, who in the space of one week had been on the receiving and delivering ends of two successful charges, answer that:

"Do away with the bayonet—Hell, no! When the right situations develop, which cannot be predicted, men trained and equipped with the bayonet add a new dimension to the battlefield."

CHAPTER 43

The Ties that Bind the Airborne

The word "paratrooper" is hedged about with misconceptions and thus there are angles about joining the jumpers that are not generally understood. Furthermore, one of the greatest benefits to a soldier from airborne duty goes almost unnoticed. Nobody is ordered or drafted into the "nylon cavalry," but for those who may volunteer, here is a remembered once-over-quickly look at jumping and jumpers.

When regulations were relaxed in 1948 to permit elderly gentlemen to go airborne, I volunteered, and soon discovered that some people thought I was going nuts. One non-jumper friend put it this way: "You won't like paratroopers—and they won't like you."

By the time I reported as chief of staff of the 11th Airborne Division at Fort Campbell, Kentucky, my feelings had become quite schizophrenic. But I could only mutter to myself, "Well, you dumb so-and-so, it's too late to back out now."

If you're not a jumper you have no place in the sun among paratroopers. Until you qualify as a parachutist they look at you with a will-he-jump question mark in their eyes. All qualified troopers wear jump wings; so that blank space on my left breast cried aloud for an explanation. But being a jumper is like being a virgin: you are or you are not. If you are not, nobody is really interested in your tedious explanation of your unfortunate status.

So I left for jump school at Fort Benning, Georgia. As frequently happened in my military career, I managed to do things the hard way, but eventually the day arrived when I hit the ground on my fifth and qualifying jump and rose to my feet all in one piece—Airborne!

In an airborne division you learn all the skills of an infantry division besides those of individual and unit airborne operations. In general anything that can be loaded into an airplane can be dropped out of it by parachute, from trucks to artillery and bulldozers. And I never ceased to be amazed at the load of stuff a man could be draped with and still jump. With so many things that can go wrong, the jump injury rate is remarkably low. The best protection is a well-trained jumper. Of course there are tragedies and comedies in jumping, often with a fine line separating them.

At one large post there was a military show with grandstands for visitors and VIPs. When a flight of planes made an exhibition paratrooper drop, there was a sudden gasp of horror. One body plummeted earthward like the proverbial stone, until—at the last second—his reserve chute ballooned and he landed.

Investigation revealed the jumper had deliberately failed to "hook up" so that his chute would not open, measured his fall by "counting seconds," then pulled his reserve. His idea was to "Wake up the show; give 'em a thrill." He did.

But don't get the idea that airborne duty consists primarily of jumping and finding new ways to risk your neck. That's only frosting on the cake. When the Korean War erupted thousands of miles away, things began to happen at Fort Campbell, too.

To the American people, there was a combat-ready airborne division at Campbell, but this was far from the truth, for it was about half-manned. Meeting the requirement to organize new units, as well as sending replacements to Korea, caused a further great disruption because officers and men taken away had to be replaced by others assembled from many sources— including the call to active duty of reservists, new recruits and draftees.

By 1 August 1950, levies on the 511th Airborne Infantry Regiment had reduced it to some 500 (normal strength was approximately 3,000). At this point, I was offered the chance to command it. I jumped at the opportunity, knowing it would be built up to strength again.

Our regiment was first scheduled to receive several thousand individual reservists for refresher training before they went to Korea as replacements. So we set out to do the best we could with the few men we had—drawing thousands of pieces of equipment, renovating barracks, doing countless other necessary administrative chores.

While we would be housekeeping for soon-to-arrive reservists, they would be serving at great sacrifice to themselves and their families. Furthermore, some would never return from Korea.

In those pressing days, I saw things I had never seen before, like lieutenants driving 2½-ton trucks, platoon sergeants sweeping out barracks, mess sergeants scrubbing garbage cans and a first sergeant mowing the lawn in front of his company. I was, and am, as proud of the way my regiment met this military requirement as of anything in my service.

It is not exactly the picture of paratroopers the newspapers paint.

In due time we received our airborne replacements, but it was months before we had a fully jump-qualified regiment. More months of unit training were necessary before we were ready for full-scale ground and airborne operations.

A special airborne problem came up one day when seven qualified jumpers "quit" by refusing to load up for a jump. They were transferred out of the airborne before sundown that day, a move which was accepted and correct policy. Usually those who don't have what it takes fail in jump school, although a few jump-qualified men do, from time to time, lose their nerve and become "quitters."

For a group to fail was unusual. It is an unhappy memory to recall those seven dejected young soldiers marching away, turned in an instant from proud paratroopers to outcasts from their regiment.

As is often the case with quitters, they were new troopers, not long out of jump school. The unusual number was due primarily to the fact that our regiment was made up almost entirely of recruit replacements. The original members—except for the stay-behind cadre—had been requisitioned for Korea. It started when one man got cold feet and quit. A buddy joined him. The first thing anybody knew, others from nearby planes saw them—and then there were seven.

You can't temporize with quitters. If you keep them on they are apt to refuse again in a plane and cause an accident, for when a man surrenders to fear his actions are unexpected and unpredictable. Besides, other jumpers will not tolerate quitters in their midst.

After being sent to Iceland for a "lost year" out of my professional life, good fortune brought me back as commander of the 505th Airborne Infantry of the 82nd Airborne Division at Fort Bragg. At the first opportunity I went out and jumped with my new regiment—and soon found myself lying full length on the ground for a moment, realizing it was a safe landing. Then, as I stood erect savoring that satisfying sensation only a jumper knows, the nearest old noncommissioned officer walked toward me, smiling, and held out his hand: "Welcome to the Five-Oh-Five, Colonel!"

That's the way the airborne was for me—if you can read between the lines the things there's no space to say. After I left the 82nd most of my remaining service was anticlimactic.

For those on active duty—now eligible to volunteer for airborne—it's time to go back to that great benefit from being a trooper which I feel has been largely overlooked.

Landing by parachute is not merely another means of transportation into battle. It's more fundamental than that. There's a close bond between the airborne soldier and his officer, because each knows the other has passed the jump test. And they continue to do so together. Each believes the other will be a good man to have around when things get sweaty—and for good reason, though they might not think about it that way.

The reason: parachute-jumping tests and hardens a soldier under stress in a way nothing short of battle can do. There are and always will be uncounted thousands of non-jumpers who are outstanding combat soldiers, yet you can't be sure who they are until the shooting starts.

But paratroopers will fight. You can bet on that. They repeatedly face danger while jumping and develop that self-discipline that conquers fear. Subconsciously each trooper knows this. That's why he has that extra cocky confidence.

If you go airborne you'll have it too.

CHAPTER 44
When Chips are Down the Will to Dare is Not Enough

When travel arrangements by military air misfired, the graduating class of the Ranger School was spared my scheduled peroration. However, a phone call from Lt. Colonel James Tucker, commander of the Florida Ranger Camp at Eglin Air Force Base, suggested I fly in commercially for an overnight visit and look around the next day. That was like a whiff of gunpowder to an old war-horse. But when my plane landed in Pensacola that evening I still did not guess the real purpose of my visit, from which would come better understanding of the combat axiom: *The will to dare is not enough.*

Colonel Tucker, with a Yul Brynner haircut, met me with Maj. Robert Frix and Capt. James Fraser—the kind of alert, dynamic officers you would expect at the Ranger School. Major Frix drove us to Captain Fraser's bachelor apartment where we found several young officers of the Ranger staff and faculty. It was a bit late for cocktails but I've always been adaptable in such matters. Besides, the dining room table was set for a sit-down dinner, which Captain Fraser masterminded in the kitchen. So it was only polite to color my glass of branch water a nice oak shade.

The steaks were smothered in mushrooms, supported by green peas, baked potato with sour cream, and asparagus tips Hollandaise. Flank protection was hot buttered garlic bread, buttressed by avocado and hearts-of-artichoke salad. Instead of dessert, Captain Fraser brought in crystal goblets filled with exotically flavored and alcohol-spiked coffee, topped with a layer of partially whipped cream—served icebox-chilled.

Then Colonel Tucker asked, "General, what do you think are basic requirements to be a successful officer?"

That question brought a kind of reflex unstudied answer: "He must want to be the best officer possible, and both like and respect soldiers with whom he serves."

Now little things puzzling me fell into place. From "The Forward Edge" articles in *ARMY*—for I had never met any of these men before—they had recognized that, in my yearning mind, I was still where they were: young active professional officers, analyzing and studying how to be better commanders and leaders of their soldiers, for whom they had the same love and respect I had always had for men in uniform. So this planned informal seminar was the real purpose of my visit.

Colonel Tucker had performed the miracle for which a poet once pleaded. For me it translated to "Backward, turn backward, O Time, in your flight, make me a company commander again, just for tonight?"

This was the common ground on which we met. I was welcomed as another company commander, back from a long reconnaissance in time to discuss our shared experience in peace and in war.

After my quickie reply to Colonel Tucker's question I gained time to think by asking a question myself. "Major Frix, what do *you* think are characteristics of a successful officer?"

"Well," he replied, "here are some of them: Ability to use subordinates, knowing when and how much to supervise. This includes the force of personality to demand standards you set and not accept below-par performance. He must always be aware of the time element, recognize when time is short but know, too, when there's no hurry—and rest his men. A good officer can communicate his ideas across clearly. With these qualities and others he must have self-discipline, be in control of himself and the situation. Finally, no officer is truly a successful leader unless he can fight—do all those things under the stress of combat."

Colonel Tucker gave me a pleased grin and said "You asked the right man. That's on Bob's side of the house in the school."

Having collected my thoughts, I said, "Here are two more ideas. First, that a successful officer must anticipate situations and plan accordingly, like a big-league shortstop. If there's a man on first and third, one out, and his team is leading 4-2 in the bottom of the seventh, the big-leaguer thinks about what he'll do if the ball is hit wide to his right, hard straight at him, a deep pop-up, or a slow roller on the grass past the pitcher. However, if a shortstop waits until the ball is hit before thinking about what to do, then—no matter how good a glove man he is or how accurate his throwing arm—

he'll always be a minor-leaguer. That's the way it is with officers, too. The successful officer must be thinking ahead."

I took another sip of that gourmet coffee concoction and asked Captain Fraser, "What's in this?"

"Sir, that's a trade secret. But when nobody else is around I'll tell you." (He did, too, but it's classified and so can't be reported here.)

"The second idea," I continued, "came from research at West Point years ago. They studied not only military men but all successful leaders—in business, religion, education, the professions of law, engineering and others. They found one clear characteristic all successful leaders have. Do any of you know what it is?"

Some answers included: professional knowledge, common sense, good judgment and personal courage—physical and moral. "Those are part of it," I said, "but they discovered the one basic quality all successful leaders had was human understanding. For how can you be a successful leader if you do not understand those you aspire to lead?"

To change the pace I said to Colonel Tucker, "Let's talk about Rangers. What is your mission, how do you go about it and how does it fit in with our discussion tonight?"

Again that Yul Brynner smile revealed his alive and questing personality. "What we're talking about," he said, "is right on the button. Because our mission is leadership development.

"The way we carry it out, in addition to normal school instruction, is to learn by doing. We make it tough, real tough, in varied and testing field exercises. That's one reason why, before students are enrolled, they must pass the physical proficiency test and the combat water survival test."

From the cocktail hour I knew they were Vietnam veterans, so I asked, "How have your graduates measured up in combat?"

"All the way!" Colonel Tucker answered promptly. "Senior commanders in Vietnam compete to get our Rangers. General Westmoreland himself, when in Vietnam, wrote to the chief of staff, 'Leadership by graduates of the Ranger course has been impressive . . .' and asked for more of them. Experience there proves our graduates are technically trained, and have that vital quality: the capacity to endure. We emphasize that here, driving them close to their physical and mental limits."

A bell rang in the file room of my memory when I heard that word *endure.*

He turned to his adjutant, Captain Utter. "George, list the kinds of graduates we have."

George Utter has the gift of brevity. "Sir," he said, "we have four kinds of graduates: distinguished graduates, who make the top grades and best showing in the course; honor graduates, who finish below them, but well above average; graduates with award, who earn the Ranger tab by meeting all standards; and graduates, who finish the course with all the training benefits but are not entitled to the Ranger tab because they failed to meet the standards."

For a brief moment we sat in silence, and my mind went back to that word *endure*.

"Colonel Tucker," I said, "you mentioned emphasis on pushing students to the limit of their endurance in field exercises, so they will know what it's like. I'm sure this brink-of-limit training is one of the primary reasons your graduates stand up so well in combat.

"This suggests a thought I've groped for a long time. We've all been in battle and know what happens there. Also, we're all paratroopers, another type of physical and mental testing— which proves the *will to dare,* an essential element in battle. But here you add the *ability to endure,* and that is quite something else.

"To dare briefly is not enough. The sudden flame of raw courage must be there when needed, but combat calls for the capacity to endure cumulative, pyramiding stresses: loss of sleep, hunger and thirst, long-continued physical effort to utter exhaustion, living with gnawing fear for yourself and the terrible strain of responsibility for lives of others—for hours, days, weeks and months. So we must endure. I see now this is the vital element your school adds. No wonder you are proud to wear the Ranger tab!"

It was a good time to stop—mandatory when I looked at my watch. It's impossible to cover all the things we kicked around and about, but two comments can be added:

- After lunch next day, my visit over, we lined up for a picture. As our jeep driver moved away Colonel Tucker said, "Come back here, Bishop. We want you in this too." I like to remember that. The hard-driving officer-soldier who demands the last ounce of strength and top performance from his Rangers was, without thinking, demonstrating the quality of human understanding. Everybody likes to get in the picture.

- All I have left now is the memory. Yet it is also more than a memory for there is the sure knowledge that never in our nation's history have we had finer soldiers; who know that to dare briefly is not enough, that you must also endure.

PART THREE

General Officers

*****General of The Army (war only)*
****Generals*
***Lieutenant Generals*
**Major Generals*
Brigadier Generals

As a rule generals are complicated people who can get things done—and that is not incompatible with the fact that there are a few who may be a bit on the unlovely side. Our guideline to their composition is the principle "by their works ye shall know them." Some specifics in this regard are detailed in the following chapters.

I hope that "reading between the lines" here (and in my book, *Follow Me,* Presidio Press, Novato, CA) will provide a better understanding of what Pulitzer Prize Winner Hanson W. Baldwin meant when he said:

"Generals are born not made, yet the influences which touch their lives unquestionably shape their careers."

For us "run of the mill" generals, being at the right place at the right time and serving with the right people—these are not inconsequential factors. Nor are these factors always chance happenings. Sure, it's all confusing—but I did not promise to make it simple . . . just to provide a background of information for your consideration.

CHAPTER 45
They Trained a Winning Army

What has happened to and within our Army during the last half century, from the end of World War I in 1918 to Vietnam in 1968, seems little known to the average American. Especially what, if any, particular factor saved our Army from complete atrophy when it was reduced to little more than a token force between the two World Wars.

The most basic statistic about the Army during this period is the tremendous expansion in numbers when fighting begins—and the disintegration of our wartime fighting machine when peace comes. For World War I, the contortion necessary to reach the great upward gyration in numbers was clearly shown by the use of "ninety-day wonders" as officers. While they made such an impression on both military men and civilians that those derisive words have become part of the language of that time, an overall examination of our military strength since 1918 casts those unjustly maligned emergency officers in a far different role.

No less an authority than Sir Winston Churchill pinned down a key fact when he said, "It remains to me a mystery as yet unexplained how the very small staffs which the United States kept during the years of peace were able not only to build up the Armies and the Air Force units, but also to find the leaders and vast staffs capable of handling enormous masses and of moving them faster and farther than masses have ever been moved in war before."

It is my purpose here to solve Sir Winston's World War II mystery. Concurrently, my eyewitness testimony will show that those so-called ninety-day wonders stand skyscraper tall in our battle heritage when their overall careers in two world wars are recorded.

One of the most basic functions of any small peacetime army is to organize, train and lead greatly expanded military forces in war. Our little regular army of the 1920s and 1930s—shunted aside, miserably equipped and supplied, even shunned and derided—performed its mission unbelievably well. Thus, the question remains: how could this small force multiply so quickly into the complicated military machine which amazed the world with its tremendous capacity for organization and leadership in World War II?

There were few regular units that in peacetime were manned at TO&E authorization. The same for our Reserve and National Guard units, our military college and school systems, the General Staff in Washington—and paper plans. But it's inherent in all these elements that the quality of their officers is the critical factor: retaining our battle know-how, developing military doctrine and an adequate training base. They were the nucleus, the hard core of leaders whose professional ability and brilliance were not appreciated until tested in the cauldron of World War II. To see the quality of this leadership in the making, it is necessary only to recall some names from the years 1921-41.

From my cadet days at the U.S. Military Academy these names come to mind: Generals of the Army Douglas MacArthur (then Brig. Gen.) and Omar Bradley (Maj.); Generals Matthew B. Ridgway (Capt.), Jacob L. Devers (Maj.), Wade H. Haislip (Maj.), Walton H. Walker (Capt.), and Williston B. Palmer (lst Lt.); Lieutenant Generals Simon B. Buckner (Maj.), Willis D. Crittenberger (Maj.), George E. Stratemeyer (Capt.), Samuel D. Sturgis Jr. (1st Lt.), Harold R. Bull (Maj.), Oscar W. Griswold (Maj.); Major Generals Robert M. Danford (Lt. Col.), Charles H. Bonesteel Jr. (Maj.), Ernest N. Harmon (Capt.), Frederick A. Irving (Capt.), Charles W. Ryder (Maj.), Leland S. Hobbs (Maj.), Vernon E. Prichard (Maj.), Emil F. Reinhardt (Maj.), Frederick E. Uhl (Maj.), Jens A. Doe (Maj.), Ernest J. Dawley (Maj.)—and a number of brigadier generals.

From my first Army station—Fort Benning, Ga.—these names stand out from the Infantry School (among many others): Generals of the Army George C. Marshall (Lt. Col.) and Dwight D. Eisenhower (Maj.); Generals J. Lawton Collins (Capt.), Joseph W. Stilwell (Maj.) and John E. Dahlquist (Capt.).

From my duty assignment at Benning—in the 29th Infantry— memory supplies even more impressive facts. All officers on duty at West Point had been graduates (a mistake since rectified), thus I had subconsciously assumed that most Army officers were West Pointers. But the opposite was true. On joining the 29th Infantry I found that only four officers higher than second lieutenant were from the Military Academy: two first lieutenants, one major and our regimental commander. Not one company commander or regimental staff officer was a graduate. Yet all were wartime officers who had been commissioned in the Regular Army after the Armistice.

Granted, this is an enriched sample. However, the officers of that time were not an average group, but were outstanding professionals with an inclination and preference for command and leadership—and they were nearly all combat veterans. Young officers entering on active duty under them could not fail to gain from their example and experience. Sure, there were some misfits, but they were being actively weeded out, though a few below-par specimens managed to hang on for years.

The point is this: soldiers can be trained relatively quickly if well commanded, but it takes years to produce a battle-ready colonel or general. Another factor is that officers of that time spent many years in company units—and there is no better training in how to command men. The result was that for our World War II expansion we had not only a plentiful supply of officers ready to step up and perform brilliantly as generals, but there were uncounted hundreds of lieutenant colonels and colonels for lower but critically important staff and command assignments, most of whom would have been outstanding generals, too, if they had had the chance.

Recently I was talking to a retired major general who had been commissioned in the Regular Army following World War I. After telling him of the wonderful professional leaders we have coming to the top in the Army today, I voiced my admiration and respect for the thousands of veteran officers from World War I (in the Reserve and National Guard, as well as in the Regular Army), who had such an indispensable part in the way our Army met the test of World War II—to the mystification of Sir Winston Churchill.

He smiled and said quietly, "Thanks, Red. A lot of people don't stop to think of that, but we never forget it was you West Pointers who set the pace and standards for us."

These veteran soldiers have never failed to give us due credit for our efforts, but it seems to me we haven't stopped to think to give them due credit in return. As an eyewitness—who served under them, alongside of them, and over a few of them—let me say for the record that they were surpassed in professional ability by no group and matched only by those with comparable battle experience.

Now we have a great reservoir of "graduates" of World War II, Korea and Vietnam—a resupply of veteran officers every ten years. The best measure of their capacity is the large number of active-duty generals today whose Regular Army careers began when they were integrated after World War II.

After reviewing the past fifty changing years it is clear there is one salient feature which has insured our continuing military ability to meet the challenge of the world's battlefields. The threatening cloud of The Bomb and other fantastic developments in hardware have been duly goggled at by prognosticators in gauging our military strength. But whatever the weapons and equipment, wars are still fought by men who use the hardware—which means that a vital requirement remains for adequate numbers of topnotch combat-experienced leaders.

No other nation today can match us in the depth and breadth of our combat-experienced officers—from lieutenants to four-star generals.

CHAPTER 46
Evaluate: Not Just Read History

It is generally recognized that professional military men should read military history. It is not so generally recognized, however, that readers should be alert to evaluate each book as to the validity of the author's research, the extent of his personal knowledge (if any), and the nature and degree of his bias—or lack of it.

For a combined case study, consider three widely varied histories of events in the Pacific during World War II in which Gen. Douglas MacArthur played a major role: *American Caesar,* by William Manchester; *Eagle Against The Sun,* by Ronald H. Spector; and *The General, MacArthur and the Man He Called 'Doc,'* by Roger Olaf Egeberg.

To illustrate the need for evaluation of opinions (as distinguished from established historical facts) here are some extracts, with particular reference to conflicting opinions about General MacArthur:

American Caesar: On the book jacket William Manchester details his view of General Douglas MacArthur's personal foibles (which he picturesquely accents), but ends with these incisive sentences: *Yet he was also endowed with great personal charm, a will of iron, and a soaring intellect. Unquestionably he was the most gifted man-at-arms this nation has produced.*

Eagle Against The Sun: From Ronald Spector's Introduction, *My own view of MacArthur is that despite his undoubted qualities of leadership, he was unsuited by temperament, character, and judgment for the positions of high command which he occupied throughout the war.* Spector also tries repeatedly to discredit MacArthur, including the Buna operation.

The General, MacArthur and the Man He Called "Doc': By Roger Egeberg, a doctor in civilian life. He was MacArthur's aide-de-camp (as a Lt. Col.) from January 1944 to the end of the war in August 1945, then on to Tokyo. After MacArthur's daring and spectacularly successful "re-connaissance in force" in the Admiralties he said to his aide, *"Doc . . . I wear this cap with all the braid . . . feel in a way that I have to . . . a trademark many of our soldiers know . . . but with the risks we take I suggest you wear a helmet."*

Roger Egeberg's personal observation book is factual and perceptive, an irreplaceable record that fills a fascinating gap in the MacArthur saga.

As to William Manchester and Ronald Spector, both were in the Marines in a combat area. Manchester served in World War II in the Pacific and had intense front line battle experience in an enlisted status, while Spector is listed as a major in the Marine Corps Reserve (now teaching history at the University of Alabama) who was in Vietnam—whether front line combat or rear area is not stated.

Both are established writers, Manchester having a great national name, authoring fourteen books in five categories: biography, history, essays, fiction, and diversion. Spector, a Senior Fulbright Scholar and contributor to scholarly journals, has authored three other histories, two on naval subjects and one on Vietnam.

American Caesar is an outstanding encyclopedic definitive biography of MacArthur, while *Eagle Against The Sun* is a broadly based overall history of World War II in the Pacific. Both are founded on comprehensive research, and cover the same ground only in assessing the place in history of one of the most dominant and dynamic military commanders in this or any other war, Gen. Douglas MacArthur.

So it's time to evaluate. My personal observations of Gen. MacArthur (previously recorded) cover brief and varied contacts over a twenty-four year period—and include service under him during World War II (1943-45) from Australia into New Guinea, and on into the Philippines. So I'll spot-check Manchester's judgments of MacArthur vis-à-vis those of Spector in an area where I have some personal knowledge and understanding.

The time frame selected covers MacArthur's truly *Great Decision:* "We shall defend Australia in New Guinea." Subsequent key implementing operations lead to the capture of Buna. Spector criticizes Buna caustically—and fails to recognize it as a strategic defeat for the Japanese from which they never recovered.

When MacArthur arrived in Australia the concept for defense was based on "The Brisbane Line"—thus conceding all of New Guinea, northern Australia and contiguous sea areas to the Japanese. MacArthur alone had the vision and understanding to see his solution. Further, he had the "iron will" (Manchester's words) to implement that daring and brilliant concept in the face of attempts to dissuade him. Manchester sees this clearly, and sums up the results of that decision this way:

> Here his long years of studying military feats of past wars were to reap spectacular harvests. Altogether he would make 87 amphibious landings, all of them successful, cutting Japanese escape routes and lines of communications. Mark S. Watson, the distinguished military analyst, would call them "ingenious and dazzling thrusts which never stopped until Japan was beaten down." Field Marshal Viscount Alanbrooke, chief of Britain's Imperial General Staff . . . wrote that MacArthur, " . . . outshone Eisenhower, Marshall and all other American and British generals including Montgomery." B. H. Liddell Hart agreed: "MacArthur was supreme among all generals. His combination of strong personality, strategic grasp, tactical skill, operative mobility, and vision put him in a class above all other allied commanders in any theatre."

In this spot check we look for some indication of why Ronald Spector found, "MacArthur unsuited . . . for the positions of high command which he occupied." A good place to start is with Spector's preliminary comments when he addressed his attention to the Australia-New Guinea area:

Spector: " . . . there was the presence in the Pacific of Gen. Douglas MacArthur . . . who had to be employed in some task commensurate with his *supposed greatness.*" (italics supplied)

Observation: This about a soldier of international renown since World War I, who had served an unprecedented five years as Chief of Staff, U.S. Army, and had headed the lost cause of Bataan-Corregidor, thus gaining first hand experience of Japanese battle methods. Could this be bias showing?

Spector: "The Navy did not share . . . admiration for MacArthur . . . and would never have entrusted the fleet to a general unschooled in the mysteries of seapower."

Observation: The brilliance of MacArthur's integration of combined army, navy and air forces in implementing his strategic decision is too well known and documented to need comment here.

Spector: When the attack on Buna in New Guinea was stalled, " . . . They lacked appropriate weapons to knock out the Japanese bunkers. Gen. Harding had repeatedly asked for tanks and more artillery, but he received nothing. Why none of MacArthur's observers saw fit to mention these things remains a mystery."

Observation: To me the mystery is how Spector failed to understand that it was not what observers may or may not have told General MacArthur—such a basic need was obvious. The problem was how to get artillery and tanks to Buna, which was surrounded by jungle and sandwiched between the Owen Stanley Mountains and shoaly sea where our navy could not operate within reach of enemy air. Finally, our air supply was limited by the low lift capacity of planes of that time. Lt. Gen. Robert L. Eichelberger, who relieved Maj. Gen. Harding at Buna, gives a graphic account of that situation in his book, *Our Jungle Road To Tokyo.*

Some comments:

- Obviously it is not possible to review three books in depth here, and provide an overall assessment of them for posterity. But that is not the objective—especially since the books are radically different in purpose and scope. Our aim is to highlight the requirement to evaluate what we read. Finally, a true grasp and understanding of historical individuals, operations and activities can be obtained only after multiple readings on the subject.

- I have read extensively about General MacArthur, and many writers in some degree cite his "arrogance." They fail to understand an intangible problem of famous leaders—and by the time frame here MacArthur had been a world famous general for twenty-five years. Yet in my limited and varied contacts I was impressed with his innate courtesy and consideration for others—but no man in his position can bend to every breeze, or talk to anyone at any time. He must remain "in command" of his time and existing situation.

- The picture here (a snapshot recently discovered in my papers) was taken by somebody the last time I saw MacArthur—at headquarters 24th Infantry Division in June 1945, on the beach at Davao, Mindanao, P.I. From left to right: Unidentified (walking); Maj. Gen. Roscoe B. Woodruff (division commander); Maj. Gen. Franklin P. Sibert (X Corps commander); Gen. Douglas MacArthur; Col. Aubrey S. Newman (division chief of staff); Lt. Col. Kenwood Ross (a brash young staff officer, in the act of saluting).

Translation: Lt. Col. Ross had walked up to pay his respects to Gen. MacArthur, and I introduced him. There was no time pressure, so the "arrogant" world famous MacArthur turned toward Ross with a quiet smile and pleasant greeting—look at the picture again, note his forthrightly extended hand. This was repeated for others who came up too. So place this happening in the record.

- Having read, in diverse degrees of interest and detail, some 200-odd historical books of various types in the past twenty five years, my basic conclusion is that an essential for such reading is an evaluation of what you read—preferably by multiple readings on the same subject. For example my evaluation of *Eagle Against The Sun* is this: A broadly researched valuable work by a naval historian whose book, unfortunately, is marred by an extreme bias against one of the dominant figures involved (MacArthur), and who on occasion finds himself at sea in his opinions about ground operations ashore.

CHAPTER 47
Bad Guy in the Black Hat

In TV Westerns it's easy to tell the good guys—they wear white hats. In any large Army headquarters it's easy to find the bad guy among all the good ones: look for the office marked "Chief of Staff." He'll be wearing a big black hat, figuratively.

The manuals are clear as to how a chief should operate, but commanding generals differ greatly in how they use him. I should know, because I was chief of staff to more generals than I have fingers, varying from one month to over two years. Five wanted me to be chief of staff; the others varied mightily in their methods—from using the chief as a whipping boy or hatchet man to a high-priced administrative flunkey.

But all had two things in common: they wanted the chief of staff to produce results, while they wore the biggest white hat around—which is as it should be. Not everybody can be a good guy, for it takes at least one hard-nosed SOB to get things done. So the chief of staff is elected.

Those generals who did not use the chief as the manuals prescribe had diverse reasons. The most basic one was, apparently, to prevent anybody from thinking the chief might be running things. There is a definite "command posture" angle concerned here, and its importance cannot be overlooked, especially if the chief is in the same age bracket as the commander.

When I was designated a division chief of staff in 1942—before inhibitions were born of age and experience—the commanding general, an outstanding soldier, was nearly twenty years my senior. Having watched my much older predecessor work, I went to see the general after I became chief and said I needed the answer to a question:

"Do you want me to operate as chief of staff, sir, or like my predecessor?"

He smiled, because he knew exactly what I was talking about. "You are my chief of staff. Do the job as you think it should be done. I'll slow you down if necessary."

There is not space for details about how the man in the big black hat operates, so we'll touch on only a few high spots. Perhaps nothing made life as chief of staff more trying than the idea back of a minor incident years later, when I was chief of another division.

A newly arrived lieutenant colonel was temporarily assigned a desk in my outer office, with instructions to orient himself on the post and in local staff procedures. A week later I asked him if he knew how to get things done in our headquarters.

"Yes, sir. I know the magic words, Colonel."

When I asked what the magic words were, he replied: "The Chief of Staff says do it."

This is one of the things that puts the big black hat on the chief of staff: what others say he said. You'll wear a black skimmer anyway, if you're to get the job done, but how you are quoted or misquoted makes your image a favorable or an unfavorable one.

What we're touching on here is that intangible, universal trouble-maker: human friction. For a closer look we'll jump forward sixteen years from the time I put on my first black hat to the day I clapped on my last one, as chief of staff of U.S. Continental Army Command.

To be the chief in such a large and complex headquarters is like having a migraine headache: those who have never suffered from one are apt to wonder how much is headache and how much psychotic affliction.

But there are some who understand.

Soon after I became chief of staff there was a conference of the six army commanders. One, who had been chief of staff to a famous general we both knew, said to me:

"Red, you have my sympathy because I was a chief myself in a high-level headquarters, under General So-and-so. You can't bat a thousand in this league. Sooner or later you'll make a mistake—and I made one.

"Of course I had to tell the Old Man, so I said, 'General, you know Christ selected Judas Iscariot as one of his disciples, and Judas became a traitor—so that was a mistake. Therefore, since even He made a mistake, maybe you'll forgive me the one I made this morning.' "

He grinned. "It's a little gimmick you might try, though I hope your boss has a better sense of humor than Old Man So-and-so, because it didn't work well for me."

The manner in which the chief works in any large headquarters follows the same principles as in a division, but the problems and daily operating procedures are vastly more complex.

Besides being an executive and a coordinator, the chief is also an administrator. A famous university president said, "The minimum qualifications of an administrator are courage, fortitude, justice, and prudence—or practical wisdom. However, for good reason, I regard patience as a delusion and a snare, and think administrators have too much of it rather than too little." There are times, however, when a chief needs a Job-like quality among his characteristics. To counteract the patience he is forced into on these occasions, it's expedient for the chief to pick his time and every now and then to really blow his top over nothing much.

This creates a certain unpredictable aura about him in the minds of staff officers, which helps him pick the time to be patient without being pushed into it.

That may sound confusing, but there's a firm idea involved.

A large part of your day's work on a high staff is based on faith in those who research the problems and prepare papers for your signature. It's impossible to have detailed knowledge about everything in the papers you sign.

In similar fashion, but from a different angle, faith is vital to a sound commander-chief relationship, for the general must have faith in his chief of staff too. Not in just seeing that papers are correct, but that he is loyal, and that the chief of staff is not as big an unnecessary hard nose with the staff as his aide tells him several (incompetent) staff officers say he is.

This brings us to personalities. Certain officers of the technical staff appear to insist as a matter of professional pride on writing their papers in a language that makes them mysterious to the lay reader.

In such cases I usually gave such a paper my best speed reading once over slightly, absorbed the idea through extrasensory perception, and asked myself, "What the hell difference does it make?"

If the answer that echoed from my subconscious was "None," I tossed the paper in my Out basket, figuring that appropriate general staff action had been taken.

Then there are two related types of staff officers, typified in my mind by the story about how to tell the difference between a psychotic and a neurotic.

The psychotic thinks two plus two is five; the neurotic knows two plus two is four—but he worries about it.

With both types my patience was short, especially since they were inclined to argue—so I tossed 'em out. At the next cocktail party I was apt to see one or both of those gents having a friendly drink with the commanding general's aide—which illustrates the need for that sound commander-chief relationship I was telling you about.

Then of course there is the staff officer who comes into your office with a clear grasp of the problem and why he is there. He is intelligent, conscientious, loyal—and his sole objective is to present the best paper possible. Also to get the matter concluded with the least trouble to the chief, and exactly the way the commanding general wants it.

Furthermore, he is agreeable to revising the paper, but will strongly marshal his reasons if he thinks the proposed revision is wrong. So you pay close attention if he disagrees with any change you suggest. With few exceptions, this was the type of officer we had at CONARC.

But even with paragons as staff officers, they still come equipped with what we call human nature; therefore the chief of staff must wear that black hat. It's not just a matter of bringing divergent views into alignment and carrying them out; you can't take all day to do it.

Finally, even though you wear a big enough black hat as chief of staff to get things done promptly and well—which includes never failing to listen enough, but not too much—there will be times when you put on the big white hat you keep locked in the safe. That's when you make out efficiency reports.

CHAPTER 48
Give Credit Where and When Due

From some forgotten source, my sometimes faulty memory tells me Napoleon originated the gambit of awarding medals and ribbons as battle decorations. Whether or not it was the little Corsican's idea, the combat-awards ploy is here to stay because it implements one of the most basic principles of command and leadership: give credit where credit is due.

I wondered what sages have said on the subject but could find nothing—until I realized that "praise" was simply a method of conveying "credit." Then I found a whole jackpot of comments. Most were in the stilted language of long ago, some extolling the value of praise (giving credit) and others warning against over abundance of praise that cheapens it.

The one of this latter type that most piqued my interest was this convoluted double negative written by the English writer and divine, Sydney Smith (1771-1845):

> Among the smaller duties of life, I hardly know any one more important than that of not praising where praise is not due. Reputation is one of the prizes for which men contend; it produces more labor and talent than twice the wealth of a country could ever rear up. It is the coin of genius, and it is the imperious duty of every man to bestow it with the most scrupulous justice and wisest economy.

A bit on the rhetorical side but it seems to me a balanced guideline. There are many angles to this matter of "getting credit," including sometimes the reprehensible "taking credit" where credit is not due . . . especially if it is robbing others of their just due. This general subject has long interested me, as evidenced by two mini "staff studies" from my files. The first one reads:

Credit Stealers

It has long been noted that the military chain of command provides people of dubious wit and integrity opportunities to "pass the buck." An altogether unadmirable phenomenon, the buck-passer will always be with us, but is usually spotted for the less-than-a-man he is. The other side of the buck-passer's coin has an equally deplorable trait, practiced by men of equally low cunning. These men are the credit stealers.

There was the platoon leader who took credit for the results of some hard thinking and work by his sergeant. There was the staff officer who took the work of a smart young assistant and presented it as his work to his boss. There was the subordinate who bypassed his boss and took a job his boss had directed him to do (and probably told him just how to do) to the boss's boss and presented it as his own idea.

It can be argued that credit stealers do not hamper the projection of the Army's business in the way the buck-passer does—even though the wrong man gets the credit, the work gets done. But if the Army's protestations of interest in the soldier as an individual mean anything, and I think they do, the credit stealers ought to get their comeuppance.

Conclusion: The man who does the work will be a better soldier if he gets credit for what he does. And what the Army wants are the best men, getting better.

Nothing in the years that have flowed by since then has changed the validity of that conclusion. My second little study is on a related theme:

Initiative vs. Credit

Some say the lack of initiative in a subordinate may be because his superior has restricted his initiative. But the subordinate must be sure he himself is not partially responsible for this restriction. The normal human being is interested in getting credit for what he does, and this includes superiors.

Suppose Lt. Yessir does a fine job of fixing up the mess hall of Co. J, and also suppose that when favorable comments are made Lt. Yessir takes the bows. Further, he discusses the matter around and about until people get the idea that Lt. Yessir is back of a lot of other improvements in Co. J—and that it's fortunate Capt. Stifle has a lieutenant so full of initiative.

Now Capt. Stifle, being human, may not feel enthusiastic about the world in general—and his battalion commander in particular— getting the idea that Yessir and not Stifle is the brains of Co. J. If Lt. Yessir was working on the orders of Capt. Stifle to "do something to fix up the mess hall"—then there is a real question about who was showing initiative, Yessir or Stifle.

Now, I am by no means saying a commander should steal credit from his junior; but I am saying that when a junior does a good job, the junior *has* received credit for it when his immediate superior sees that job. The subordinate should not go around claiming credit, for to do so may well, and with some reason, make his immediate superior leery of future displays of "initiative."

When a staff officer does a good job, much of the credit should quite naturally go to the commander. The young man is supposed to be working for and under the direction of his commander. But, con- versely, good commanders give due credit to the fine staff officers that serve them.

Some will say "credit" and "initiative" should be in no way connected. Maybe so—theoretically. But it's a good idea to remem- ber that even the finest soldier, inspired by the highest sense of duty, still feels the pull of human nature, and may, perhaps without realiz- ing it, give way to that pull.

Conclusion: The pure theoretical idealists will shout back at me, "But that is not right; it ought never be that way!" True, my friends, but what we are trying to find out here is what the facts of life really are—not what they should be in a military millennium where human nature has been eliminated.

Those little thoughts about one aspect of the human element in mili- tary service were published in the old *Infantry Journal* (January, 1948, and January, 1949), signed "Colonel Riposte." They stemmed from my hobby of constructing "Cerebrations" for the *IJ,* based on day-to-day ob- servations during my active-duty years.

A fundamental method of "giving credit" is to go look at a job that has been well done. Just as "a carpenter likes to show his chips," good soldiers like to have their superiors recognize the fine work they have done. One of the indispensable ways to do this is to "go see," because when you see the chips, so to speak, the carpenter knows he has received a measure of credit.

In my company-commander days—those wonderful five years with Co. G, 26th Infantry; Cos. F and D, 19th Infantry—I considered it one of my most important duties to make frequent inspections of barracks, with particular attention to squad rooms, supply room, kitchen, mess hall and garbage areas. It was a means of giving credit to the men who kept these areas "ready for inspection." Too often "command supervision" is thought of only in the narrow sense of correcting errors, but it is a poor commander who inspects with that limited view.

Other comments are:

- I like to think that, in general, I paid my debts to good soldiers by giving them the credit that was their due. But one of the greatest regrets of my military service is that, in the brief time I was in command of the 34th Infantry before entering combat, I failed to check personally on preparations for awarding battle decorations. I tried to follow up later (after returning to our division from the hospital), but have had to live with the fact there were surely some who deserved recognition for gallantry in action and who did not get it.

- An old Chinese proverb reads: "When you paint a dragon you paint his skin: it is difficult to paint the bones. When you know a man, you know his face but not his heart."

  True enough, as far as it goes, but what men do opens windows to their hearts. Thus, how a commander recognizes and gives credit for work well done is like an X-ray into a corner of his heart that reveals a facet of what kind of leader he is.

- One of my interesting conclusions in retrospect is that those most avid in "getting credit" themselves were more likely to be remiss in giving due credit. A related angle was this intriguing observation:

  When fine soldiers were alert to reward others, this sometimes brought credit to themselves with recognition they might not otherwise have received. Or to switch a metaphor: the bread of credit you cast upon the waters today for others may remind your boss to float some bread your way, too. However, this could put your motive in question, if the credit you pass on is not well founded.

- Perhaps I am making something complex out of the simple guideline: do unto others as you would they should do unto you in giving credit. But whether you call it simple or complex, when selection boards meet to choose military men for promotion their primary source of information is the credit placed in their records by others.

CHAPTER 49
Neither Cross of Gold Nor Crown
of Thorns

One of the finest articles ever published in ARMY Magazine was "Three Gold Leaves" (Nov. 1963) by Maj. Hugh Davidson. When he witnessed the promotion in the Pentagon of three majors to lieutenant colonels, he noticed the discarded majors' leaves were all regulation—but differed widely. One pair was strictly government issue of gold gilt; another pair was of freshly shined brass; and the third pair had the dull rich sheen of gold plate.

After thinking about this, he made these points:

- Those leaves reflected the personalities and professional postures of the three former majors, who were different in many ways.
- All were outstanding officers, each in his own fashion.

Selective promotion is usually a many-splendored thing, or many-bittered thing—depending on whether the lightning strikes you or the other fellow. There is one often overlooked angle about selective promotions that should be understood by all officers: the system that makes it possible for one man to jump over another in rank also makes it possible for the man jumped over to end up on top. It's not the "hare and tortoise" idea, but a matter of basic worth, ability to grow, and staying power.

Perhaps the best illustration of this is in the career of the officer featured on the cover of the same issue of ARMY in which Major Davidson's article appears: General George C. Marshall. He reached the absolute top not just because he was selected over others, but because when others stepped ahead of him on the career road—and many did— General Marshall retained his sense of perspective and simply continued to be the best soldier he knew how.

An incident in General Marshall's career was recalled to my mind by Major Davidson's statement that the three majors selected for promotion were all graduates of "the same famous military college," while he himself was not. Yet he is able to stand back and view this objectively in a fine well-reasoned conclusion to his article when he says, "Only fools would credit their success to the accidental parallels of schools, branches, career patterns and assignments."

General Marshall was not a graduate of that "famous military college" either yet he reached the top, as others have, by selective promotion over those who were. I was stationed at Schofield Barracks in Hawaii before World War II when he visited there soon after he became Chief of Staff of the Army. All officers at Schofield, then the Army's largest post, were assembled in the Engineer Theatre for General Marshall to speak to us.

He made a fine talk, but the thing I remember most clearly is the way he concluded. He said he was not a graduate of "that famous military college," but that he could not leave the platform without acknowledging his debt to those who were: that he would not stand before us as Chief of Staff if he had not received their support and help through the years.

Whether or not you wear the school tie of this famous military college is an often misunderstood and sometimes misrepresented factor in career advancement. When I retired in 1960 one of my final responsibilities was to complete efficiency reports on subordinates. While doing this I remembered outstanding officers who had previously served under me.

This led to the idea of writing letters to The Adjutant General of the Army, requesting the letters be filed with the efficiency records of officers concerned. The officers had to be exceptional, and my knowledge of them definite, to justify such a procedure. After much thought I wrote letters on only two officers, both lieutenant colonels—and neither was a graduate of that college, though I was.

As to selective promotion, I had extensive personal experience with this from above, below and sideways. It is like playing leap frog, because the man who makes the first jump is not necessarily going to end up in front.

Eight months before Pearl Harbor I was a company commander, and eight months after Pearl Harbor I was chief of staff of our division as a colonel. On the day I received my eagles I also received a telephone call of congratulations from an older lieutenant colonel, an officer who had been some eight years senior to me and whom I admired and respected greatly. My reply, I am happy to report, included this statement:

"It is my opinion I will still be wearing these eagles when you are a major general."

And he was—for eight years.

Of course wartime emergencies accent this seesaw in rank, but it takes place in peacetime too. There are many reasons for this, including luck of the draw of assignments and rating officers and other special circumstances. But the biggest factor is the true worth of an officer, *especially the capacity to grow.* Many fine company and battalion commanders are not so good as regimental commanders; and some outstanding colonels have reached their top potential. These things show up in the overall record in time. Those who make the big jump to stars have almost always been tested by adversity, and proved their mettle in the way they faced early disappointments.

Which brings us to one of the most basic factors in career advancement: It is necessary to strive to succeed—but if promotion in itself means too much, that can be a severe handicap. High rank is only one of many worthwhile goals in military service, and is more likely to be achieved by those who recognize this. After World War II a decorated colonel, who had been an outstanding combat regimental commander, said it this way:

"I don't envy these battle-virgin generals wearing staff stars. They will never know whether or not they could command a regiment in battle—but I know, because I did!"

The system of selective promotion in the Army cuts three ways: it undoubtedly inspires the best efforts of many fine officers, but a few of those who get that early jump tend to think they have it made—and many who were jumped fall into the error of being disgruntled or unduly discouraged.

When all of the facts and factors mentioned above are considered, it becomes clear that professional competence—ability to grow, and staying power—all rest on the cornerstone of an objective professional attitude.

Perhaps it was more than fortunate chance that included Major Davidson's "Three Gold Leaves" in the same issue of ARMY with Mr. Spore's "Marshall, The Tempering Years." The articles are as different when closely examined as were the majors' leaves, yet both teach the same invaluable lesson. If I were starting my military career tomorrow I would consider myself fortunate to have them as a guide in forming a sound, well-balanced professional attitude as the key to success and satisfaction in the military service—including the realization that rank should not be borne aloft as a cross of gold nor worn as a crown of thorns.

CHAPTER 50
Importance of the Point of View

The view you get of anything depends on where you sit. In military situations, conflicting opinions often result when people are separated geographically, or their duties and responsibilities vary widely. Thus, your opinion may depend on whether you have a rear-area viewpoint, a front-line view or observe from the flank. There are countless other viewpoints, too.

Here are three case histories where viewpoints were basic considerations. The incidents occurred during the campaign in the Southern Philippines of World War II. My observation post was as chief of staff of the 24th Infantry Division.

This was jungle fighting, and most roads were little more than trails. Since jungle growth crowded these winding dirt roads, poor visibility caused several jeep and truck accidents. After our division commander's jeep had to detour into the undergrowth to avoid a speeding truck, he issued a warning through command channels.

Soon thereafter, the CG's jeep again narrowly avoided an accident when his driver took quick evasive action. So the CG published a policy directive which read like this:

"Speeding motor vehicles on the primitive roads in our division area continue to be a serious traffic hazard. To correct this situation the following policy is announced:

"Military police will patrol the roads. Drivers who violate speeding restrictions, or otherwise endanger traffic, will be considered to have shown an inability to control their vehicles. In an effort to find a job for which they are better suited they will be assigned to front-line infantry companies."

This resulted in telephone calls from regimental commanders to me

along these lines, "Red, about that new policy of assigning traffic violators to infantry regiments. Do you think the CG would rescind that? Assignment to front-line infantry outfits is not punishment—it's an honor!"
The CG didn't rescind the policy. But that was academic, because
motor vehicles were suddenly brought under complete control. In retrospect, it is clear that the divergent viewpoints of the CG, the regimental
commanders and vehicle operators were all valid—from where each sat.
Thus, their actions were consistent with the situation as they saw it.

Then we had the case of the psychiatrist from higher headquarters
who came down "to visit the troops." As he traversed our area the regimental commanders called me again.

"Red," they said, "will you get this so-and-so psychiatrist outa my
area—and keep him out!"

We were suffering casualties, and the going had been heavy for weeks.
In one regiment, all front-line company and battalion commanders except
one had been killed or wounded. But battle morale was excellent.

Then the psychiatrist arrived, and his approach in talking to men was:
"It's sure tough here. No rest, and so many casualties. Have any of your
friends been killed? You're under a terrible strain. How do you feel?"

Put that way, they didn't feel so good—and we did get that guy outa
there. His viewpoint appeared to be one of clinical interest for his own
enlightenment, with no regard for how his questions might affect others.

Our regimental commanders had a radically different idea. Their men
were oriented to an aggressive fighting viewpoint: to get the job done in
spite of fatigue and stress from long combat. To change that around to taking inventory of their troubles and hardships was a serious matter.

The most interesting viewpoint situation within my experience was
the one involving black soldiers in our Mindanao operation. Since this
was before integration, we had no blacks in our division until an order
from X Corps attached some to us. It happened this way.

There were black units among corps troops, and some soldiers had
been convicted of offenses which merited confinement at hard labor. It is
usual practice that when troops are scheduled for active operations to sus-
pend confinement of men in the guardhouse, except those guilty of major
crimes. In this way, the guardhouse does not serve as a haven to avoid
combat.

Our corps commander suspended confinement for his corps troops,
but not hard labor. That's how our division got some black soldiers from

the guardhouse—as the corps CG directed that their hard labor would be in the form of burying enemy dead with front-line infantry battalions. Burying enemy dead, especially in the tropics where Nature's processes are rapid, can be a heavy and onerous job. So, this time, there were no viewpoint telephone calls from regimental commanders; the principle is similar to the case of traffic violators, but something new was added—a self-interest viewpoint.

Some days later, the Japanese launched a few large rockets, one landing in the perimeter of an infantry battalion at night. Several men were killed, and two or three of the burial detail wounded. Soon thereafter, we got a query from Eighth Army, wanting to know why black soldiers were among the wounded in our latest casualty report since we had no black units.

When the Eighth Army CG heard the explanation, he ordered our special burial detail returned to their parent units immediately—where, of course, they would not be in active combat. Since it was all right for hundreds, even thousands of 24th Division soldiers to be killed and wounded, why had our army commander taken such strong exception to the names of two or three black soldiers on our casualty report? What was his viewpoint?

Again, it's the question of where you sit. The CG was a long way from those dead enemy soldiers in need of burial, so they were no problem to him. But if some sharp newsman had seen that casualty report and discovered the unusual situation, *that* could quickly have bounced back on him.

Our army CG was sensitive about unfavorable publicity—with political repercussions likely to follow—and he understood the viewpoint of newsmen looking for a story. They were in the "man bites dog" business, alert for some unusual incident—however small and inconsequential—to hang a story on. Those wounded black soldiers could be made into a "story" by raising questions of "discrimination" and "persecution." Also, by searching out members of the burial detail, it might be possible to blow it up real good.

In this situation, the viewpoint which interested me most was that of the hard-labor burial detail when ordered out of the battle area. Some men asked to be assigned to our infantry regiments, so they could remain with them. They had developed the battle-pride viewpoint of combat soldiers that comes from shared danger.

The importance of viewpoints in our Army permeates all we do.

Morale is a matter of viewpoint, and disagreements are often a question of "Whose ox is being gored?"—a self interest view-point, the most pervasive of all. Some added comments are:

- Sending those traffic violators and that hard labor burial detail to front-line units stems from an old and basic viewpoint: When men on soft jobs fail to meet desired standards, transfer them to less cushy duties. There's a lot to be said for the idea, including the fact that it is effective command action. That's what Maj. Gen. Charles P. Stone did in Vietnam in the "saluting incident" ["Charley Stone: Maverick," by Martin Blumenson, ARMY, June 1969] which one newsman, applying his "man bites dog" viewpoint, transformed into a "story" that misled a lot of uninformed people and some who should have known better.

- Every military problem and situation results in differing opinions, because each man is a creature of his own viewpoint, largely determined by where he sits. All too often the best interests of the military service and the public welfare are not the controlling viewpoints they should be.

- The term "a good soldier" means one who has a good view-point, who looks at the Army from the angle of a trained, efficient professional. That's why a well-trained unit has high esprit—another word for viewpoint.

- When you disagree with somebody, consider the problem from where *he* sits. Sometimes this leads to the discovery that *you* have the wrong viewpoint.

- One of the most fascinating experiences in the Army is to see how the viewpoint of a commander is reflected in his unit. In fact, during World War II, the heroic viewpoint of one man shaped the viewpoint of a nation, and changed the history of the world, when Sir Winston Churchill made his magnificent speech that ended with "we shall never surrender!"

CHAPTER 51
"Think Time" is Vital in Command

When reporting on duty at Ft. Benning, Ga., in 1925, my advance planning was limited to, "Carry out orders and perform all tasks assigned— no sweat." In other words, assume somebody will tell you what to do, then cross that bridge when you come to it.

That was a workable policy for new lieutenants in an era made safe for democracy by World War I, with a small, well-officered Army and those wonderful old Army veteran sergeants. This was especially true at a time when somebody had to die or retire for you to gain a file on the way to the twin bars of a captain some fifteen to seventeen years in the future.

But life was far from stultified professionally. Our 29th Infantry Regiment put on demonstrations for Infantry School classes, and the program included an annual two-week field encampment. On one encampment, about an hour after dark, I heard several shots fired nearby where a narrow brush-bordered dirt road passed through a wooded area.

On inquiry I discovered that an "enraged husband" exercise had been engineered by several members of the company officers' class. One imaginative student had approached another (a self-proclaimed Casanova) along these lines:

"I've got a date out here tonight, but she has brought along a friend and three is a crowd. How about helping me out—though, to be fair, you should know the friend's estranged husband is very jealous."

In due course the two of them approached a parked car on that narrow dirt road in the wooded area. Then, suddenly, a figure jumped out of the darkness from behind the car, and shouted, "So you are the so-and-so who's been running around with my wife," and opened fire with a pistol—loaded with blanks.

But, instead of taking evasive action by a rush into the roadside brush, Casanova (tipped off in advance) produced his own pistol and returned the fire—also with blanks. Now it was the surprised "husband's" turn, and he beat a frantic strategic retreat through the brambles and brush into the friendly dark woods.

There is no reason good training cannot include some fun on the side. That is the way it was then, but, for me, mostly under programs and on schedules founded on thinking by others.

Anyway, by early spring 1941, I was a company commander in the 19th Infantry at Schofield Barracks, Hawaii, and very happy in that status. Then, suddenly, change-of-duty orders assigned me assistant chief of staff, G2, of the Hawaiian Division, while still a captain.

All other principal staff officers were older and of higher rank, had been to the Command and General Staff School at Ft. Leavenworth, Kan., and exuded an almost visible aura of knowing the answer to everything, and of pitying those who did not. I had never been to Leavenworth, knew little of staff work—and from the angle of some of their noses they sniffed my aura of ignorance.

I had not yet discovered that this indefinable attitude of disapproval was a standard general staff professional posture. Not being sure what else to do, I began reading books, manuals, files, orders and otherwise bending every effort to learn my new job.

After about ten days, I was at my desk at five o'clock one evening when, as usual, I heard the slow measured tread of dignified footsteps in the hallway. I knew this was the fine old chief of staff on his daily promenade homeward.

I looked up to see him pass my door, for I both liked and respected him, but this day the tempo of his footsteps changed and he turned toward my doorway. As I came hastily to my feet, he let his steely blue eyes rest on me a contemplative moment before he said:

"Newman, every day when I pass this door I see you talking on the phone, pushing a pencil as though in a hurry, or reading with a worried frown on your face."

He tapped the side of his knee gently with the braided riding crop he always carried.

"In fact," he said, "I'm beginning to worry about you a little—and to wonder if we have got the right man up here."

The braided riding crop continued to tap.

"Now," he continued, "if some of the time when I come by here I find you smoking a cigarette and looking out the window, then I would be encouraged—and think maybe some general staff work was getting done."

The riding crop stopped tapping. "You think that over," he said, and his measured footsteps resumed their dignified parade toward the stairway.

I did think about it, at much length and with tremendous benefit to myself and, perhaps, some benefit to the military service in the nearly 20 years' active duty that remained to me.

My old chief of staff meant, among other things:

- When you are reading, writing, talking or listening you are not thinking in the clear sense necessary for a general staff officer to separate main issues from unimportant details.
- At general staff level you cannot know all about everything, so squirreling away masses of information you may never need is a stupid waste of time.
- A general staff officer will fail if he simply fires shot-gun blasts of mental effort hoping thereby to do his job. He must aim the rifle of his mind at *selected* targets, and to do this the first thinking must be toward selecting things to work on.
- Therefore, stop. Look out the window now and then, and let your mind stand away from problems to see them in perspective, to select those areas to which you will direct your efforts.
- Finally, the most important duty of a general staff officer is not just to work skillfully, even selectively, at matters brought to him for resolution or coordination, *but to reflect on matters he should be working on that nobody else has thought about yet.*

While the little experience above deals only with my initiation into general staff duty, let me add quickly that the principles apply to all officers and NCOs, no matter what their levels or duty assignments.

Of all the ways this principle can be applied, from the squad on up, none known to me beats the thinking of Adm. Horatio Nelson before the climactic battle of Trafalgar. Nelson knew that a great combined fleet had been assembled by Napoleon to destroy the English fleet, thus forcing England to its knees and enabling Napoleon to bring all of Europe under his control.

It was standard practice at that time for hostile fleets to sail in line opposite each other, cannonading one another until one prevailed. In such a battle the outgunned English seemed likely to lose. So Admiral Nelson assembled all his ship captains and briefed them on a simple but radically different plan for the certain-to-come battle at some future date. When the great naval confrontation came, with the fleets sailing in lines parallel to each other, Nelson suddenly turned his fleet directly into Napoleon's combined fleets about one-third back from the head of the enemy line. In this carefully thought-out maneuver the prevailing wind kept the hostile leading portion out of the battle, while the whole weight of the English fleet fell on and destroyed the trailing body of the combined fleet.

Thus, one man, by looking through the window of his mind into the future with imaginative advance planning, changed the whole course of history—because that was the beginning of the end for the great Napoleon.

I shall be forever grateful to Col. Earle Wilson for directing my attention to this "look out the window principle" of thinking as you progress upward in rank and broader responsibilities. My 15 years' service in nine companies (commanding three of them, in six regiments) laid a solid foundation of *understanding* of the Army and the people in it.

But that "window principle" was the catalyst that enabled me to go—in about 15 months—from a captain commanding an infantry company to an eagle colonel as chief of staff, 24th Infantry Division, in July, 1942.

Of course, other factors were involved, too, like being in the right place at the right time. Anyway, these comments seem in order:

- With the exercise of authority goes the responsibility to think, to "look out the window" with your mind free to rove. This should be planned, otherwise you will surely be caught up in the treadmill of routine inconsequentials, most of which someone else should be doing for you.
- Some like to ruminate in bathtubs; Bernard Baruch made park benches well-known cerebrating places; some officers begin the day with an hour free from appointments, others end the day that way — to think free from the push of people and pull of paper problems. Some (I am one of them) like a second or "thinking cup" of coffee at breakfast, relatively free from interruptions, to review plans for the day.
- But whatever your method, free yourself periodically from the

involuntary mental sleepwalking that the press of duties and events tend to invoke, and do some voluntary planned and controlled thinking, looking beyond your desk, out the window to where the troops are and the action is, toward tomorrow and the future.

CHAPTER 52
Lady Luck often Works in Strange Ways

Mark Twain is sometimes credited with having said, "Everybody talks about the weather, but nobody does anything about it." That's the way it is with luck, too, especially as it affects military assignments and promotions. This suggests the question: Can anything be done about Lady Luck and her capricious influence on military careers?

My dictionary says that luck is that which happens by chance; that chance is the unknown or undefined course of events not subject to calculation; opportunity. To see how Lady Luck operates we'll look at some chance circumstances in military life.

Of course, there are stories about mistaken identity, like the colonel recommended for a combat star, which an Army chief of staff vetoed because he thought it was for another man of the same-sounding name. Then, on a trip overseas, the chief met the colonel, realized his mistake, and the colonel eventually retired as a four-star general.

Or tales about being in the right place at the right time—about able soldiers, from privates to generals, who fill combat vacancies when the man higher up is wounded, killed, relieved, or promoted. A World War II brigadier who took over a division when the CG was wounded, and pinned on a second star, has a career total of eight Purple Hearts. One view could be that this is proof he lived with Lady Luck. He also sounds like a fighting battle commander to me—so maybe that had something to do with his luck, too.

Among other "lucky" themes is the one about "you-have-to-know-the-right-people." Since they would know you, that could cut two ways. Whether justified or not, it's only human to damn Lady Luck as a faithless floozy, and I could list some real gems she's pulled on me. But here are two incidents which reveal overlooked facets of her character.

After landing on Leyte in 1944, my regiment pushed halfway across the island and on the way I was seriously wounded. The conventional approach would have been to bemoan the fact that I fell only weeks before there was an opening for a brigadier general, and to cuss my luck for not being there to get the star. But that needs further examination.

Consider my landing on Red Beach. Four waves were stalled there, so I moved inland to clear the impasse. In doing this I stepped over the lower legs of the sprawled body of the gallant commander of Item Company, 1st Lt. Howell Barrow—who had fallen with a bullet through his head. A fine young staff officer, Captain Wai, was among those who followed—and died. Others fell on Red Beach, in fighting across the swamp behind it, and in the Japanese counterattack that night, while I continued on untouched. Lady Luck was at my side when I needed her.

As we fought our way to Jaro, happy chance led me by the hand. Not only did my skin remain whole, but every maneuver worked—until we ran into the Japanese 41st Infantry Regiment. Impatient, I pushed my luck too far and was among the first to get it. But that wasn't just bad luck; it was also poor judgment.

After the medics took me apart and put me together, the surgeon handed me a cookie-sized piece of steel retrieved from my middle. "Colonel," he said, "you're living on borrowed time. Another half inch and you'd have been dead in two minutes."

That steel hit a tough web pistol belt before it got to me, so Lady Luck saved me from paying a higher price for an unnecessary risk. Also, maybe I would have pulled some dumb stunt and been relieved, or maybe they would have picked the other guy for that star anyway, or I might have got myself killed. So maybe Lady Luck was more than kind to pull me out of the ball game.

About six weeks later, a fellow patient on the evacuation transport headed home was the maddest man I saw in World War II. When I could walk well enough to make it to the sun deck, we occupied adjacent chairs. His bitterness was showing, and pretty soon it boiled over.

He had been commissioned a second lieutenant, then shipped out in the early Attu operation. There he was wounded, decorated, and evacuated. After returning to duty he was in the Kwajalein assault, and was again wounded, decorated, and evacuated. Then—you guessed it! He got it for the third time, on Leyte.

Now, after three campaigns, three wounds and three decorations, he was returning to the States, still a second lieutenant, while many of those commissioned with him had not left home or heard a shot fired. But they were first lieutenants. Of all the blasted luck! Since it might help a little to know he had company, I was about to tell him the sad story of my broken romance with Lady Luck, when two patients came walking slowly down the deck.

One had his forearm in a cast and sling. His other arm was linked through that of his companion, who walked slowly in odd, short steps. When arm-sling helped his partner into a deck chair we got the picture, and saw the depression in the left side of his forehead where a sliver of enemy steel had smashed in to blind that fine-looking young man for life.

My second lieutenant friend said nothing more about his blasted luck, and I didn't mention mine. In fact, since that day I've not complained much about Lady Luck; when I start feeling unhappy because chance has been unkind, I remember that young man with the dent in the side of his forehead, his eyes turned upward to the warmth of a sun he could not see.

Strangely enough, it's not in war you hear most of the complaints about Lady Luck as a no-good hussy who bestows her favors on others. We have peacetime laments about not getting promoted, getting jobs we don't want, trouble with our bosses and other administrative misadventures. Actually, there seems to be less unfortunate chance than is alleged, because, too often to be "luck" alone, the best professional officers end up under the better bosses in the most desirable jobs.

I attended a cocktail party some years ago that was hosted by Adm. Jerauld Wright, then Commander in Chief, Atlantic, and Supreme Allied Commander, Atlantic. One of his guests said, "Admiral, I hear you're going to Washington for several weeks."

"Yes," the admiral replied, "I'm on an SDB board."

I asked, "What's an SDB board?"

"Well," he said, deadpan, "it's the board that selects flag officers. Every Navy captain not selected for admiral says it's because Some Dumb Bastard on the board didn't like him. So I call it an SDB board."

The idea that Lady Luck enters the picture is obviously true in some measure. Selections are matters of opinion, so it is illogical to assume that no matter who is on the board there would be no change in names selected. But only a few marginal names would change. Officers who depend on Lady Luck to give them a marginal selection are unlikely to find themselves among the "best qualified."

The way chance operates is complex and interrelated with everything in our personal and professional lives. It is impossible to classify the lady's whims and caprices. Perhaps, however, these comments may point the way toward better coexistence:

- There is such a thing as luck in a military career. Sometimes this has far-reaching results, but closer examination reveals an interesting angle: happy chance can produce favorable circumstances, but the "lucky" man is the one who has the perception to see the opportunity, and the ability to take advantage of it.
- Things don't come out even in uniform any more than in civil life, but the best soldiers of all ranks don't dwell on good or bad luck. They meet unfortunate chance as a natural obstacle to be overcome with assiduous effort, and view favorable circumstances for what they are: opportunities to be exploited with energy and skill.
- When Lady Luck lets you down, remember the good breaks you've had and realize how much luckier you are than so many others. Over the years since World War II, when I have felt abused by Fate or betrayed by Lady Luck, I've thought back to that young soldier in the deck chair, with the dent in the side of his forehead. Then the rocks in my road become pebbles to be taken in stride.

CHAPTER 53
Importance of Rank on the Job

In my recruit year in the Army I learned some specialized things about the place of military rank in uniform, such as: "Rank among second lieutenants is like virtue among practitioners of the world's oldest profession—nonexistent." Another slant was the old question: "Would you rather be a colonel with an eagle on your shoulder or a private with a chicken on your knee?"

That query, however, must have a fallacy in it, because my observation over the years did not confirm it as a mutually exclusive "either-or" proposition.

I also learned there was a blockading "hump" in military promotions, which consisted of a large number of officers commissioned in a short space of time during World War I. Further, I was behind that "hump," therefore could not expect to be a captain for some seventeen years—because promotions depended on vacancies, not just length of service and time in grade.

Resignations were rare, and it was a healthy peacetime Army with few deaths or physical retirements. Also the law required 30 years' service for retirement—and most officers stayed in to the then mandatory retirement age of 64 years.

Perhaps these factors explained why there seemed to be less preoccupation with rank then, than now. At least, that is the way it seemed to me. The rank of the man on the job was often below that specified in Tables of Organization. In my regiment several first lieutenants commanded companies, two majors commanded battalions, and one of our regimental commanders was a lieutenant colonel.

The question arises: how important, as a factor in getting the job done, is it for an officer to hold the proper rank for his duty assignment?

Or, expressed another way, which comes first: the job, the man or the rank? Here are several case histories, within my past personal purview, where that angle was a consideration.

Fortunately, the promotion law was changed in 1935 when I had just over ten years' service, thus making me an instant captain. Five years later I was still a captain but in a positions vacancy for lieutenant colonel, as G2 of the old "square" Hawaiian Division in early 1941. So I know from personal experience that the lack of normal military rank for an assignment is a handicap in getting the job done.

The 7 December 1941 attack on Pearl Harbor and our subsequent mobilization produced a totally different rank progression. In July, 1942, by then a six-months-in-grade lieutenant colonel as G2, 24th Infantry Division in Hawaii, I was designated in orders as division chief of staff.

That produced a special situation, because I was next to the bottom-ranking lieutenant colonel in the division. Three older lieutenant colonel section chiefs on our division staff were veterans of World War I, with eight years' more service. Whether I was the best man for the job could be debated, and probably was—but I was in the saddle with the title.

As might be expected, a senior staff section chief promptly questioned one of my administrative orders. So I listened, then declined to change my directive. He appealed it to the commanding general, who sustained my decision.

However, I remained on good terms with that officer—especially after my "spot promotion" to eagle colonel came through by wire from Washington a couple of days later. It was important that the man on that job, under those circumstances, have the proper rank.

Of course, this was in a war environment, because "spot promotions" like that in peacetime would really open up a can of unhappy, unhealthy and very wiggly worms.

More than a year and a half later, in the Southwest Pacific Theater, our division was preparing for an amphibious operation in New Guinea. Our headquarters commandant was a relatively newly joined officer, a pleasant and agreeable major.

By this time (as I learned many years later), some of the staff referred to me as "The Great Red Father," while others preferred a less mellow redheaded term. Thus, what I decided should be done about the headquarters commandant no doubt gave more credence to the views of the latter group.

Anyway, I asked the division commander's clearance to replace the major, and he said, "Why—and who do you want to replace him?"

My reply was to the effect that with him as headquarters commandant I was being pulled into administrative matters that, as chief of staff, I should not have to worry about. Further, in combat this would seriously interfere with my proper function as chief of staff.

As to a replacement, I wanted 1st Lt. Hightower—to include putting in a request for his immediate promotion to captain. I well knew my CG would not okay hijacking a key major replacement from some staff section or one of our lower units. But, after some thought, he approved my proposed solution. For the record, Captain Hightower was a fine headquarters commandant in the Tanehmerah-Hollandia operation that followed.

This points up the fact that it takes more than Table of Organization rank to cut the mustard. This is a particularly critical fact of life in combat, because the first requirement—truly a matter of life and death—is that the man must be up to the job. But the right rank helps.

In time of peace there is a different set of rules, with no on-the-job "spot promotions," thus a different situation.

In the summer of 1950 I was promoted from chief of staff, 11th Airborne Division, to command the 511th Airborne Infantry—a happy change.

By this time in my military life cycle it had become clear I was neither a One-Man Army or Superman. So my first concern was to observe and evaluate the men in key positions on whom I must depend in the command of our regiment.

The S3 was leaving, a major's billet, so I wanted the best possible replacement. This called to mind an outstanding captain who had commanded division headquarters company when I was chief of staff but who was being reassigned to another Army post. It was a pressure time (beginning of the "Korean Police Action"), so when I requested him for my regimental S3 his orders were changed. And Capt. "Bud" Parson made a truly superior operations officer for our regiment.

Other changes came in time. The regimental adjutant was given the company command he wanted, and his replacement was more on my wave length—a factor not to be overlooked, especially when you work closely together every day.

When the regimental executive officer received change-of-station

orders, I brought in a major as "exec"—rather than one of two lieutenant colonel battalion commanders. Rank is a many-splendored thing, in
its place, but it is not an inviolate strait-jacket in making assignments. It
is, however, almost always unwise to assign a man to a spot lower than
his rank.

Nine months later I was kidnapped, kicking and squealing, for an
overseas staff assignment in Iceland. To those who made that decision I
guess it was just another personnel action, although it was an unhappy
change for me. But you don't have to like your duty assignment, just do it
the best you can.

Some comments are:

- Military rank is an essential factor in military command, but it is
not a substitute for the ability of the man to do the job. The job
must come first, then comes the right man to do the job—and with
the proper rank he can do the job better. A fascinating case history
of command in combat is that of Task Force Kingston in Korea,
where a second lieutenant exercised control over a major, three
captains and several first lieutenants. Sure, it is a most unusual case
that grew out of a special situation. For the details read *Masters of
the Art of Command* (by Martin Blumenson and James L. Stokes-
bury, Houghton Mifflin Co., Boston).

- Obviously, if you do not have the right man for the job, you go out
and try to get him—as I did for Captain Parson. But that is like
picking players in a professional football draft: in most cases somebody else gets the star player you want. So you usually end up like
that man who searched the world over for his fortune, without
success—then found diamonds in his own backyard.

- There are a lot of undiscovered diamonds in our Army, waiting to
be found and polished to display their brilliance. So it is not
enough just to fill your assignment spots with the best men available, with due consideration for ability and rank. Also involved is
your perception to see below the surface, to shape and polish the
hidden brilliance there into the right man for the job to which you
assign him.

- One of the greatest satisfactions of my years in retirement has been
to follow the shining careers of some fine soldiers who once served
under me. And I like to think that, just possibly, I may have helped
a little in the polishing process.

CHAPTER 54
What Are Generals Made Of?

A short item in the March issue of *ARMY* concludes that "general officers really know how to put a guy in his place." This reminds me of another polarized generalization: "Sugar and spice and everything nice—that's what little girls are made of." Which suggests the question, "What are generals made of?"

Soon after pinning on my first star I visited Fort Benning and walked into the officers' club bar where several members were sampling the merchandise. An older colonel introduced me around and insisted on buying the first drink to "baptize that new star." He then told this story:

Some years ago in London [the colonel began] a famous British combat unit from World War I held a reunion. Among those present were two brigadiers and an old sergeant major, all retired. After reliving their battle days, when the brigadiers were subalterns and the sergeant major a soldier in ranks, they got around to personal matters.

"I married after the war," one brigadier said, "and I'm proud of my son. He's a famous brain surgeon."

"I married after the war too," the other brigadier said. "My son is a distinguished lawyer. King's counsel, you know."

When they looked toward the old sergeant major he said, "I've got a son, a career military man. He's now a brigadier."

After a pause one brigadier said, "Sergeant Major, remembering the old days, it's hard to think of you as a married man."

"Well," the sergeant major replied blandly, "You're right. I've never been married."

Maybe there's a thread of truth in this parable about the sergeant major's son, but a single thread is not a true sample of whole cloth. That "sugar and spice and everything nice" is not the whole story about what little girls are made of, either.

There are no established specifications for general officers, so we'll take the biblical approach: "By their works ye shall know them." This translates into: What they do—as cadets at West Point, as Army officers, and after they reach star rank—reveals what generals are made of.

I knew seven cadets at West Point who were first captains of the regiment in their last year (1921-28). All later became generals. These, too, were also first captains in their day: General John J. Pershing, Douglas MacArthur and William C. Westmoreland, among others.

But these were exceptional men who "had everything," and they do not set the pattern for average general officer composition. For example, while cadet first captains always stand well academically, academic excellence is not necessary to be a general. Yet the popular myth that the last man in a class is as likely to be a general as the top man is not true, either. In 35 classes (1907–38) 21 of the top 35 became generals, compared to only two of the last 35.

The superintendent during my first year was Brig. Gen. MacArthur, who compiled the highest grades ever scored by a cadet: an unbelievable 98-plus average. He was followed as superintendent by Maj. Gen. Fred W. Sladen, who required five years to graduate. Yet both had outstanding battle records and each, in his way, was the personification of a general.

The great comedian and cowboy philosopher, Will Rogers, visited the U.S. Military Academy in the early 1920s and talked to cadets in the gymnasium one weekend. Also present were post officers and their wives, including the distinguished and austere General Sladen. Mr. Rogers convulsed his audience, even drawing a wintry smile from General Sladen, when he said: "One thing I don't understand about West Point is why they send a man here to make you fellers do in four years what it took him five to do."

In World War II in France, three great American armies lined up abreast in one of the climactic battles of world history: First Army, Third Army and Ninth Army. They were commanded by Gen. Courtney H. Hodges, who failed academically at West Point, enlisted in the Army and rose from the ranks; Gen. George S. Patton, who needed five years to graduate; and Gen. William H. Simpson, who finished 101 in his class of 103.

The class of 1915—the one "stars fell on"—produced 60 generals from 164 members, including Generals Dwight D. Eisenhower and Omar N. Bradley. They were the right age when World War II greatly increased the number of generals needed. Of those 60 generals, 29 came from the top third of the class, 17 from the middle third and 14 from the bottom third. Apparently those with above-average academic records are more likely to wear stars but, clearly, this is not a controlling factor.

Most cadets of my time who later became general officers were members of athletic squads. But the reverse was not true, for many great athletes never wear stars.

However, cadets who were athletes, had good academic records and wore chevrons of military rank in their senior year, were excellent general officer candidates. But they were still only candidates. Many would never reach star rank. Further, there were others whose cadet records gave little indication of the high rank they would later attain. What made the difference?

In retrospect, it's possible to see the significance of certain happenings which revealed latent qualities in some cadets that would bring them stars. Like the day a cadet in my company jostled another, knocking him off the sidewalk as we walked out for dinner formation. The jostled cadet said in an even, quiet tone, "Don't do that again."

The next day the same thing happened—obviously planned—except this time there was an instant fight. The jostled cadet was never jostled again—by anybody.

Is it coincidence that the jostled cadet—who was no athlete, below average in academic standing, and held no high cadet rank—reached three-star rank?

One year the football team left West Point by train for the Army-Navy game. It was before breakfast, but the corps streamed down the hill to the station with traditional fervor. After the train left, cadets started back to their company parades for the usual march to breakfast. In so doing they were passing the mess hall entrance when one cadet stepped from the moving hundreds and ran up the steps.

"Come on!" he shouted, swinging his arm in an inviting gesture, "time to eat!" And he pushed through the doors into the mess hall.

Some followed quickly, then the mass of them filed in the mess hall, talking and laughing, except a few who returned to their company parades as they were supposed to do. One cadet stood watching this development, then hurried into the mess hall. There he pushed his way through the milling crowd to the table of the first captain who was not present, having left with the football team.

Stopping in the aisle by the first captain's table, the cadet talked briefly to another, who went into the inner mess hall to play his part there, while the first cadet jumped up to stand in the first captain's chair, "At-ten-TIONN!" his voice rolled out in drill field tone.

The hum of voices died down and the mess hall grew silent. "Think what you are doing. Don't get the Corps in trouble before the Navy game!" he said. "Go back to your companies and march down."

Without hesitation, he jumped from the chair and walked quickly out of the mess hall. Some followed him, then all filed out to march back in formation.

What more is there to know about the cadet who led them in and the cadet who led them out? Both were members of varsity sports squads, both stood in the top third of their class and both held fairly high cadet rank. But was it these things which, years later, resulted in their selection as permanent major generals—two of only sixteen men from their class of 245 to reach that rank? Or did they have other unmeasurable qualities?

More memories from those years crowd forward, but it's time for some comments:

- Knowing which cadets would later become generals, was there anything distinctive about them as a group? Yes. While they were liked and respected and got along well with others, they were not hail-fellow-well-met types. There always seemed an intangible aloofness about them, a quiet self control in manner and bearing.

- Another quality, a vital requirement, was that they stood on their own feet and were not easily pushed around, mentally or physically. There were also other characteristics, not recognizable from cadet records, which an officer must have to reach star rank.

- Stress situations are limited in cadet life, but years of service develop and test an officer's judgment, human understanding and—as President Richard Nixon said of the attributes of a leader in his greeting to King Hussein—"Courage, wisdom, and moderation." An officer measures up and grows, or fades—depending on what he is, not his IQ, his athletic ability, what school he went to, or whether he rose from the ranks.

To Be Noted: WHERE THEY STOOD

Much has been written about the fact that Gen. Douglas Mac-Arthur graduated at the head of his West Point class, with an unsurpassed academic record. Which raises the question: How did other famed leaders stand?

Gen. Robert E. Lee graduated No. 2 out of 46—and received no demerits in his four years. Gen. U. S. Grant was 21st of 39, Gen. Thomas J. (Stonewall) Jackson was 17th of 59 in a brilliant class that included George B. McClellan, Jesse L. Reno, Ambrose P. Hill, George E. Pickett, David R. Jones, and others.

Gen. George A. Custer who, after a gallant Civil War record, died in an Indian massacre, graduated last in his class of 34. Gen. Philip H. (Little Phil) Sheridan, another famed Union commander, finished 34th of 52. Gen. William T. (War Is Hell!) Sherman was 6th of 42.

General of the Armies John J. Pershing finished 30th of 77, and Gen. Charles P. Summerall was 6th of 42.

Other more modern great names graduated: Dwight D. Eisenhower, 61st of 164; Omar N. Bradley, 44th of 164; George S. Patton Jr., 46th of 103; James A. Van Fleet, 92nd of 164; Robert L. Eichelberger, 68th of 103; Maxwell D. Taylor, fourth of 102; Hoyt S. Vandenberg, 240th of 261; Matthew B. Ridgway, 56th of 139; Harold K. Johnson, 232nd of 347 and William C. Westmoreland, 112th of 276.

I believe it's clear that controlling factors in the rise to general officer rank are intangible personal qualities. To learn more about what these characteristics are let us take another look backward, this time observing officers in the Army who later reached star rank.

On my first post there were many future generals, including officers in my regiment like Maj. Oscar W. Griswold, Captains Withers A. Burress and Andrew D. Bruce, and 1st Lieutenants Reuben E. Jenkins and William B. Kean. All five would become lieutenant generals.

The indefinable mantle of leadership rested on them then—if you had the perception to see it. The key word is *professionalism.* They were interested in every soldier and everything about their units. While there was a difference in personalities, they were well liked and respected—yet always seemed to stand a little aloof, like the cadets who later reached top rank.

They also had a special quality personified by another officer at Fort Benning at that time, Capt. J. Lawton Collins. His outstanding characteristic was *dedication* to the military profession, which I believe was the cornerstone of his rise to be chief of staff of the Army.

What's the difference between professionalism and dedication? It's somewhat like the reported difference between sex and love: sex is a hunger, and love the sauce that makes the hunger keener. In an analogous sense, military dedication is the sauce that intensifies and gives continuity and enduring purpose to daily professionalism.

Several years later the company officers class at the Infantry School was being instructed in firing at airborne targets. This included shooting .22 caliber rifles on a 1,000-inch range at small black sleeves on a panel that moved laterally across our front.

The instructor was Maj. Claudius M. ("Spec") Easley, who divided us into squad-size groups. Each squad would fire at one panel, shooting at sleeves on the left edge as it moved left, then at those on the right edge as it moved right. This required "leading" in the air ahead of the moving panel.

One lieutenant decided to find out where his shots were hitting, so he fired at a sleeve on the trailing edge. Sure enough, a bullet hole appeared in that sleeve, and the lieutenant looked up with a pleased smile and chuckle.

"Hold it! Stop where you are!" came the sharp command from Maj. Easley. He stared at the pleased lieutenant, who lost his smile, and the major continued. "It's never smart to disobey orders. Some wise guy scored a hit on that trailing edge sleeve. He and I know who he is. Don't do it again."

Both the wise guy lieutenant, who figured how to identify his hit, and the alert major who caught him at it, reached general officer rank. Were they, in different ways, revealing qualities that helped them win stars?

To Be Noted: TRAINING FOR STARS

> The modern pentathlon event in the Olympic games, sometimes called military pentathlon—patterned after the military pentathlon of the original Olympic games in ancient Greece—is little known to the American public. It consists of the 300-meter free-style swim, pistol shooting, dueling sword fencing, 5,000-meter cross country steeplechase ride, and 4,000-meter cross country run.
>
> When first included in modern Olympic games it was based on

skills required in battle of a courier of that time. He would start on horseback to deliver his message; when his horse was killed he would continue on foot; faced with a river obstacle, he would swim it; and fight his way with sword and pistol.

In the period 1924-36 only Army officers made the American team (civilians tried and failed; some have made it since, also men from other services). Since I was on the 1928 team, it's interesting to look back and see what kind of military careers those officers had later.

The 1924 team: two became generals, one was an infantry regimental commander in battle, one retired a colonel—his career unknown to me. The 1928 team: all four became generals (including the alternate, as competing teams were reduced to three). The 1932 team: one became a general, one commanded an infantry regiment in battle, one was killed in combat as chief of staff of an armored division. The 1936 team: two became generals, one commanded an infantry regiment in battle.

When in Germany (1944-46) I met a member of the German 1928 team. He said two of them were division commanders in World War II, the third was killed early in the war as an infantry regimental commander.

In 1912, when the event was first included in modern Olympic games, a member of the American team was the future Gen. George S. Patton Jr.

In Hawaii in the late 1930s we had a ball of fire as regimental executive of the 19th Infantry. All officers knew him as an outstanding soldier but one who could be real rough around the edges. Thus, company commanders in my battalion were not happy to learn that the regimental executive, Lt. Col. Clarence R. Huebner, would command us temporarily for our two-week encampment on the towed target range.

But we never had a pleasanter two weeks, because we got on the ball and had things shipshape from the first day. He raised hell only when things were not up to snuff; thus his reputation of demanding high professional standards served to produce those standards without further command action by him. This is a quality common to many officers who later wear stars. Further, I'm sure it was an important element in the continued brilliant career of Lt. Gen. Clarence R. Huebner, retired.

After Pearl Harbor a company of another regiment, participating in a field exercise, returned to its bivouac area from a march over mountain trails. As tired, dusty men were breaking out mess gear for supper, the first sergeant reported to the captain with a soldier who had abandoned his rifle on the mountain trail.

"Why did you leave it there?" the captain asked.

"Sir, it was heavy and I was tired."

"Do you remember where you left it?"

"Yes, sir."

The captain looked at the soldier, then said quietly, "Go back and get it—now."

As the soldier stood, irresolute, the first sergeant said, "Does the captain mean after supper?"

"No," the captain said, "I mean *now*. Tell the mess sergeant to save supper for him when he gets back—with his rifle."

That captain, who was Lt. James L. Dalton in my company at Plattsburg Barracks, became one of the finest combat regimental commanders of World War II. He was promoted to general officer rank in combat, then killed on Luzon. He had the quiet iron in his soul that most officers who would later wear stars always seemed to have. Not senseless harshness but a steely refusal to accept the unacceptable—like a soldier who abandoned his weapon.

But don't think future generals are always grim and never relax. The reverse is true, like the drink-and-smell golf foursome at Baguio in the Philippines 40 years ago. This was a handicapping method adopted by four lieutenants: a 75 shooter, two who were 85, and the fourth a 95. It worked this way:

One caddy carried a bottle of bourbon in his bag of clubs, another a bottle of scotch, and still another a water glass with a hefty size drink marked off on it. To be sure everybody started even, they had a measured drink all around on the first tee, neat. Then the winner of each hole took a measured drink—choice of bourbon or scotch—while others smelled the bottle.

When the 75 shooter won four holes he was cut down to size. Then the 85 boys alternated several drinks, and the foursome ended the nine holes within one stroke of each other. The efficacy of the method proved, we adjourned to the 19th hole.

Three of that foursome are now retired generals. To avoid giving the impression that familiarity with bottles is in itself a help toward gaining stars, it should be added that another lieutenant in Baguio at the time—known as One-Drink So-and-so—was the only one to reach four-star rank.

In general, a goody-goody reputation—no wine, women, song, cussing or smoking—did not lead to stars. Officers whose high professional attainments on duty were combined with a balanced life off duty—characterized by moderation—seemed to wear better, last longer and rise higher.

Finally, over the years, it became clear that an officer was not selected for star rank on a sudden eleventh hour burst of efficiency. Those who reached the top had long careers of dedicated service—of getting better each year, constantly striving and growing. This was typified by four officers with whom I served (1949-51) in the 11th Airborne Division: Ben Harrell, Theodore J. Conway, George R. Mather and Albert O. Connor. The first three became four-star generals, and the last one reached three-star rank. They were "on the way" then and obviously had been for years. They had the professionalism, drive and personal attitude that only sustained dedication can develop—along with the all important capacity to grow.

So what makes generals tick?

- The sooner a young officer develops a professional attitude, the more likely he is to wear stars. Just as Rome wasn't built in a day, the complex characteristics and professional know-how that leads to stars requires years to mature.
- Self-confidence is an essential requirement. If you don't believe in yourself, how can you expect others to? The foundation of self-confidence is knowledge which, like uranium, develops a chain reaction after you acquire enough of it: the more you learn, the more you want to know. Most future generals had this type of mental radioactivity, and the aura of confidence that stems from it.
- No two people are exactly alike, so no two generals can ever be the same. But all need a certain amount of steel in their souls, or as retired Japanese Army chief of staff, Gen. Ichiji Sugita, once expressed it to me, "To a general a chin is as important as a brain."
- That steel in the soul—as do wine, women and song—requires restraint, judgment and moderation. The awareness of others that the steel is there will usually make its use unnecessary.

- On the other hand, the bulldozer approach—without a sense of humor or compassion for others, and no toleration for human error— is the classic mistake of trying to push instead of lead. Officers with this approach seldom get to wear stars.

CHAPTER 55
Character is the Arbiter

It's clear there is no formula, based on measurable qualities, that leads to star rank, but there are patterns in what people do and how they react to situations.

In my first year as a cadet, our brilliant young superintendent, Brig. Gen. Douglas MacArthur, was already a living legend. On the infrequent occasions we saw him, the rainbow of ribbons on his chest reflected his gallant World War I battle record and, somehow, emphasized the great void between us. It seemed impossible that this gap in years and distinction could be bridged by any kind of personal touch.

When news circulated that our "Supe" would bring a bride to the historic red-brick house facing the parade ground, it all seemed remote and impersonal to us. Then each cadet received an individually packaged piece of the general's wedding cake.

Some will say this personal touch of a piece of wedding cake to every cadet was an isolated incident, unrelated to Gen. MacArthur's military career. They are wrong on both counts, for I saw him apply the same principle—reaching out for contact with those under him—at a critical time during World War II in the Southwest Pacific. (That's another and longer story.)

In the early 1930s the Hawaiian Division was commanded by one of the Army's great combat soldiers, Maj. Gen. Halstead Dorey (Distinguished Service Cross, Distinguished Service Medal, four awards of the Silver Star and four of the Purple Heart). On a certain payday night—always a busy time for the division's military police—my friend and fellow lieutenant, Paul MacLaughlin, was the MP duty officer.

One of the "customers" brought to MP headquarters was a soldier in an exhilarated condition. While waiting his turn for Paul to handle his case, the soldier was parked on the "mourners' bench," a heavy, pew-like seat with side arms at both ends. But he would not stay put, making a loud nuisance of himself, including barging into Paul's office a couple of times.

Finally, Paul decided the soldier's obnoxious behavior was a put-on to harass the MPs. So he ordered the man's wrist handcuffed to an arm of the mourners' bench, thus anchoring him in place. Within minutes, Gen. Dorey walked in the door of MP headquarters.

Everybody snapped to rigid attention—except the culprit cuffed to the arm of the mourners' bench—and a tense silence settled as the distinguished old general stopped in the hallway, leaning on a gold-headed cane. Lt. MacLaughlin came out of his office and halted at attention. From the vantage point of nearly forty years of service, the grizzled, war-crippled old soldier looked around him, his tired battle-wise eyes taking in the situation.

The now suddenly unexhilarated soldier, anchored to the oak arm by his steel cuff, was the first to break the tableau.

"General," he said in a piteously meek voice, lifting his hand to rattle the handcuff against the oak bench arm, "I don't deserve this!"

After looking at the soldier a moment, then glancing around at the desk sergeant and the motionless MPs, Gen. Dorey turned to Paul and said, "Lieutenant, I don't know what happened here before I came in. You must keep in mind, however, that if a man is unnecessarily and unjustly manacled, the iron on his arm may enter his heart."

When the general turned and walked out as quietly as he had entered, Paul looked at the mourners' bench and said, "It didn't work, did it?"

The rumpled soldier lifted his shoulders in a little philosophical shrug. "Well, Lieutenant, it was worth a try."

Gen. Dorey had the perception to see the obvious difference between the rowdy payday celebrant and the neatly uniformed MPs; also, the human understanding to visualize what happened before he arrived, and to see through the act put on for his benefit. Further, he had the wisdom to avoid a cheap display of indignation over a handcuffed soldier without knowing the facts, which would have damaged the standing of a fine young officer and thus impaired the discipline of a key element of his command. On the other hand, he made it clear to all present that he viewed use of forcible restraint as a very serious matter.

In World War II, my division—in Australia to train for a major operation in New Guinea and camped in the intermittently wooded countryside—received word of a coming visit by our Sixth Army commander, Lt. Gen. Walter Krueger. The grapevine also circulated a broader supplementary warning: Gen. Krueger was a real tough cookie, and he specialized in checking unit messes.

When Gen. Krueger arrived, he more than lived up to advance billing; hard-eyed and grim, he wasted few words. In one of the early companies he visited he headed straight for the mess before the first lieutenant in command could report.

When the company commander arrived on the double the general and his party were near the kitchen garbage pit. The general pointed at several fragments of food scattered on the ground and asked, "Lieutenant, what's your explanation for that?"

"Sir," the young officer replied, "we didn't expect you for another half hour."

There was a stunned silence at this, the most classic wrong answer of which I have any knowledge, especially when given to Gen. Krueger. But the general's comment is a classic, too.

"Lieutenant," he said, "you don't run this mess for me. You run it for the men in your company."

General Krueger did not develop his feeling of responsibility for the well-being of those under him after he pinned on stars. Rather, it is one of the primary qualities which made him a general, and a major factor in his outstanding success in that grade.

In a high headquarters where I served after the war, we got a new four-star commander with a great national name. One day, his chief of staff sat in on a scheduled ten-minute briefing for the CG by a lieutenant colonel. There were carefully prepared charts, and the briefing officer was extremely well informed on his subject.

"That's all," the general finally interrupted, "your ten minutes are up."

"Sir," the briefing officer said in some agitation, "I've not yet covered the main issue on which a decision is needed."

"I know," the general said, "but your ten minutes are up." And he reached for the paper he had been studying when the briefing started.

This left it for the chief of staff to take over. In his office the chief explained to the crestfallen briefing officer that the general's time was valuable, that he could never accomplish his diverse responsibilities unless he budgeted his time. The chief also said that, hereafter, the briefer should be less concerned with displaying his own broad knowledge of the subject and proceed directly to the pertinent facts and factors necessary for a decision.

That general knew the story would circulate through his headquarters over cups of coffee, thus broadcasting the idea he would not tolerate verbosity that wasted his time. This matter of time becomes a growing problem the higher you go, not only because duties are more complex but also because so many more people are pressing to take up your limited time unnecessarily.

Any officer who fails to control and organize his time is unlikely to wear stars. That is why the generals you meet always seem time-conscious. It is also why many of them appear abrupt and unapproachable.

Some star comments are:

- It is universally agreed that every man in ranks is a human being, yet there is a vocal element who would have you believe most *generals* are not. But that is untrue, as I think these footnotes to the past indicate. Further, like everybody else, they are afflicted with all the frailties of human nature.

- To offset these frailties, those who rise to star rank need other strong qualities, which may explain why some are considered curious people—or, anyway, complex personalities. There is, however, one overriding quality they must have, which these incidents reveal and which a study at West Point years ago listed as an essential quality for leadership: human understanding.

- Shakespeare said, "The evil that men do lives after them; the good is oft interred with their bones." The hard side of generals, along with their frailties as viewed after the fact by second-guessing writers, receive wide publicity. But their human side often lies buried in unnoticed silence.

Any analysis of what generals are made of would be incomplete without a closer look at some freewheeling attributes, as well as a glimpse of clay feet. Not long after receiving my first star, I attended a small cocktail hour for eight or ten generals. When the conversation turned to outstanding officers in line for promotion to star status, the name of one colonel was mentioned as a sure bet for selection.

"No," a brigadier said, "Col. So-and-so will never make it. He's got a court-martial on his record."

The senior officer present, a three-star army commander, turned around to remark, "Oh, I wouldn't say that, because I've got a court on my record, too!"

That general was no once-in-a-lifetime case, for I've heard of two other generals with courts-martial in their files, and a four-star general whose record included a reprimand. Their disciplinary misadventures certainly were no help; in fact, those officers had to be particularly outstanding to overcome black marks against them from their salad days. I think, however, that the same obstreperous qualities that got them into hot water as young officers were, when brought under control, a factor in their eventual selection for stars.

Since the majority of colonels eligible for selection are qualified to become general officers, we come back again to that basic question: What characteristics lift the "best qualified" above many other outstanding professional soldiers? Recently I learned of a little happening which is revealing. I knew the two general officers concerned, and this happening highlights intangible facets of their characters worth noting.

The occasion was the birthday of a division commander. His headquarters officers decided to give him a surprise party, so, to set the stage, his chief of staff invited the CG and his lady for informal end-of-day cocktails—with no reference to birthdays. Thus, it was after dark when the colonel was informed by phone that everything was ready.

"General," the colonel said, "that call reported a riot in progress down at the rock quarry swimming pool!"

The general promptly grabbed his hat and took off with the colonel for the scene of the riot. On arrival at the incline leading down to the pool, which was a water-filled old quarry fitted out with a swimming float and other pool equipment, the general jumped from the car. His chief then turned off the car lights.

"Turn on the damned lights! I can't see a thing!" the general shouted.

Whereupon the whole pool area was suddenly flooded with lights, as officers of his headquarters and their ladies sang "Happy birthday!"

This was the kickoff to a fine picnic-type party. Among others present was the assistant division commander, still in a body cast because he had a fractured vertebra. This injury resulted from a parachute jump, when a gusty wind had blown him out of the drop zone to land in a ditch.

Now, as the surprise party drew to its close, the division commander produced a surprise of his own. He rose to his feet and announced, "In the airborne, everybody follows their leader!"

He then climbed up the "high dive" tower and plunged down into the pool—clothes and all. Naturally, the officers, including some who had never before ventured to make the high dive, followed their leader and splashed down amid much laughter, punctuated by appropriate squeals from wives as their husbands took off.

Suddenly, the division surgeon shouted, "Don't let him jump—he'll kill himself—he can't swim in that cast!"

His shout came too late, for the awkward figure of the assistant division commander, sheathed in the rigid body cast, crashed down into the pool from the high dive. When they fished him out, grinning and sputtering but without further damage, that buttoned up the party.

Many inferences can be drawn about what intangible qualities in the two generals were revealed by that splashing finale. They faced quite different challenges, yet each, in his way, turned circumstances to his advantage and came away one-up. Some may cluck about senior officers in such an off-trail maneuver, but both of those generals were successful combat commanders, and battle leaders don't come in pantywaist models.

In the mid-1950s, while in Germany, I went to a social function for American officers working on documenting the history of World War II. Also present were senior generals of the old Wehrmacht. I was impressed with those German generals I met, who were not Nazi or SS types but regular army professionals.

One of them was a rather small, bald man who seemed to take himself seriously. Since he was standing quietly alone, I moved over to talk with him. On getting close enough to read his name tag I discovered he was Col. Gen. Kurt Zeitzler, chief of the Army General Staff under Hitler, 1942-44.

After a little mutual back-scratching about professional military leadership on both sides, I asked, "How did you pick generals in the old professional Wehrmacht?"

"Character!" he said without a moment's hesitation, holding up a finger to emphasize his point, and repeating, "Character—without that, you have nothing!"

He then went on to make clear that intangible qualities were what they looked for as the foundation on which to build military leadership. We may not think of it that way, but these same intangibles are reflected in our efficiency reports, too—especially in written evaluations under

"Remarks." An officer is not rated in a vacuum solely on his drillfield performance, but on what kind of man he is: his character. Make no mistake; when you see years of efficiency reports on an officer, by many raters, the outlines come clear: as a strong character, as a weak character, or a middle-of-the-road good officer.

One of the most penetrating descriptions of a man I've ever read was, "he did his best in everything." This was in a biography of General of the Armies John J. Pershing, said about the young Pershing by one of his contemporaries. He didn't get the name "Black Jack" for nothing, either, which reflects another facet of his character.

Sometimes one of the primary characteristics which pushed a man to general officer status may get him in trouble—which was the case with Brig. Gen. Francis T. Dodd. I knew him as a cadet and admired him greatly, for he impressed me then as a future general. A fine-looking forceful personality, self-confident and much respected. It was his very boldness and positive character that, in an unwary moment, resulted in his being seized by North Korean POWs in Korea, leading to his reduction to the grade of colonel.

Granted, Frank Dodd got beaned by an unexpected fast inside pitch while crowding the plate, but it seems to me he has more than paid for that. Now, nearly 20 years later, his name is on the retired list as a colonel. I respectfully suggest that it would be in the best interest of the military service and our country if a senator from Texas—where Frank lives now—initiated a bill to restore Francis Townsend Dodd to the rank of brigadier general on the retired list. But for that one momentary lapse, resulting from his own fearlessness, I think he would have reached multistar rank.*

This emphasized another intangible aspect of general officer status: that strong driving personality characteristics lift an officer to star level, and are vital to his success in that grade. Yet those same qualities often bring down criticism on his head. There are endless incidents to verify this contradictory situation, perhaps the most overt and publicized being

---

*Years later (in some measure sparked by this published item) administrative action, initiated by friends, restored Frank Dodd's rank to Brig. Gen. on the retired list—unfortunately, however, by then he was deceased.

that of the "Patton soldier-slapping incident." The explosive nature of that great battle captain, which made the regrettable incident possible, was also a vital element in making General Patton one of the only two American generals in the last 100 years who can be classed as a true military genius.

At best, we've been able to make only spot checks into this complex and evanescent subject of who get to be generals, and why. Every officer of experience has his memory library of things he has seen general officers do, before and after they pinned on stars, especially how they reacted to various situations. Thus, each experienced reader can conduct his own analysis, using his personally assembled empirical factors.

Of course, I'm out on a limb by writing about such an explosively controversial subject, to which there can never be any one approved answer. It is not the first time, however, that I have stuck my neck out and, I hope, not the last. My final comments are:

- Chance circumstances often play a decisive part in raising any one officer to star rank—as well as blocking the road for others. Almost always, the real comers, those who have everything, overcome bad breaks and forge their own opportunities. This opens a whole new field of case histories, many of them difficult to describe. For those who feel abused by fate, it is well to remember that some of our greatest soldiers reached the top because they stayed in there pitching in the face of adversity. Fate has a way of evening things up in the long run.
- No one has a better chance to evaluate your ability than the man you work for, and he's the one who writes your efficiency report. Further, those with the best opportunities to evaluate an officer's overall career are those who see all his efficiency reports and the papers related to them. Finally, those who can best evaluate all colonels in the zone of consideration—in relation to each other—are experienced older officers of balanced judgment who see all of their efficiency reports. That's what the board of generals do who, by law, select colonels for nomination to the Senate for promotion.
- This system means that those nominated for general officer rank are the colonels who, in the consensus of those in the best position to know, are best qualified to wear stars. We have so many superbly qualified colonels that it is very hard to choose among them. I know, because I was a member of such a board of ten major gen-

erals, chaired by a lieutenant general. It is not a matter of adding up overall efficiency index scores. You try to see the man, not just pieces of paper. In my view, it's the colonels who have the right kind of strong intangibles whose ability, character and leadership qualities give them the edge.

- This is the system used in peacetime for selecting up to two-star generals. Selections for three and four stars are quite different in nature, and I am not sure I understand all I know about that, except that there's a political angle—but this analysis has already complicated itself enough. Besides, it is a good idea when pontificating to stick to things about which you have personal knowledge, and I was never tapped for enrollment in the multi-star fraternity.

- There are many kinds of generals—peacetime generals, wartime generals, staff generals and command generals, technical services generals and other highly specialized generals—even space age generals. Each type has its own demanding requirements which differ from others, but the same basic character qualities are common to them all. The best summary known to me is the poem by Rudyard Kipling, titled "If—." I would like to add, however—in the light of my story in the preceding chapter about two brigadiers and the old British sergeant major—that Kipling forgot to include the idea about the sergeant major's son. In my opinion, it is an intangible not to be overlooked—but don't overdo it. If you're too nice to be true, everybody may love you, but you'll probably never be a general.

- For those officers who aspire to stars, I congratulate you on setting yourself that goal; work toward it, but don't bet your happiness you'll get there. The road has too many unpredictable twists and turns. Yet nobody ever climbed the mountain who didn't try. Make yourself a 30-year drill schedule of duty assignments that best fits in with your planned route to professional advancement, but keep it flexible. Study successful leaders under whom you serve, and learn from them. Also read biographies of great soldiers, but not merely about their battles and achievements; look for the intangibles which were the foundation of their success. Finally, remember that to emulate great leaders, past or present, does not mean to copy or ape them. Study yourself, too, so that you put on only those shoes—and characteristics—which fit you.

Everything considered, what are generals made of? They're made of some qualities they were born with, but, in large measure, their success depends on what kind of personal and professional characters they develop for themselves—and a smile from Lady Luck.

CHAPTER 56
Characteristics that Make Up Character

An ambitious reader has written me for guidance on how to get efficiency reports that would insure his selection to general officer rank. He had read my study of case histories ("What Are Generals Made Of?" ARMY, July and August 1969), so apparently my conclusion that "Character is the Arbiter" was not definitive enough for him. This suggests searching for some recognizable elements of character—which we can call characteristics of character.

One great soldier, Gen. Joseph W. Stilwell, put it this way: "A good commander is a man of high character (this is the most important attribute). . . . He must have moral backbone (this stems from high character). . . . He must be accessible, human, humble, forbearing. . . ."

These characteristics are not easy to grasp and hold. We need the desire to reach for them, and must also see clearly what it is we are reaching for.

One of the greatest leaders in our nation's history is also recognized as one of the finest characters who ever lived. During his second inaugural address as President he said, "with malice toward none, with charity for all." On another occasion he said, "If I were to try to read, much less answer, all the attacks made on me, this shop might as well be closed for any other business. I do the very best I know how—the very best I can; and I mean to keep doing so until the end. If the end brings me out all right, what is said against me won't amount to anything. If the end brings me out wrong, ten angels swearing I was right would make no difference."

Those two majestic characteristics of Abraham Lincoln's character were basic elements of his enduring strength and inspiring leadership. Yet they are simple principles, within reach of all of us.

Another foundation characteristic of character is loyalty: loyalty to

259

yourself and to your fellow soldiers, to your leaders, to your unit and to our country. There are countless ways this characteristic of character is evidenced. But you must be loyal in your heart, and in fact; it cannot be counterfeited.

Then there is the characteristic expressed in the Golden Rule: treat others as you would like to be treated. For soldiers this translates, "Lead others as you would like to be led." Or, "Follow others as you would like to be followed."

There are many more characteristics of good character—like honesty, integrity, industriousness and the like—but we have gone far enough to see an obvious fact: A man of good character is a man to be trusted and emulated. That is why a good character is the cornerstone of your military career.

It must be emphasized, however, that a good personal character will not in itself lift you to high rank. There must also be high military competence and a good professional character—which calls for additional characteristics. Some of these qualities, if not all of them, can be developed, even though they do not come naturally to you at first.

My battalion commander in the 31st Infantry, Manila, P.I. (1929-30) came up with an idea that enabled me to see that others thought I was lacking in an essential element of an officer's military character. Each of the 18 officers in this battalion received 17 mimeographed slips, with the name of an officer typed at the top of each slip—one for each other officer in the battalion.

Under each name was a list of characteristics on which officers of that time were rated on their efficiency reports, including: intelligence, judgment, loyalty, force, cooperation, common sense and tact. Accompanying the package of slips was this directive, signed by Maj. Irving Engleman:

"In order to help me evaluate fairly the officers of our battalion when their efficiency reports reach me, it is desired you use the attached slips to make your own personal evaluation of these officers. Under the officer's name, you will rate him from 1 to 5 in each of the rating qualities shown. You will then return the slips, *unsigned,* by handing them to me personally."

After all the slips had been returned to him, Maj. Engleman assembled them in name groups and sent them to us for our information. Thus, I got the 16 slips with my name on them, made out by the 16 officers evaluating me—which showed they considered me lacking in *force.* This was a surprise, because I knew I could be an SOB when necessary; but since others did not realize I had this characteristic, the logical thing to do was make the trait more obvious.

Apparently my efforts in this regard were fairly successful. While I have no documentary proof, consider this conversation in my retired home several years ago.

Three businessmen in civil life, who served under me in World War II—one each at company, regimental and division staff level—stopped by for a surprise social visit. When we were on our second drink, thus well into cutting up old memories, the former division staff officer took the floor.

"Do you know," he asked me, "what we called you around division headquarters when you were chief of staff?"

"Well," I temporized, "I'm not sure. Would you like to tell me?"

"Yes," he said, like a man delivering a long overdue message. "We called you that redheaded SOB." Except he didn't abbreviate it.

This shows that, if you work at it, you can change the characteristics of your professional character. Like if you are not born one, you can become a self-appointed one—but I hope I was a fair and reasonable one and not the unadulterated kind.

When I was deputy commandant (Army) at the Armed Forces Staff College, I had an unusual opportunity to gain added insight into the professional characteristics that lead to successful military careers. The obvious question was: Since students at AFSC had been selected as the finest young officers of their age and rank brackets, what kind of people were they?

The best answer came from AFSC faculty members. Under college procedure each Army faculty member was adviser to five or six Army students. To assist me in preparing academic reports, these faculty advisers filled out a rating form on students under them, which included two significant questions:.

Question: Does he seek responsibility? Yes or No.

Answer: In the four classes while I was at AFSC, which included some 250 students, in the case of *only one man* was the answer *no*.

Question: Does he work best as a chief, as an Indian, or equally well at both?

Answer: This one amazed me, for I thought, "These are the hotshots, so we'll have lots of chiefs." But *only two* were rated as working best as chiefs. Both were technical specialists, overage for the class and below par for the course. *Only one* (the same man who did not seek responsibility) was rated best as an Indian, and he also was below AFSC standards.

Thus of 250 Army students 247 were rated as seeking responsibility and working equally well as chief or Indian. This makes sense. There will always be superiors above you as well as subordinates below you. Hence, for well-rounded effectiveness you must be able to work yourself as well as to direct others.

There are endless variations to the professional characteristics that successful commanders and leaders need—and high-level staff officers, too. But these are enough to show the nature and type of qualities required. Here are added comments which may be helpful to those beginning military careers:

- A man is not born with a good or bad character, but when he matures his character is what he is. Many things go into this: early environment, parents and home life, community and friends—but these are only influences. Each thinking man is the architect and builder of his own personal and professional character, a forming and remodeling process that must never stop.

- Some may say that a good character is too simple a base to support the complex demands of military life. But I believe with a biographer of William Ewart Gladstone, four times British prime minister, that, "Simplicity of character is no hindrance to the subtlety of intellect."

- The importance of character to a soldier is summed up in this quotation from the article, "Faithful to Our Trust," in the December 1954 issue of *Combat Forces Journal* (now ARMY): "It is the inner man and not the outer trappings of uniform that makes the soldier the strong right arm of Democracy." Similarly, it is the inner man—his impulses, motivations and drives—that forms the foundation on which to build a successful military career.

- Finally, this point must remain sharp and clear: You can have the character of a saint and still fail as a soldier, unless you also have the high military competence that professional success demands.

CHAPTER 57
Care and Feeding of VIPs

Visitations by VIPs, as distinguished from inspections—though the two often overlap—are part of the Army. Like it or not, Very Important Persons are here to stay. To relax and take advantage of their visits requires an understanding of the hazards involved. There is no middle ground: you'll either look good, or you'll smell.

Nothing in my years as chief of staff to various generals caused me more sweat and exasperation than trying to make sure that visiting VIPs were handled without the occasion being marred by some stupid or ridiculous incident. To this day I have a type dream I call my "VIP and C/S Nightmare." No two are the same, but there's always some high-ranking visitor coming and I'm busy checking other matters until the last minute. Then I discover something about to go wrong with the VIP visit, which I try frantically to avoid—as it would embarrass our CG to have *that* happen.

Just as I've got things under control something else really louses up the formation. After the publicly embarrassing scene ends my CG walks over and says in an aggrieved but quietly controlled voice, "Well, Red, you let me down again."

These traumatic dreams are less frequent in recent years, as actual events recede into the misty past. Perhaps it will clarify the types of hazards inherent in VIP visits if we examine two case histories.

During World War II Mrs. Franklin Delano Roosevelt visited Australia—and the wife of the Commander in Chief is a VIP by any yardstick. She was scheduled to visit our division, and asked that arrangements be made for her to address the troops. This was the first VIP visit of major-league caliber for which I was responsible—and it was educational.

As chief of staff I examined plans for the event. Since our distinguished visitor would arrive by staff car, with an escort from higher headquarters, our responsibility was limited to preparations for her talk to the troops. There were three primary requirements: get the troops there; install loudspeakers; provide a reviewing stand type of platform from which she would speak. I therefore:

- Asked the G3 officer if he had checked the bridge on a dirt road over which half the troops would move to the assembly area. He said, "Yes."
- Directed that two loudspeakers be installed and checked periodically until zero hour.
- Gave the headquarters commandant detailed instructions for building the platform on which Mrs. Roosevelt would stand—even drew a sketch, showing steps up and a guard rail.

The evening before the event there seemed no duty more important for the chief of staff than to check plans on the ground, with these results:

- The critical bridge on the dirt road was impassable. The staff officer had not said *when* he checked it, and a recent rain had washed it out. (Troops re-routed.)
- Only one loudspeaker installed and tested. (Orders issued for another to go in that night.)
- The speaker's "platform" consisted of two layers of quartermaster ration boxes, each box wobbly, covered with a canvas tarp so you couldn't see the cracks between them—and our elderly First Lady was supposed to walk on *that* in ladies' heels! The "stair" was another ration box, quite tippy. And no guard rail.

"Sir, it would be a waste of good lumber to—" the responsible officer began, before he was interrupted (rather rudely, perhaps) with orders to personally supervise building the speaker's stand as directed, by lantern light that night.

And everything went off fine.

The lesson was clear, but the puzzle remains: Why do otherwise able officers so often regard VIP visits as routine drill formations? There are always angles that are not routine (like a loudspeaker failure) which are definitely *not* routine when vital to the purpose of the formation.

During the next sixteen years I experienced many visitations by VIPs, and there seems no end to things that can snafu them. Like the messing arrangements for an army G3 which misfired, so that he made

his inspection without breakfast—with predictable results. Or when daylight saving time brought in a VIP an hour before he was expected, then
substitute staff-car drivers got lost. Or the MP who ticketed several Congressional cars in their reserved area; and a VIP's personal flag at half
staff during an honor guard ceremony—because it came loose from the
staff and slipped down against the bearer's hands.

So when I became chief of staff of the U.S. Continental Army Command on my last duty assignment, the parade of VIPs through Fort Monroe didn't add to my peace of mind.

Some months after my arrival we received a visit by the Chief of
Staff of the Army, General Maxwell D. Taylor. Plans were simple: he
would talk to all officers in the post theater at 0800, then get a briefing in
the G3 war room—escorted informally to both places by the CG himself,
General Bruce C. Clarke. There seemed no sweat in sight.

So word went out to the post commander and to the secretary of the
general staff to be sure the theater was policed, open, and ready. Of
course, that should have been enough. But I decided to look in at the theater an hour ahead of time, just in case.

When I arrived at 0700 several soldiers were waiting, locked out, unable to clean the place after the late movie the preceding evening. And no
officer present. Further, outside the theater there was a perplexing mess.
After sending out an SOS for the keys, the post commander, and the secretary of the general staff, I demoted myself to sergeant and took charge
of the detail.

What made outside the theater perplexing was the sheet of ice covering the front steps and cement walk—in which was frozen an unattractive
mosaic of cigarette butts and other debris from the late-show crowd of the
night before. This had the police detail stumped, including me—until a
flash of genius suggested copious sprinklings of that salt-like stuff used
on ice to keep people from slipping.

Fortunately one man present knew where there was a supply of it.
The key finally arrived—but no officers—and by two minutes before
0800 the situation was under control.

Then a staff car rounded the corner and from it the shortest, fattest
soldier ever encased in a uniform struggled out and waddled to the rear
door. There he began to wrestle a large concrete urn from the back seat—
a ponderous sand-filled receptacle for cigarette butts.

With the CG and our VIP due momentarily I was acutely aware of a well-known fact: General Taylor kept himself trim and immaculate, and fat soldiers were anathema to him. My imagination pictured the ridiculous spectacle of this monstrously obese soldier rolling his absurd concrete hoop up the sidewalk under the cool and scathing stare of the Chief of Staff.

So I came to life in my best sergeant's vocabulary: "Shut that condemned door, get your overstuffed anatomy back in the car—and take off!" Or words to that effect.

Seconds after the startled staff-car driver pulled away, the multi-starred VIP car rounded the corner and pulled up to the curb. Generals Taylor and Clarke walked calmly over the neat sprinklings of salt-like stuff on the ice—never guessing the white splotches spangled here and there camouflaged butts, gum wrappers, and other things frozen hard in the ice.

The only damage from that VIP visit was to the jangled nerves of an old staff officer, and the loosened tail feathers of a couple of colonels. If General Taylor chances to read this, it will be his first inkling of the frantic scene that transpired immediately preceding his calm arrival.

This is enough history from which to draw some conclusions:

- Having seen good and bad handling of VIPs over the years—from all angles, including visiting as a VIP myself—I know that standards vary greatly. To overdo it is just as bad taste as poor hospitality.
- The best way to handle the VIP situation—with courtesy, military efficiency, and proper protocol— is to put the right officer in charge. (When I did that at CONARC my VIP worries were over.)
- Visiting VIPs come to see the situation, *and to help*—thus are happy to receive well considered requests for aid in their fields. They should be welcomed as friends at court with influence and power—for that's what they are.
- Most VIPs are inspectors too. Thus a VIP who meets sloppy housekeeping arrangements for himself, and whose visit is fouled up administratively, will think overall standards are poor—and in most cases he will be correct. On the other hand, it's misguided thinking to believe a red carpet reception formation will cover up a poorly trained command.
- Finally, though men in ranks don't seem to realize this: visiting VIPs are the soldier's friends.

CHAPTER 58

Stars: Little Hard Pieces of Metal

The English poet and critic Samuel Taylor Coleridge said, "To most men, experience is like the stern lights of a ship, which illumine only the track it has passed." In one sense that describes me, with my life-cycle ship headed for a not-distant horizon.

It also reminds me I have on file a paper stern light that provides glimpses back down the track of my active-duty years. This is a shoe box full of small clips, notes, quotes and 3 " x 5 " notebook jottings that I collected as an aide-memoire over many years. So at my favorite time of day yesterday, with a liberal libation of bourbon as a sundown toddy, I leafed through this trove of paper slips—tracing the track of the past, supplemented by the stern lights of memory.

Maybe the fact I am reading *American Caesar,* a book about General Douglas MacArthur by William Manchester, focused my attention on the appreciable number of these paper hindsights that referred to the nature of star-wearers. In particular, Mr. Manchester zeros in on—and I think unduly accents—General MacArthur's personality foibles.

Perhaps selected items about star-wearers, gleaned from my shoe-box paper trail to yesterday, can supplement my earlier discussion ("What Are Generals Made Of?"), especially their personalities, and what it is like to deal with them.

As a place to start consider this definition of *hubris:* "The insolence of office, the arrogance of power." Thus the question: did the composer of that definition have generals in mind?

Other related notations included: "His attitude is like that of a man from Texas who went to Harvard, then joined the Marines." Also, reference the boat carried on a Navy ship: if it belongs to the captain, it is the

Captain's Gig; but if the same boat on the same ship belongs to an admiral, it is the Admiral's Barge.

Another series of notes concerned rather esoteric aspects of military rank, like this one: "What price rank? Mark Twain said, 'It is better to be a young June Bug than an old Bird of Paradise.' "

Other related notes included: "Senior officers should be treated like senior officers—and they should act like them." Clipped to that was this item: "One reason Congress puts a limit on the number of generals and flag officers is the pressure to get a star-wearer to head every important project or activity. Reason: even though he may not be better qualified technically than available colonels, the presence of a star has a certain catalytic effect."

My interpretation of that comes out this way: the proximity of a general facilitates action, without materially contributing to it.

Another note to myself read: "When you see two officers of the same grade (from lieutenant to colonel) walking down the street, the one on the right may not be the senior. But if they are generals, wearing the same number of stars, it is a good bet the one on the right is senior by date of rank. Reason: general officers often command others wearing the same number of stars; so date of rank can be a major consideration among them."

An interesting footnote to history, illustrating how far-reaching this can be, is that when the five-star rank was established during World War II, Gen. George C. Marshall's date of rank as chief of staff of the Army was one day earlier than that of General MacArthur. This fixed their rank status.

Another classification of stern-light notes deals with "generalship." That might be defined as "high-level command and leadership." This includes aspects in the exercise of authority not usually faced at lower levels.

One note quotes S. L. A. Marshall with this intriguing thought: "Generalship, in its least understood aspect, is often a form of super-salesmanship." A field manual of my day put it this way: "Generalship is the art and science of adopting doctrine successfully to the situation at hand."

Another facet was expressed by Gen. Dwight D. Eisenhower at the Armed Forces Staff College in 1948. He said "Mere knowledge itself is probably the least of the available factors you will apply in war. Knowledge can be gotten many places, but good sense and breadth of vision are the things for which we are striving here."

The following slant about high level modus operandi appeared in a newspaper:

Soon after Gen. Marshall assumed his duties as secretary of state, an assistant secretary of state received an important message from a capital abroad and went in to Secretary Marshall's office, handed him the telegram, gave him time to read it, then said, "Mr. Secretary, what shall we do?"

Marshall looked him straight in the eye and replied, "Never ask me such a question. You tell me what I am supposed to do. That is what you are paid for. I am paid to decide whether I will do what you tell me, or find someone else to tell me otherwise."

Two more intangibles were expressed by famous generals. Field Marshall Bernard L. Montgomery of Alamein, when commanding British Forces in North Africa, had a picture of Marshal Erwin Rommel on the wall of his battle van. When asked why, he said, "I look at his picture and keep wondering to myself, what would I do in this situation if I were Rommel."

Gen. George Washington wrote, "Do not suffer your good nature, when an application is made, to say yes when you ought to say no. Remember it is a public not a private cause that is to be injured or benefited by your choice."

A jotted note on a piece of air mail envelope reads: "Have noticed that generals who call their superiors by their first names are those who are most stiff-necked in such matters when so addressed by their own juniors."

Another group of paper stern lights concerned personality points to ponder—like the time Adm. John Sidney McLain, as a captain, with Adm. Ernest J. King aboard, was trying to get his ship out of San Francisco harbor under adverse winds and tide, and having a tough time.

Finally Admiral King came out and said, "McLain, what in hell are you trying to do?"

"Admiral," the then Captain McLain replied, "I am trying to turn this (censored) ship around. If you will stay in your cabin, I will do it."

Admiral King was McLain's firm backer from that time on.

The grapevine also produced this note about Maj. Gen. Ernest N. (Old Gravel Voice) Harmon, one of the great combat commanders of World War II.

"The best way to handle Ernie," one of his aides said later, "was to keep him on the move; otherwise he would get into everything, opening doors, etc."

On wide-ranging inspections the general always said to the local CO, "Get out in front and lead me." One day when being so led he said to the company commander, "Lieutenant, where are you from?"

"Texas, sir."

"Well," Ernie said, "that explains it. I knew there was something about you I didn't like. Texas, huh?"

The lieutenant wheeled around and said, "Sir, stand at attention when you say that word!"

That left the general a bit taken aback but pleased, too. That kind of reaction, from one combat soldier to another, was something he understood—the kind of thing, had their positions been reversed, he might have done.

Of course, I found other records of humor, too, like the incident involving a multi-starred general in the Pentagon. After returning from a trip to the Middle East, via Africa going and Europe coming back, he made this jocular pontifical announcement:

"I have circumscribed half the world in two weeks."

His enlisted aide, who heard him say this, was soon reported as proclaiming to all and sundry, "Me and the general has circumcised half the world the last two weeks."

Funny, sure, but it illustrates a constant problem for star-wearers: complications that result when they are quoted incorrectly—or out of context.

Two added comments are:

- Considering the above as a whole (and other star twinkles revealed in the stern lights of my shoe box), the overall picture of generals, in the eye of the public, seems to be of split personalities, changing with changing situations. Some apparently liken them to Dr. Jekylls and Mr. Hydes, while others simply diagnose them as mildly schizophrenic.

  However it could be that to handle complex situations requires complex people, which could have something to do with how they got there. As previously stated my former aide, who is somewhat of a semanticist, categorized them as "curious people." Apparently that is a widely held view—and my former aide should know, as he is now one of them.

• In my view, it is not all that complicated. Soon after I pinned on my second star, a senior colonel's wife, whose husband might or might not be retired in that grade, congratulated me. My reply included, "When I reached up and touched the new stars on my collar they were just hard little pieces of metal, cold to the touch, not worth all the heartbreak the lack of them sometimes seems to bring. I am exactly the same man now I was before pinning them on. So never forget that the most important stars in your husband's life are those he sees in your eyes when you look at him."

Anyway, that is how it was for me then—and still is.

CHAPTER 59
Your Professional Posture Can Help or Hurt You

Doctors develop their bedside manner, lawyers cultivate their legal approach, ministers wear their man-of-the-cloth aura and, as professional men, each develops a professional posture appropriate to his business and suiting him as an individual. Every military man also has a professional posture—good, bad or indifferent—which either helps or hurts him. This includes his appearance, personality and manner, even his tone of voice and mental attitude.

To consider all characteristics of a well rounded professional posture requires more space than is available here. So we'll limit this inquiry to the visual aspects of a good professional image and look back down the years for case histories as guidelines.

The best-dressed officer I have ever seen was Maj. Gen. Fred W. Sladen, the Superintendent at West Point during my last three years there. His uniforms were perfectly fitted and always freshly pressed, with brass and leather buffed and shined to a high gloss. He moved in a precise unhurried manner. The visual impact of his professional posture inspired instant respect.

Gen. George S. Patton Jr. was famous for his "blood and guts" posture. He wore two ivory-handled pistols, riding breeches, highly polished boots and a lacquered helmet liner, while stars gleamed from collar tabs, shoulders and helmet. When General Patton arrived anywhere there was never any question about who he was.

In one sense he and Gen. Sladen were alike—they were immaculately groomed. However, in another respect they were far apart, for Gen. Sladen was strictly regulation, while Gen. Patton was nonregulation. Yet each was outstanding in his way. If either had tried to adopt the visual image of the other, the effect would not have been the same—your posture must fit you, not ape someone else's.

On the Pacific side of World War II another great commander established his visual professional posture—gold-braided cap, open collar shirt and corncob pipe. Like General Patton, but with his own distinctive flair, Gen. Douglas MacArthur created a visual image that both identified him instantly and fitted his personality, much as General Patton's pistols and riding boots swank produced the right eye appeal for him.

These great soldiers did not acquire their style after they became famous leaders. Old pictures show General MacArthur smoking a corncob pipe as a captain, so it was not just a corny gesture—he liked corncob pipes. Nor was his uniform cap innovation new for him. I was in the troop officers equitation course of the Cavalry School at Fort Riley, Kan., when General MacArthur stopped there, en route to assume his duties as the youngest Chief of Staff in our Army's history.

As he walked down the aisle to the stage in the post theatre to address the assembled officers, he was a military fashion plate to remember. His knee-length cordovan riding boots were well worn, but polished to a rich low-gloss sheen. His pink riding breeches and green blouse fitted him to perfection but, like General Patton, he was carefully non-regulation. At that time regulations called for a white shirt and black tie with the open collar green blouse—but he was wearing a light coffee colored shirt and a dark maroon tie.

The effect was eye-catching, but harmonious. Whether he ever wore that uniform anywhere else I do not know, but it was just right for him at that time and place.

One of the great battle sagas of our history was the way Gen. Matthew B. Ridgway arrived in Korea when our Army had taken a terrific battering there, and turned it around from desperate defense to calculated attack. He created for himself the same kind of visual impact as had Generals Patton and MacArthur. But Gen. Ridgway's trademark was a steel helmet and a couple of live hand grenades attached to his battle dress in front of and just below his shoulders.

During World War II, General Eisenhower was in overall command in Europe, but at the international level rather than as a battle leader. So pistols and grenades would not have been appropriate appurtenances to establish his professional posture. But he also adopted a visual means of identifying himself on sight. To do this, he cut off the skirt of the regulation blouse, thus creating the Eisenhower jacket.

More recently, we knew the visual trademark of a half-smoked cigar for Gen. Curtis E. LeMay when he commanded the Strategic Air Command and, later, as Air Force Chief of Staff. He was a most forceful commander, so it would be absurd to say the cigar gave him his clout—that came from the dynamic personality of the man himself. But the cigar was a gimmick that did help identify him in the public mind—and to men in uniform as well.

On the other hand, one of our most illustrious military men was known for his lack of trademark and idiosyncratic flair. General of the Army Omar N. Bradley was strictly GI, known with affection and respect as "the soldier's general"—and you can't get any better professional posture than that.

Another of our great names of more recent time is that of Gen. Maxwell D. Taylor, a tremendous soldier in battle and in high level command. In many ways, he resembled General MacArthur more than any of the others, but he eschewed visual trademarks like those of Generals MacArthur, Patton, Ridgway, Eisenhower and LeMay. His professional posture was not the same as General Bradley's "soldier's soldier" plainness. Rather, he typified the highest professionalism of an officer, immaculately groomed like General Sladen, strictly regulation and with the incisive mental qualities of the intellectual he is.

Many years ago someone (his name now lost in the misty past) told me of a high level official social function in Washington, attended by Gen. Peyton C. March, Chief of Staff during World War I; General of the Armies John J. Pershing, Chief of Staff after that war; and Maj. Gen. Douglas MacArthur, later to become Chief of Staff.

All were in uniform: General March, erect and slender with a neatly trimmed beard and white hair, wore the high collar uniform of World War I, tailored from the rough cloth of enlisted uniforms; General Pershing, squarely built but not fleshy, was wearing his clipped military mustache and immaculate uniform of pinks and greens with riding breeches and boots; General MacArthur, clean shaven and youthful was in a white doeskin mess jacket with gold shoulder knots.

The interesting thing, my informant said, was that while they were so different in dress and general appearance, no one of the three stood out above the others—each had the bearing and professional posture of men who reach the very top in our Army, as all three of them did. Further, each man reflected his own time and personality, and was himself:

relaxed, yet not casual; an alert manner combined with self-confidence and authority, yet without arrogance.

These comments seem relevant:

* Every soldier should develop a well-rounded professional posture. An important element of this posture is your appearance—what others see when they see you.

* Some great commanders have included trademarks in their visual image which identified them in the public eye—such varied things as ivory-handled pistols and highly polished riding boots; a gold braided cap and corn cob pipe; live hand grenades dangling from battle dress; a uniform specially designed by turning a military blouse into a jacket, and a half-smoked cigar. But these things came naturally to them and were compatible with their own personalities as well as the situation around them.

* Did I have a visual trademark in my professional posture? Yes—the one I was born with. As one sports reporter said when writing about a basketball game in Atlanta in 1921: "Clemson College trotted one Newman on the floor, the possessor of a particularly violent crop of red hair." But I never tried to develop a gimmick to publicize my image because, for me, it would have come out phony. Unless you are a MacArthur, a Patton or a Ridgway, and the flair comes naturally, it is far better to leave posture trademarks alone—I can think of nothing sillier than an Army full of officers, each trying to flaunt some different "look at me" gimmick.

* But I do emphatically believe every officer should give careful attention to his professional posture—which includes his visual appearance. In this connection I think of three men: Maj. Gen. Fred W. Sladen, General of the Armies John J. Pershing (who delivered the graduation address to my West Point class), and Gen. Maxwell D. Taylor. Each of them was the very epitome of an officer in the immaculateness of his dress meticulous compliance with existing regulations, an outstanding military bearing—and no gimmicks. They typify the visual professional posture to which every officer can aspire. And you take a "giant step" toward being a good officer when, every day in every way, you look like one.

CHAPTER 60
. . . Some Rain Must Fall

It was after I was promoted to major general while in Germany that I developed Newman's Theory of Rank Relativity: *It's not only among company and field grades that life gets complicated, because on occasion human perversity and professional adversity are common to all ranks—from bars to stars.* A second star was a definite career milestone, but it did not lead to my idea of military heaven. My new assignment was as G1 (Assistant Chief of Staff, Personnel) at Headquarters U.S. Army Europe (USAREUR) in Heidelberg, and thus I was a staff officer, just as I had been for most of the preceding 15 years. But just as a soldier digs a latrine when ordered to—and a good one—it behooved me to give my best to the latrine-like chore of administrative paperwork.

Serving in a theater headquarters for the first time provided a closer look at some of the bigger stars in the military firmament. My basic observation is this: they reached their exalted positions because they had outstanding ability.

But it is equally true that they had many special problems and harassments. Circumstances beyond their control, including mistakes by their subordinates, sometimes made it easy for journalistic sharpshooters to take advantage of a fundamental idea I once heard expressed by one of the Army's fine old field soldiers who was equally effective as a cocktail circuit storyteller.

Soon after I put on my first star he cornered me, glass in hand, with some pointers on the art of being a general—ending with this admonition, slightly edited here: "Red, never forget: the higher the monkey climbs up the tree, the more of his behind you can see."

I do not quote this casually. It brings out a salient point G1 has to keep in mind, for his mistakes are exposed to public view more often than those of other general staff officers. But to me the most disconcerting thing about this was that the behind of a staff officer is not as interesting a journalistic target as that of his boss, so newspapers and magazines aim their arrows at the target higher up the tree.

But enough of this high-level philosophy. . . .

Like my tour as a military police lieutenant in Hawaii during the early thirties, most of my time in G1 was taken up with troubles and minutiae, and it was truly educational. The big things, with a few notable exceptions, were no real problem.

Before citing cases, let me say two things: (1) As a major general who had made every effort to specialize in being a field soldier, I was not involved in such things willingly—but it was my assigned duty; and (2) If some of these things sound childish, let me be the first to assure you they were. In fact, let me quote Demosthenes: "It is impossible, I say, to have a high and noble spirit while engaged in petty and mean employment."

I got letters and phone calls and visits from all kinds of people—generals, officers, enlisted men, civilians—many of them wanting something that, in good conscience, I could not grant. *And they knew it.*

One interesting letter from an officer asked for assignment to an area where there was a severe shortage of family housing. Thus some officers were unable to have their families with them. But this one would "be perfectly satisfied with two adjacent apartments," adding, "I do not think it fair to let the fact my family has increased only from seven to eight children to interfere with my career."

Like everybody else, however, he got a reply. With a postage stamp, you can put a general staff officer to work.

For no particular reason, that reminds me of staff inspection reports made by teams sent out from Headquarters USAREUR to look for things that needed correcting. These reports were fine and did much good but, occasionally, included off-beat items. Like this extract from one report: "Some American female civilian employees [DA, Red Cross, and Special Services] have low morale, and it appears this is in large part the result of difficulty in making friends with American males, who seem to prefer the company of German females. I recommend G1 study the problem of morale among American females."

So G1 studied this problem, with all of its implications, and generated this staff comment: "Local commanders may take such action in this regard as they consider appropriate. Much advice on this subject has been received subsequent to distribution of the inspection report, but its originality is greater than its usefulness."

A fine organization was developed in USAREUR called "Men of the Chapel." It was run not by chaplains (though they were members) but by officers and enlisted soldiers who wanted periodically to meet for lunch or dinner and hear a speaker on some worthwhile subject related to better Christian living.

At one of these meetings I was the speaker, assigned the subject "Faith in Our World."

In my talk I pointed out that if all human beings in the world were removed from it, but everything else remained—money, roads, buildings, machines, forests, oceans, and mountains—there would be nothing left to have faith in.

Thus, to me, faith in our world meant faith in the people in it—and that each of us should be sure we were worthy of faith in us by all with whom we served.

I talked with more feeling than my audience knew, because at this time I was looking on the unlovely face of disloyalty. The worst kind, since the motivation was professional character assassination for personal gain. This can take as many forms in the service as it does in civilian life, but the underlying principle remains the same: an effort to polish your own apple by telling distorted tales about others.

I am happy to say that only twice in my long service did I see real disloyalty, though you smell it more easily than you can see it, for it is a tenuous, nauseous, poisonous miasma difficult to meet face to face. An innocent victim can have an invisible knife in his back and not know he is that professional miracle: a walking dead man.

Of course a lot of fine G1 business was done in my Heidelberg office by my section's outstanding officers. Day after day, week after week, for two years—the unromantic but vital business of G1 so necessary in any large force.

But important as my job was, I had a bellyful of G1 activities by the time my tour in Europe ended. I was glad to turn over my responsibilities for Boy Scouts, school teachers, sale of alcoholic beverages, policy for post exchanges, Solomon for civilian employees and Civil Service regulations, sale of life insurance (also cars and about everything else, if trouble was involved), replies to Congressional letters, the Meistersinger contest, safety programs (on and off duty), morale indicators (like VD rates), policy supervision of welfare funds (who gets the next bowling alleys?)—and of course policy supervision and implementation of assignments of virtually every officer, enlisted soldier, and civilian employee of USAREUR, plus things like housing problems (no dogs in apartment buildings), official greeter for do-good visitors (regardless of sex), also dispenser of oil on troubled waters resulting from off-duty contacts between playboys and bunnies of all nationalities, so long as one was American.

In summary and in brief: Anything that concerned people and caused trouble was likely to be branded a G1 baby in need of a diaper change.

What does all this add up to? Both stars and bars are only small pieces of metal pinned on uniforms, and the men who wear them—or intermediate rank insignia—are equally subject to the grinding wear of human frictions. There are good jobs and bad jobs in the stellar ranks just as there are in the bar grades—and, often, divided opinion as to which is which.

Expressed in another way, weeds grow in every pasture, so don't be fooled by that nice green look on the other side of the rank fence. When you get there, if you do, be careful—or you'll find yourself chewing more bitter nettles in the star pasture than you did in the bar barnyard.

Therefore, you young fellows looking up the rank ladder should not get the idea that the higher you climb the more everything comes up roses. It's not all rain or all sunshine in any one grade. As your rank and compensations go higher, so do the complexities, frustrations, and responsibilities.

Thus, while wearing bars or leaves, never make the mistake of envying a man who is wearing eagles or stars. If you cut the military mustard, and Fate is kind, you may some day stand where he is—but he knows, sadly, he can never again stand where you are.

CHAPTER 61
In Command Use Power Wisely

In the past, when commenting on matters within the experience of my active-duty years, I have not trod on ground eschewed by angels. So maybe it is time to live dangerously for a change.

My encyclopedic dictionary defines *arrogate* this way: "To claim or take surreptitiously or without right; to assume, usurp." The noun is *arrogation;* thus, undue exercise of authority by an individual is the arrogation of power, which tends to be both cumulative and addictive. It becomes dangerous unless checked.

In 1955 I was privileged to sit in on a fascinating discussion of this problem. The occasion was a three-day meeting at a small country resort (in Germany near Stuttgart) with about forty members of the old German regular army, the *Wehrmacht*. Of those present more than half were former Wehrmacht generals and the others were chaplains. They had invited a representative from headquarters, U.S. Army, Europe, to be present, and as G1, I was that representative.

The purpose of the meeting was to discuss ways and means to insure that never again could any individual arrogate to himself such power as Adolf Hitler had done.

The former German generals and chaplains were somber. They asked me how the United States had avoided such arrogation of power while Germany had fallen into that trap, resulting in two disastrous wars.

My reply stressed two points:
* Germans had been schooled for generations in respect for and obedience to authority in a nation headed by one powerful man. Otto von Bismarck and Kaiser Wilhelm II had preceded Hitler.

    On the other hand, our Constitution prevented such concentration of power in one man by creating the checks and balances of a nationally elected president, a two-house, regionally elected Congress and the Supreme Court. Further, procedures were included for removal from office of any man, including the president.

* Under our Constitution, the source of all money for governmental operations is Congress. Even our president can operate only with money authorized by Congress. Without money nothing can happen; thus, there can be no national arrogation of power by an individual.

But I did not tell them that the principle of arrogation of power existed at lower levels under our system and that this could lead to unfortunate results. Nor did I tell them that, in my opinion and contrary to belief, civilian executives in our military system were more likely to exceed their authority than their counterparts in uniform.

In fact at that time, I was facing just such a development. The problem: arrogation of power by civilians over the interior manning of my G1 office.

Among the staff branch chiefs under me was the chief of civilian personnel. This was an important responsibility, exercising general staff supervision over all Department of Army civilians in USAREUR. Normally this would be a colonel's job but it was then held by an exceptionally able lieutenant colonel.

Soon after taking over as G1, I flew back to the Pentagon, where the chief of civilian personnel for the Army (a civilian) buttonholed me. He thought that the chief of civilian personnel in my office should be a civilian.

After considering this, I replied that I could not agree. He then said, "This may not be the end of it."

Following my return to Heidelberg, a letter arrived for the commander in chief, USAREUR, signed by the G1, U.S. Army, in the Pentagon. It stated the view that the chief of civilian personnel in my office should be a civilian.

The commander in chief replied that he could not agree. His letter also included reasons on which his opinion was based.

In about six months (with a new G1 in the Pentagon and a new commander in USAREUR) a similar letter arrived, signed by the new G1 in the Pentagon. This letter received the same reply, signed by the new commander in USAREUR.

Several months later, the assistant secretary of the Army for personnel visited Heidelberg. At the official luncheon for him he was seated on the right of our commander, while I was across and down one seat.

During the luncheon, he addressed a question to me by name. While I do not remember how the question was worded, I do remember my answer.

"Sir," I said, "if that is leading to whether or not a civilian should be chief of the civilian personnel branch in my office, then I cannot agree. Two reasons for this are fundamental.

"Since I have many and varied responsibilities, it does not appear organizationally sound for me to be the first managerial connecting link between Department of Army civilians and the military.

"In a war situation this becomes doubly important. If war comes unexpectedly, I know the officer will remain on the job, but how can I be sure the civilian will? Further, in war the officer will be far better able to cope effectively, without coming to me for detailed guidance at a time when I am overwhelmed with other problems.

"Finally," I concluded, "there has been no criticism of how my civilian personnel branch functions. In fact two commanders in chief have, in the recent past, stated in writing to the Pentagon that they do not want any change in the present organization of my office."

The assistant secretary of the Army smiled slightly, and nodded his head. After lunch he came up to me and said, "General, as far as I am concerned you can keep your present staff organization."

But that was not the end of it. A month or so later a letter from the Pentagon to our commander in chief, signed by the G1, U.S. Army, contained this directive: "The assistant secretary of defense for manpower and reserve affairs directs that the chief, civilian personnel in the G1 office of USAREUR be a civilian, not a military officer."

In my view, this was an arrogation of power that would adversely affect the functioning of G1, especially in the event of a sudden war in Europe. Further, I do not believe that, in establishing the Office of the Secretary of Defense, Congress envisioned that his office would arrogate authority to bypass the secretary of the Army (as represented by his assistant secretary), the chief of staff, U.S. Army (as represented by his G1), the commander in chief of an overseas theater and a general staff section chief to direct that section chief how to man his office in a potential war zone.

During my last year in the Army, as chief of staff of the U.S. Continental Army Command, I received a telephone call from the secretary of the Army. This was a surprise, since I had met him only once.

"Newman," he said, "are you available to sit on a board of officers to select colonels for promotion to brigadier general?"

"Sir," was my reply, "I will ask General Clarke."

"I am not asking General Clarke," he said sharply. "I am asking you."

After a slight pause to collect my thoughts I replied, "Sir, if an office is well-organized it will continue to function effectively in the absence of any one man. My office is well-organized."

"All right," the secretary said. "Tell General Clarke you will be a member of the General Officer Selection Board in the Pentagon for 30 days."

To me, it was almost unthinkable to order the chief of staff to a four-star general away from his headquarters for 30 days without even consulting the commanding general.

These comments seem relevant:

- The two selected arrogation-of-authority incidents may not appear earthshaking in themselves. But as specific case histories they illustrate a dangerous tendency—the arrogation of authority by civilian executives in military matters over and beyond the scope intended in the laws establishing their positions.

- There can never be any question that our country is ruled and controlled by civilians and I would not have it otherwise. During my active-duty years, the military careers of two service chiefs were curtailed when they would not publicly espouse views contrary to their professional opinions. This was right and proper on both sides: the military maintained that essential quality, their professional integrity; the civilians asserted and exercised their power and control.

  (During more than 25 years in retirement I have discovered that the American public thinks military men in uniform "run the Pentagon." But the reverse is true—civilians in mufti do, and properly so.)

- Arrogation of power can occur not only at the top, but downward at lower echelons. It does not matter whether a man in authority wears civilian or military pants; his exercise of power must be limited to that within his legal job description.

  As with many aspects of our national security, this can never be regulated by a computer or fully stated in words to cover all circumstances.

The answer must come from common sense, intelligence, good judgment and self-imposed restraint by the individuals who wear the pants.

CHAPTER 62
Sublimest Word is Duty

The recent letter from a distinguished multistarred general said, "You have quoted many people about duty and it is impossible to quote them all. However, the quote that influenced me over the years is on a plaque in each of the four barracks at The Citadel, by Gen. Robert E. Lee: "Duty is the sublimest word in the English language."

When his letter arrived I was reviewing my copy of *Black Jack Pershing* (by Richard O'Conner, Doubleday & Co.), a biography of General of the Armies John J. Pershing, which, from many angles, limns duty as the cornerstone of his unparalleled career. To our younger generation he is largely a shadowy historical figure, so I'll try to brighten that image with personalized glimpses of his devotion to duty, as gleaned from the book.

He stood No. 17 in discipline at the U.S. Military Academy, and graduated 30th scholastically in the 1886 class of 77 members but was selected as First Captain in cadet rank by the authorities and elected president of his class. In the face of those statistics, how could that be?

Robert Lee Bullard, in the class ahead (who commanded the Second Army in France under him), said "Plain in word, sane and direct in action, he applied himself to duty and all work with a manifest purpose."

A classmate of Pershing said it this way, "He always did his best in everything." These echoes from his cadet days indicate clearly that duty was his guiding star—and duty calls for your "best in everything."

Lt. Pershing was assigned to the 6th Cavalry in Apache country in campaigns against the Apache chiefs, and acquitted himself admirably. Here we also see an unexpected facet of his sense of duty. At West Point he agonized over his French studies, having a limited aptitude for languages. Yet he devoted himself to learning the Indian dialects from the "tame" Indians, a task very few officers assumed as a duty obligation.

On a winter march through the Dakotas his troops were caught in a blizzard that had taken many lives in the area. But Lt. Pershing had equipped his men with overcoats, felt oversocks and overshoes. Further, he made sure his troopers muffled their faces with towels, pegged down their tents securely and had cooked meals during the blizzard. Years later a veteran of that time said, "That's the kind of officer he was, always thinking of his men."

Translation: meticulous and tireless attention to duty, reaching out beyond routine requirements.

He had been an instructor at West Point less than a year when war with Spain broke out. But his sense of duty impelled him to seek combat, and he went to Cuba with the 10th Cavalry. Post battle reports tell the story: Maj. J. T. Wint, his squadron commander, informed the adjutant general's office that Pershing, "was with the Second Squadron . . . and during its advance on San Juan Hill conducted himself in a most gallant and efficient manner." Col. Baldwin, his regimental commander cited Pershing for "untiring energy, faithfulness and gallantry during this engagement." His brigade commander, Gen. S. B. M. Young declared Pershing was "the coolest man under fire I ever saw."

Not surprisingly, Pershing was awarded the Silver Star for gallantry in action, breveted major of volunteers and promoted to captain in the regular Army. Ordered back to Washington, he came to the favorable notice of Secretary of War Elihu Root, who "found that Pershing was the rare officer who could carry out a directive and assume responsibility without buck passing."

Translation: he had good judgment, and recognized his duty to accept responsibility.

In late 1899 he sailed for the Philippines, to Zamboanga on Mindanao, where he remained "for the best part of the next 14 years, campaigning against the toughest jungle fighters in the world." His campaign to pacify the fanatic Moros was a classic blend of force and restraint, patience and harsh action, with compassionate human understanding. The following factors are relevant:

- He learned to speak Moro dialects, to read Arabic, studied the texts of the Koran, and mingled on friendly terms with "tame" Moros in the coastal towns.
- Amazingly, a Moro sultan asked Captain Pershing to be the adopted father of his wife, and later the sultan and his court con-

ferred an unprecedented honor on him: he was consecrated a *datu* of the Moros of Bayan. Never before and never again would a Christian be made a Moro prince.

- En route to the United States in 1906, he was promoted from captain to brigadier general, arousing media allegations of favoritism since he was married to a senator's daughter. Actually, President Theodore Roosevelt first considered this before Pershing even met his wife. Also there was ample precedent: Leonard Wood from captain in the Medical Corps; Tasker H. Bliss from major in the Commissary Department; Albert L. Mills from cavalry captain— all to the rank of brigadier general. Explanation: the President could nominate outstanding officers to be brigadier generals, but not to lower ranks. And Brigadier Pershing was sent back to the Philippines.

- Years of "pacification" remained. One result was the recommendation by Capt. George Charlton of the Philippine Scouts that Gen. Pershing be awarded the Medal of Honor. But the general wrote the War Department that he did not believe his actions were "such as to entitle me to be decorated with the Medal of Honor. . . ." I went to that part of the line because my presence was necessary."

  In other words, he felt he should not receive the Medal of Honor for going where duty called him.

- General Pershing returned to the states in late 1913, with headquarters in San Francisco. When trouble with Mexico developed he entrained with two regiments for the border in Texas, and the situation dragged on.

The morning of 27 August 1916 an orderly arrived at his office with a telegram. At General Pershing's request, the orderly read the devastating news: the old wooden structure housing his family at the Presidio had burned, his wife and three daughters (ages nine, seven and three) had died—only his six-year-old son, Warren, survived.

Intimates who knew him as a devoted husband and loving father understood the extent of his torment, even feared he might lose his mind. But he met his personal duty for the funeral; his maiden sister, May, and married sister, Mrs. D. M. Butler, took charge of six-year-old Warren, and General Pershing returned to his place of duty on the border.

He no longer looked younger than his years, his graying hair turned white within weeks, and his mouth became the grim line shown in World

War I pictures. When Pancho Villa made his surprise attack across the border at Columbus, and President Woodrow Wilson directed the Punitive Expedition into Mexico, Secretary of War Newton D. Baker asked Gen. Winfield Scott and his deputy, Gen. Bliss, who should command the expedition. "Pershing," they replied in unison.

His professional handling of this touchy diplomatic situation and frustrating expedition—strictly on duty lines, without any play for publicity—are history. When the United States entered World War I in early 1917, "Black Jack" Pershing—now a major general—was designated commanding general of forces to be sent to France. Like his Mexican expedition, General Pershing's tremendous operations in France are history, under mission-type orders, including: "you are directed to cooperate with the forces of other countries against the enemy; but the underlying idea must be kept in view that the forces of the United States are a separate and distinct component of the combined forces, the identity of which must be preserved."

General Pershing's struggles to establish the integrity of the American Army in France were as great as his battle achievements. He came under tremendous pressure to distribute his forces among English and French commands—beyond reasonable limits—as opposed to operating under a recognized American command. But his orders were clear; thus, so was his duty. Colonel Mott (his liaison officer with the French) said, "The wear and tear on the man was something enormous, and the tension lasted 18 months without a day's respite."

On one occasion when Marshals Ferdinand Foch and Henri Petain (France) and Douglas Haig (England) failed to get Gen. Pershing to back off from what he considered his duty, the top political leaders (Georges Clemenceau of France, David Lloyd George of England and Vittorio Orlando of Italy) joined the other three, and Gen. Pershing heard Lord Milner "in a stage whisper behind his hand" tell Lloyd George, "It is no use. You cannot budge him."

Finally, General Pershing rose to say, "Gentlemen, I have thought this program over very deliberately and will not be coerced"—and walked out. He knew this could set forces in motion to relieve him of command. But like a poet once said, "He saw his duty, a dead sure thing"—so he accepted that personal risk in the line of duty. And history proved him right.

Two comments:

- One vital requirement of duty is loyalty to subordinates. General Pershing revealed such loyalty in dramatic fashion by releasing his chief of staff, James G. Harbord, for a line command that Harbord needed (and wanted) for combat experience. (Similarly, I benefited from such loyalty from my World War II commander, Maj. Gen. Frederick A. Irving.)
- It would be interesting to know if Pershing himself knew of Gen. Robert E. Lee's thought, "Duty is the sublimest word in the English language." General of the Armies John J. Pershing had many and varied attributes, but to me his unmatched career can be thus summed up in three words, *duty in action*—and there is no better guideline for young leaders in our troubled world today.

CHAPTER 63
Great White Father, Soldier's General, Jumping Joe

We read and hear much about eminent battle leaders like Generals of the Army Douglas MacArthur and Omar Bradley, and Generals George Patton, Walter Krueger, Matthew Ridgway, James Van Fleet, and Maxwell Taylor. But we read and hear little about combat commanders at lower levels whose battlefield leadership was so vital in the famous victories which made lustrous the names of their higher commanders.

One of these magnificent soldiers was Major General Joseph P. Cleland, unknown to the American public—but whose image glows in the memories of all ranks who served with him. That this extended to the top is clear from the handwritten letter to Joe when he retired, on the distinctive office stationery of the Chief of Staff, U.S. Army:

"I want you to have a special message of admiration and respect for your gallant and conspicuously superior service. It was a privilege to share some of it with you. . . . (signed) M. Ridgway."

Joe and I were classmates at West Point (1925), and fellow lieutenants in the Philippines who later shared a 5-gallon keg of Prohibition "Georgia corn" as students at The Infantry School. It was also my privilege years later to serve directly under him. Now, since Joseph Pringle Cleland has answered his Last Roll Call, I have access to letters and documents related to his military career.

The best way to preserve his image is in the words of those who knew him, and to record some of his actions that were characteristic. General Theodore J. Conway, USA Retired said:

"For Infantry second lieutenants fortunate enough to serve at Fort Benning, in the early thirties, First Lieutenant Joe Cleland was their 'most unforgettable character.' Scoutmaster, whip of the Fort Benning Hunt, post handball champion—but more importantly, he was 'father' and friend to second lieutenants. He inspired all of us who came in contact with him by his unforgettable personal example."

In World War II Joe commanded one of four regiments that landed abreast on Luzon in General MacArthur's famed "return" to the Philippines. After his regiment had fought its way inland to a key objective the rough and tough Sixth Army commander, Lieutenant General Walter Krueger, walked up to Joe on the battlefield and said:

"Colonel, I am going to make you a general." There is no harder and prouder way to win a star.

After World War II Joe reverted to the grade of colonel and in 1950 volunteered for Airborne. On completing Jump School at Fort Benning, he commanded the 504th Airborne Infantry at Fort Bragg, N.C.

As Christmas neared, Joe issued orders that no married man living at home with his family on or near Fort Bragg would be detailed on guard Christmas Eve or Christmas Day. Then on Christmas Eve he called for his jeep to inspect sentries on post.

Later that night the jeep driver returned alone to his regimental commander's home with a message. "Mrs. Cleland," the driver reported, "The Colonel said he will not be home until morning."

Then he continued, "You are not going to believe this. The Colonel found a man on post whose family is here at Bragg. So he relieved the sentry, took the sentry's rifle to walk post himself, and had me drive the soldier to his home and family."

When Florence told me about this she added, "It did not surprise me that much. It is the kind of thing Joe would do."

In 1951 he again pinned on a star as Assistant Division Commander, 82nd Airborne Division. Brigadier General Cleland became known as "Jumping Joe," always ready to jump with his troopers.

He had another name too, inspired by his beautiful head of prematurely gray hair: "The Great White Father." That, along with the fact it was his 50th birthday, gave point to the Division Band's choice of music when they serenaded him outside his tent during field maneuvers with "Darling you are growing old—Silver threads among the gold . . ."

Joe recognized the reference to his age and gray hair. When they finished he walked briskly to his nearby jeep, climbed in and stood on the rear end, then executed a backward somersault to land balanced on his feet on the ground.

"Well," he said, turning a wide grin toward the band, "any you young fellows want to try that?"

It is such unexpected little things that build legends, and Joe was a legend in his own time. His physical stamina was a never ending source of wonder—like his ability to do Airborne push-ups on first one arm, then the other.

In June 1952 Major General Joseph P. Cleland assumed command of the 40th Infantry Division in Korea. His service in the Korean War is reflected in the words of those who were there.

General James A. Van Fleet, USA Ret, commander of the Eighth U.S. Army in Korea:

"Joe had the ability, dedication, warmth, and engaging personality to advance his outfit from the bottom rating to the top. Joe's morale was contagious, and soon the Cleland outfit bristled with it.

"I wish the Army had more Joe Clelands."

Extract of letter from Lieutenant General (now General, Ret) I. D. White, commander of X Corps in Korea:

"Your officers and men always knew you were looking out for their welfare, while welding their unit into a great fighting team. They, as I, were proud to be associated with you. I speak for thousands when I say you were their constant inspiration."

Extract of letter to Mrs. Florence Cleland, from an Infantry soldier in Korea:

"What a wonderful, sincere, humble, unselfish and thoughtful man your husband is. His officers and men believe in him, and that is the highest praise a commander can receive."

Extract from letter to Joe from another 40th Division soldier, written from a VA hospital:

"I was talking to a nurse here and told her about you being a 'Soldier's General' and how you came up to our outpost and patted me on the back. It wasn't for anything really outstanding, but I'll never forget that."

A former staff officer from Joe's division wrote me about him. Among other things, he said when Joe moved his division into the line it was heavily committed. Soon thereafter he assigned every headquarters staff officer a front line company to inspect.

Each officer was given a list of things to look for that required him to cover every foot of that company's dispositions. Thus the staff officers— from adjutant types to chaplains and logisticians—learned about life in the front lines. That made them better staff officers. Also, the troops were happy to have the rear echelon see and understand their problems.

Joe's former staff officer also said that when the late Jim Lucas, Scripps Howard Pulitzer award-winning reporter, arrived in Korea he visited the 40th Infantry Division. The word was Lucas planned a series of critical stories like those about Lieutenant General John C. H. "Courthouse" Lee in World War II.

Unperturbed, Joe Cleland provided the distinguished journalist with transportation, an enlisted guide, and carte blanche to go anywhere and talk to anybody. When he returned Lucas took the Public Information Officer aside and said:

"What is with your division commander?"

Cautious, the PIO asked what he meant. Lucas said, "In other units when you ask people what the division conmander is like—particularly if you ask junior officers—they tell you he is the biggest SOB they know."

What puzzled Jim Lucas was that when he posed that question in the 40th Infantry Division—and sometimes before he asked—young officers would say, in effect, "Let me tell you about the great man who commands our division."

Joe's former staff officer answered that question by Lucas this way: "Why was he so well loved? I suspect the ultimate test of a man is when someone is shooting at him.

"To be led, then, by a man who truly knows his job; who is adamant that others know and perform their jobs in a superior manner; who demands you be treated with respect and intelligence; who in every thought, word, and deed manifests concern for your welfare and safety, who gets down on his knees daily (Joe attended Mass every day at 5:00 P.M.) and prays to God for your safe return home—well, wouldn't you love that man?"

Now we come to this, on the letterhead of the 40th Infantry Division, 19 April 1953:

Subject: Letter of Farewell

To: Major General Joseph P. Cleland

As you leave the 40th "Fireball" Division we, the men and officers, want you to know we are proud to have served under your command. From positions at Kumhwa to the rice paddies of Kap-Yong, along the main line of resistance at Sand Bag Castle, Heartbreak Ridge and the Punch Bowl, and now in Nambakchon, we have been with you. Together we have endured the bitter cold of the Korean winter and stifling dust and heat of summer.

Your leadership and thorough training by which you indoctrinated us, your care for our well being, and your constant presence on the main line of resistance, in our camps, and on hard marches during training, have inspired us.

We shall never forget the effort you made to come among us day and night, always cheerful, encouraging and confident. Especially did this touch us at Christmas, when the enemy boasted he would attack us . . . .

Regretfully, we say goodbye, God speed, and success to you. May we soon serve together again.

FROM THE MEN AND OFFICERS OF THE "FIREBALL" DIVISION

When Joe returned from overseas he commanded the XVIII Airborne Corps at Fort Bragg. After assuming command he assembled his staff, the commanders and staffs of his two divisions, and separate unit commanders. To these key officers he summarized his policies.

One policy was a high standard of physical fitness. He added that a man could not be physically fit if he was heavily overweight, so he would not tolerate fat soldiers. What gave this instant relevancy was the presence in the front row of one division commander, a friend and classmate (also a major general), who was heavily overweight.

When the conference ended the heavyweight major general (classmate and friend) walked up to Corps Commander Cleland and said quietly, "I heard what you said, Joe."

"Yes," was the equally quiet reply, "and that is what I mean too, Wayne."

No sweat, no problem. Joe lived by the standards he set, and expected others to do the same. An extract from an efficiency report on Major General Cleland reads:

"A polished, gentlemanly, magnetic officer whose courteous manner belies the aggressive, courageous and resolute character of the man."

Another facet of his personality is best expressed in this quote from W. A. Nance: "No man can be a great leader unless he takes a genuine joy in the success of those under him." No officer known to me approached Joe in this regard.

That does not mean he lacked the necessary iron in his soul, be-cause (with regret) he would relieve any officer who failed to meet his standards. Further, he could be and was sternly demanding when the occasion required it. But when you are deeply and sincerely interested in the success of your subordinates, your demands result in their finest efforts—which in turn brings success to them.

Thus it is not entirely accident that the 40th Division of that time has spawned an inordinate number of generals. Among them was the first major general from the class of 1951 at West Point, who was a platoon leader under Joe in Korea.

Now a footnote to history. The 40th Infantry Division was in re-serve in the Kap-Yong area when Joe assumed command. One day while looking for a training site he discovered an old tent where a Ko-rean man, thread-bare and thin, was holding school with small chil-dren sitting on boxes. Instantly, Joe was moved to help them in their pitiful efforts to prepare themselves for the future. So he decided to build them a school.

Back at his headquarters, he initiated a "helmet collection" in the division that produced sixteen thousand dollars. A former architect in the division designed the school building, to be built with locally available materials which the helmet fund paid for. The division engi-neers built the school as a training project, including a first aid room the division medics equipped.

Enough money was left to buy a rice mill and a saw mill to help the school be self sufficient. General Cleland named the school for Ser-geant First Class Kenneth Kaiser, first member of the 40th Division killed in Korea.

Before the division returned to the line the school was dedicated and turned over for the children of Kap-Yong. After the division was in the line Joe received a phone message that the national police were going to take over the building for a police headquarters.

Joe's reaction typifies him. He called in his Civil Affairs Officer and directed him to back track that message until he found who issued the take-over order. The officer was then to deliver this message: "The 40th Infantry Division bought the materials and built that school for the children of Kap-Yong. Before they will let it be taken away from those children, the same hands that contributed the money and built the school will tear it down plank by plank and stone from stone."

Twenty years later Joe was invited to return for the 20th Anniversary ceremony at the Sergeant Kaiser School in Kap-Yong. Unfortunately, failing health kept him home but one of his former staff officers in Korea did go. He told me, "I could hardly believe how it had grown—what a fine physical plant now stands there!"

The story of that school symbolizes the kind of man, officer and leader Joe Cleland was. For more than twenty years the school he brought into being has helped toward a better life for uncounted hundreds of Korean children—and will continue to do so.

In his professional career as an officer he helped toward a better future countless officers and men who served with him. As with the school in Kap-Yong, the Joe Cleland influence has expanded with the years because the standards and ideas he so dynamically espoused are passed on in their turn by others who served under him.

The late General Creighton W. Abrams, when Chief of Staff, U.S. Army once said at a meeting of his senior commanders, "Every man has pride. Build on it. Never destroy it. Do nothing to demean it." That was the essence of Joe Cleland's leadership technique and his life.

Our top level battle commanders were justly famous because they called the signals that led to victories. But like great quarterbacks, they needed highly skilled and dynamic men to carry the ball to implement those signals—and Joseph Pringle Cleland, in peace and in the cauldron of combat, proved himself one of the best of those battle ball carrier leaders. Joe was one of a kind. All of the great ones are.

It is unfortunate the American people read and hear so little about these indispensable links in the military chain of command that control the shield which protects our country.

CHAPTER 64
Let Me Hear No Ragged Shots

In the fall of 1921 an Old Grad "whose course on earth was run" came home to his final "resting place" in the West Point Cemetery near historic Old Cadet Chapel. The memory of that long-ago day in the cemetery was revived by a telephone conversation with my friend Lt. Gen. William P. Yarborough, USA, Ret., because I was a member of the cadet firing squad in the grave-side ceremony for the Old Grad.

Eight of us new plebes were instructed in what to do, and drilled in how to do it. It was emphasized that at "Aim!" our trigger fingers would be inside of and pressed against the *forward* part of the trigger guard—thus *not* in contact with the trigger. At the command "Fire!" our fingers would snap back on the triggers—thus insuring a volley of eight shots at the same instant. No vagrant ragged shots would mar the rhythm of this simple but impressive ceremony.

There was a career guideline in that firing squad all those years ago, but I did not have the perception to see it then. Now, sitting on the bench, no longer in the game, the lesson comes clear: a certain professional attitude on which to found a military career.

It is like the way mountain climbers explain why they climb each mountain: "because it is there." For a true mountain climber does not scale the heights in the hope of reward; it is there and he is there, and there is an inward urge to meet the challenge.

Similarly, when a true professional soldier faces a military task, of whatever nature, it is there and he is there, and he has an inward urge to prepare for and do it just right, without hope of reward—"because it is there" (firing squad or whatever).

Recently, however, a grapevine message has sifted down from the active ranks about an unhappy variation from the "because it is there" motivation principle. It concerns voluntary retirement after 20 years of service. As with most grapevine transmissions, it comes via several sources, including:

- From newly retired officers in my area.
- From a retired four-star general about his contacts with officers on active duty.
- A recent unclassified study included this phrase, "the anxieties related to promotions now rampant in the Army."
- When the condominium apartments in which I live needed a resident manager, a small advertisement in a military newspaper brought 52 applications, many of them officers who had requested early retirement.

Various considerations influence the ambivalence in the professional attitude of officers who opt for "early out." The prerequisite factor, however, is the law which permits retirement after 20 or more years of service. This leads to the "two careers" idea, which dilutes the single-minded professional approach in those "going all the way for 30."

An especially unhappy angle in this grapevine situation report is that some of our best officers are retiring prematurely because of what they view as an unduly rigid career-management pattern that they believe closes the door to future promotions after certain "breakpoints."

Rightly or wrongly, this grapevine intelligence indicates that the consensus among a number of active-duty officers sees this pattern:

- Selection for the Command and General Staff College (CGSC) requires successful command of a company or battery, and outstanding efficiency reports in "good assignments."
- Selection for battalion command requires CGSC, and a fine efficiency record in another type of good assignment, such as higher level staff experience.
- Selection for one of the senior service colleges (SSC) requires all of the above, plus outstanding performance as a battalion commander (only some 40 percent of those who command are selected), and only about 50 percent of those *not* selected for a top-level college will make colonel—which comes at about 21-22 years' service.
- Selection for brigadier general is made about 24-25 years' service in the usual case. And this is the point at which a problem develops for some valuable officers, which did not exist in my day. And I feel it should not now, in 1985.

The problem (says the grapevine) is that when they realize there are no stars in their future, some fine officers decide there is little reason for not retiring at that time. Apparently, this reaction is in some measure true for officers who fail to make any of the career breakpoints and have qualified for retirement. Such an attitude must surely affect motivation, which is unfortunate, and need not be for a true soldier.

Even more regrettable is the feeling of "failure" in some combat and support officers who do not surmount some of the breakpoints in their career road. In particular, how could this be for a colonel with 25 years' service, if no stars fell on him?

To me, to feel too good to serve as a colonel in the U.S. Army is most difficult to understand, because I served in that grade for a full ten years. So let me go back to the phone conversation I had with Lt. Gen. William P. Yarborough—which reminded me of my membership on that long-ago firing squad at West point.

General Yarborough was the son-in-law of one of the finest old Army officers and gentlemen it was my privilege to know: Col. William B. (Wild Bill) Tuttle. When the three of us served together on the same post (Carlisle Barracks, 1947-49) Wild Bill used to refer to his lieutenant colonel son-in-law as "Recruit Yarborough" (in recognition of the fact the younger Yarborough was a combat-decorated veteran with seven battle stars on his World War II campaign ribbon, and a legend in the early history of airborne).

So when, recently, I talked with Gen. Yarborough I could not resist asking about that memorable old Army soldier, Col. Wild Bill, although I was afraid of the probably sad news reply.

"Well, Red, he has answered his last roll call," and he paused as though undecided whether to continue, but added: "As he neared the end I had to lean close and listen carefully to hear his whisper, 'Yarborough, when they fire those three volleys over my grave, I don't want to hear any ragged shots.' "

That is the way it had always been for Wild Bill, a truly dedicated soldier, who lived by the grandly simple career principle that every task should be approached in the best way to insure its completion in a highly professional manner. That hope of reward, in the form of increased rank, could affect his professional dedication as a proud soldier never entered his mind. Thus he wanted "no ragged shots" in his last military formation.

That brought back my memory of the careful instruction and training given to the firing squad at West Point that insured three professional volleys.

What finer principle to live by than "no ragged shots" in every military task? So it seems in order to comment on Col. Wild Bill Tuttle's majestic guideline, as related to the grapevine report that some active-duty officers look at their careers in the light of promotion expectations, and consequent early voluntary retirement. Hence these thoughts:

- Some will say, "What you know about Army officers today and how they feel is based on hearsay that you can not authenticate, and you are long removed from the scene. So go back to your sunset toddies and gilded memories; you just don't understand our modern Army." Well, maybe so. But about that career pattern—how else could careers develop more logically and fairly?

- There are indeed many things beyond my ken, but the real foundations of military careers do not change: professionalism, dedication, human understanding, duty as distinguished from self-interest—and pride as distinguished from false pride.

- Many officers do retire voluntarily under the 20-year law but, in the view of this old soldier on the sidelines, they lose, and the Army and our country lose in the process. Our country loses because these "early outs" have, by experience and training, reached the highest point of their value to the service—assuming they do not allow false pride to sour their professionalism. Also, the total paid in retirement to "short-timers" is much greater *per year of service rendered.*

- These premature voluntary retirees lose in knowing deep in their hearts they did not "stay the course." Also, it just might be that those who leave early because their promotion prospects (they think) are limited by the breakpoints idea—well, maybe having that idea all along lessened the motivation that leads to promotions. And the difference in retired pay *for life* between 50 percent retired pay at 20 years and 75 percent at 30 years *at time of retirement* is by no means as unimportant as some believe when the time comes to live on it.

- Finally, just as active-duty officers can feel I do not understand the modern Army, by the same reasoning they do not understand what comes after their years in uniform. Nobody can say whether or not a shoe fits you but yourself, and the same applies in deciding on the nature and length of the military career you choose. So these comments may bring down some denunciatory noncurrencies on my head.

But no one can refute my certain knowledge that, if I were beginning a military career today with the benefit of hindsight, my selection would be to go for 30 years, with Col. Wild Bill Tuttle's motto of "no ragged shots"—and let promotions and stars fall where they may.

CHAPTER 65
Stepping Out of the Active Ranks

For every career serviceman, the day will come when he retires—maybe early at his own request, perhaps reluctantly under mandatory regulations. The day you leave the Army, like the day you enter it, means stepping through a one-way door in time into a new life. The day came for me on 31 March 1960. Looking back at that time may reveal some angles of interest to others.

My last assignment was in U.S. Continental Army Command headquarters at Fort Monroe, Va. There was a symbolism in our surroundings there which suggests a lesson. We lived with relics and traditions of the past, yet looked to the future with its ever-changing developments. You could walk around the post and read the story of military evolution and progress from before the time of George Washington. The key word was *change.*

Fort Monroe is on the site of the first fortifications built by English-speaking people in North America, where defenses of many types have been built and rebuilt for over 300 years. Its central feature is an old fortress of massive hand-hewn stone walls, in a centuries-old design, surrounded by a medieval type moat.

From the top of the fortress battlements Civil War soldiers watched the ex-*Merrimack* and the *Monitor* make history. Nearby, concrete-and-steel reinforced casemates of more recent times stand empty, their great seacoast defense guns outdated by airpower. Now, planes shuttle from Monroe to the Pentagon and to Army posts and headquarters across the nation.

Outside the old fortress are modern office buildings. But the biggest changes were not visible to the eye. They were there in papers of great importance to the security of our country inside those modern offices, handled by brilliant young staff officers—for the present and imaginative future.

Near Monroe are the four-star Navy headquarters in Norfolk and four-star Tactical Air Command at Langley Air Force Base, with inter-service coordination as never before. The nuclear age had arrived, and the space age dawned, with more changes for military operations not yet imagined.

As I stepped from the active ranks I was part of this passage of time in constant evolution and change.

Soldiers of all ranks are the most vital element in the Army, but time and change overtake them too. As we serve our span of years we carry the torch proudly, but the day will come—as it did for me—to pass the flame to younger bodies and better time-oriented minds.

The traditional retirement ceremony is a review, but I asked that the departure honor guard, with the artillery salute of 13 guns for my rank, be my retirement review. I also requested that "Auld Lang Syne" be omitted from the band's medley, and the great Infantry song, "Rodger Young," be played instead. ("Rodger Young . . . fought and died for the men he marched among. . . .")

With H-hour at 0815, officers and their families were there to see us off. As I stood at salute for the last time, with smoke belching from cannon muzzles as familiar sounds boomed out, my heart was full—and satisfied.

Then, suddenly, the military ceremony was over and I was shaking hands with friends as in a trance. After all those years, for the Army and the fine men in uniform I loved, this was goodbye.

The final touch to make my last ceremony perfect was added when the three soldiers from my office in the Command Building stepped forward to shake hands before I got in the car to leave. Of all the memories of my last leave-taking, that pleases me most.

Fortunately, my wife and I had planned for our new life. After considering several areas, we decided to live in Florida, and had spent a number of vacations there. So we not only had many Sarasota friends, but had bought a home on Longboat Key. We did not drive away from Fort Monroe to look for a house to live in, and hope to make friends in civil life. We already had both.

When you decide to make the Army your career, you also plan for that career in advance. Similarly, there are decisions and plans for leaving the Army too—which only you can make. Do you want a job? If so, what kind and where? Do you want to rent or buy a house? To own your own home, *free and clear,* is a tremendous move toward a successful retirement, which means a well-considered savings plan on active duty to make that possible.

Now, in retirement, I see on TV and read in public prints about activities in the Army in which I served so long, and my heart swells with pride. If I had a son I could wish nothing better for him than a career in the professional U.S. Army.

Also, for those who do not plan to make it a career, a tour of duty in uniform will be a maturing and broadening experience of much value in later life. Especially in learning how to understand and work in harmony with others, a basic requirement for success in any business or profession.

You will, of course, have to adjust to civilian life after retirement. It's a new world, with a different set of values and customs, but full of fine, friendly people. After a lifetime in uniform, being addressed as "Mister" by many civilians came as a surprise. Almost always, those who do this simply think you are out of the Army, thus hold no rank. Of course, you are subject to call to duty in an emergency, within the capabilities of dimming eyes and age-slowed muscles, and are entitled to your rank by law. It's well to remember, though, that no law requires others to address you by that rank.

An Army friend of mine, a retired colonel, had an interesting experience. The wife of one of his civilian neighbors, a retired doctor, made a point of addressing the colonel as "Mister"—which annoyed the colonel's wife. After a time, however, she came up with a solution, by making a point of addressing the doctor as "Mister"—which annoyed the doctor's wife. Now they are friends—and call each other's spouses by their first names.

This little contretemps does not mean that such superficial conflicts in customs are a retirement hazard. On the contrary, if you begin your residence in a civilian community with such an approach, you've got the wrong idea. Just relax, and join the thousands of retired soldiers living happily among civilian friends.

Some comments are:

- Each retirement is an individual case, involving personal and professional angles. Two common mistakes concern the attitudes of retirees: some retire early because they are disgruntled; others are disgruntled because they can't stay in longer. Both are exercises in futility.

• Consider the case of the soldier—officer or enlisted—who completes 20 years of service with the attitude: *first we had the Old Army, then we had the New Army, now we've got This Here Thing today.* With that attitude he'll be as unhappy in retirement as in uniform. The approved solution is to stop looking over your shoulder to yesterday; get with it today, and remember if you go for 30 years, your retired pay for the rest of your life will be 50 percent higher than if you call it quits at 20, possibly more if your rank increases.

• At the other extreme is an old colonel I once knew who reached the then mandatory retirement age of 64 with no plans for the future, so he retired bitter with the Army because of his own lack of forethought. Alfred Lord Tennyson had an idea which can be adapted as a guideline this way: "Sunset and Evening Star, and one clear call for me. There'll be no moaning at the bar when I put out to sea in retirement—because I've charted my course in advance."

CHAPTER 66
60th Reunion at West Point

"The shadows are lengthening for me. . . ." These wonderfully descriptive words are from Gen. Douglas MacArthur's famous talk to cadets of the U.S. Military Academy on his last visit to West Point, after he had become an octogenarian. When my class entered as plebes on 1 July 1921, our superintendent was Brig. Gen. Douglas MacArthur. In May 1985, the West Point class of 1925 assembled for our 60th reunion, with 15 octogenarians present of 245 who graduated—which sparked this musing reverie.

Octogenarian MacArthur had been cadet first captain and president of his class; one of our 15 octogenarians was Maj. Gen. Charles E. Saltzman, our cadet first captain and class president.

Another classmate, Brig. Gen. James K. "Mike" DeArmond, put our collective feelings into a freewheeling lyric on a scroll, which we signed as a memento for our president Charlie. The story told by the verses spans 60 years of service and several wars, beginning with the time "our alma mater spawned us to the fray."

If you do not have what it takes, West Point cannot give it to you. It does give you a good start, as well as the obligation to live up to its standards.

As I looked at our beautiful parade ground and impressive gray stone buildings against the backdrop of craggy mountains, within a great bend in the storied Hudson River, the inspiration and mystique of "The Long Gray Line" lifted my heart with pride in having started my life in uniform here.

But other thoughts came also, putting West Point in perspective in relation to the overall Army. Here are some of them:

• General John J. Pershing's chief of staff in France during World

War I was Brig. Gen. James G. Harbord, cited as "the best appointment he [Pershing] ever made. No more valuable man served in the American Expeditionary Force." Gen. Harbord was not a U.S. Military Academy graduate.

- Gen. Dwight D. Eisenhower named Gen. Walter Bedell Smith, not a West Pointer, as his chief of staff.
- Gen. Douglas MacArthur selected Lt. Gen. Richard K. Sutherland, also not a West Pointer, as his World War II chief of staff.
- Gen. MacArthur asked for Lt. Gen. Walter Krueger to command Sixth Army. Gen. Krueger selected Col. (later Brig. Gen.) George Decker for his chief of staff, who would in due course become chief of staff, U.S. Army. Neither was from West Point.
- Gen. George C. Marshall, chief of staff, U.S. Army, during World War II, did not go to West Point.
- The present chairman, Joint Chiefs of Staff, Gen. John W. Vessey Jr., entered federal service as an enlisted National Guardsman and received a battlefield commission during World War II. Thus, like countless others, he "rose from the ranks."

So my pride as a member of The Long Gray Line is in perspective. But no words can describe my feelings as the four-abreast column of graduates, in order of seniority by graduation dates, marched to music by the West Point band across The Plain to the Sylvanus Thayer monument (honoring "the father of the U.S. Military Academy") for final ceremonies.

We then assembled, by class markers, for the Corps of Cadets to pass in review for us. As I looked around and at the marching cadets, things were different in some ways from our day—but unchanged in substance and mission.

The preceding day, we 15 octogenarians went on a conducted tour of the post. At the cadet chapel, the world-renowned organ boomed out our alma mater. Memory supplied the words:

> Let duty be well performed,
> Honor be e'er untarned,
> Country be ever armed . . .

Not just for West Pointers, not just for men in uniform, those lines set the mission for all Americans in a troubled and uncertain world.

As we followed our schedule, the class of 1935 held their 50th reunion. This included ceremonies at the Soldier's Monument, an impressive memorial conceived and funded by the classes of 1935 and 1936. These ceremonies included a reading from the scriptures by my former lieutenant (Company G, 26th Infantry) and lifetime friend, Brig. Gen. Lester L. Wheeler. He concluded this way:

> We are assembled here in this hallowed place, our "rock-bound highland home," to once again honor members of our immortal Long Gray Line who can say (as did Saint Paul in his second epistle to Timothy): "I have fought a good fight, I have finished my course, I have kept the faith."

That states the fundamental mission of every member of our armed forces, wherever located or from whatever source obtained.

In searching for a symbolic idea to end these musings about West Point, our armed forces and the America we are dedicated to defend, my mind turned to the 1984 Army-Navy football game. I had watched it on television, and the past came flooding back as I viewed the opening ceremonies. After the game, I went to my desk and penciled this thought to remember:

> When the twilight is here, you can stand on shaky legs in front of the television in your living room—as I did today, right hand over my heart—and participate in absentia in the opening ceremony of the Army-Navy football game of 1984.

On the screen gleamed the colorful picture of an erect young military figure in navy-blue uniform and white cap, standing at the microphone on one edge of the field. As his resonant voice rolled out those magnificent words "Oh, say can you see!" a tremendous American flag, custom-made to the size of the football field, was gradually unrolled to cover it, thus bringing to vivid visual life the words "whose broad stripes and bright stars."

On one side of the tiered stands, rank on rank of gray-uniformed West Point cadets stood at rigid attention, hands at the salute, as they looked across at the tiered stands of the U.S. Naval Academy, also at meticulous salute. . . .

If, at that moment, the Celestial Bugler had blown taps for me, it would have been a proud and symbolic finale to my life as a soldier. Three comments:

- Memorials, pageantry, ceremonies, uniforms and disciplined control are all basic elements of military life—not just West Point parades. Regardless of our service branch or where or how we enter military service, we fight for the same objective under the same symbol, our Stars and Stripes.

- The most meaningful addition to the West Point scene since our day is the Soldier's Monument, bearing these words on its massive base: **TO THE AMERICAN SOLDIER.** Atop the base, done in bronze, is a dramatic group of three American front-line fighting men. Their animated alert postures and the symbolic forward arm swing are silent reminders that, without soldiers, those other monuments to famous leaders would not be there.

- When the colors passed during the review, time turned back. I was a member of the cadet Color Guard for two years, and memory flashed from cadet years to active duty to retirement. As I stood with my classmates where it all began for us, this paraphrase of a poem I once read somewhere in the dim past came clear:

What matter the cost—in peacetime effort, in wartime stress and strain, family separations and finally the coping years in retirement—we would do it again.

We have lived, we have loved, we have strived, we have endured, we have served . . . we have known.

Epilogue

So now we have come, in retirement, to the end of my back trail—on active duty in uniform—examining the twisting challenging and fascinating, sometimes frustrating, always interesting road that led to stars for me and all of those other hundreds within the era of my ken and observation.

But the end of the active duty road inexorably arrives, and I must add one more thought about that eventuality. Everybody likes to climb the ladder of success. However, things do not come out even for everybody—but how well lady luck and the promotion system has treated you should not cloud the end of a soldier's career. Accordingly, when the time comes to get out of the ball game—in military service or in civilian life—I suggest this guideline:

SAVOR THE SUNSET

To be retired
But not tired
Of living
Is a wonderful thing.
I've had my fling
Of giving
Youth its swing,

And do not repent
How I spent
The sunrise
And bright skies.
In the fading embers
Of sunset my heart remembers,
And is content.

Aubrey S. Newman

APPENDIX A
Summary of
Administrative Procedures for
Selecting General Officers

An old Chinese saying states, "It is easy to find a thousand men, but hard to find a general." However that is not the real problem in the U.S. Army—to find enough *average* generals—because World War II proved our school system (the best in the world) and training programs provided more than enough qualified colonels available when much larger numbers of generals were required. So our problem becomes how to select the *best qualified* from our reservoir of fine colonels.

The peacetime machinery for promotion to General Officer rank is simple, under laws passed by the Congress. It is based on a system of Selection Boards for one and two-star generals, like the one on which I served to pick colonels to be nominated for one-star rank as Brigadier Generals. The Board consisted of 10 Major Generals chaired by a Lieutenant General, relieved from all other duties for 30 days and assembled in the pentagon to review the records of all eligible colonels. These records are detailed and extensive, with regular efficiency reports and supplementary documents, from citations and other favorable papers to disciplinary actions (if any).

For one and two-star ranks in peacetime, promotion action must begin with a Selection Board. The "chosen few" names then go up the chain of command to the Commander in Chief, our President, for approval and nomination to the Senate of the United States for promotion.

Notice that while this procedure permits "selection out" of names on the way up for final promotion by the Senate (and this happens sometimes), no names can be "inserted in" that were passed over by the Board. I cannot think of a better or more fair system—though no system can be perfect that must, of necessity, be based on one man's opinion of another.

311

As to selection to three and four-star ranks: I did not serve at that rarefied level, thus have no comments in the premises.

For wartime General Officers the situation is totally different, and includes "spot" promotions to meet existing situations. However experience, personal and professional qualities and other factors were the same on which stars depended in peacetime—though chance played its part in being at the right place at the right time. The primary difference was that stress of war brought these qualities to the surface more quickly in some men.

APPENDIX B
Medal of Honor Citation
for Private Harold H. Moon Jr.

Rank and organization: Private, Company G, 34th Infantry, 24th Infantry Division. *Place and date:* Pawing, Leyte, Philippine Islands, 21 October 1944. *Entered service at:* Gardena, Calif. *Birth:* Albuquerque, N. Mex. *G.O. No.:* 104, 15 November 1945. *Citation:* He fought with conspicuous gallantry and intrepidity when powerful Japanese counterblows were being struck in a desperate effort to annihilate a newly won beachhead. In a forward position, armed with a sub-machine gun, he met the brunt of a strong, well-supported night attack which quickly enveloped his platoon's flanks. Many men in nearby positions were killed or injured, and Private Moon was wounded as his fox hole became the immediate object of a concentration of mortar and machine-gun fire. Nevertheless, he maintained his stand, poured deadly fire into the enemy, daringly exposed himself to hostile fire time after time to exhort and inspire what American troops were left in the immediate area. A Japanese officer, covered by machine-gun fire and hidden by an embankment, attempted to knock out his position with grenades, but Private Moon, after protracted and skillful maneuvering killed him. When the enemy advanced a light machine gun to within 20 yards of the shattered perimeter and fired with telling effects on the remnants of the platoon, he stood up to locate the gun and remained exposed while calling back range corrections to friendly mortars which knocked out the weapon. A little later he killed two Japanese as they charged an aid man. By dawn his position, the focal point of the attack for more than 4 hours, was virtually surrounded. In a fanatical effort to reduce it and kill its defender, an entire platoon charged with fixed bayonets. Firing from a sitting position, Private Moon calmly emptied his magazine into the advancing horde, killing 18 and repulsing the attack. In a final display of bravery, he stood up to throw a grenade at a machine gun which had opened fire on the right flank. He was hit and instantly killed, falling in the position from which he had not been driven by the fiercest enemy action. Nearly 200 dead Japanese were found within 100 yards of his fox hole. The continued tenacity, combat sagacity, and magnificent heroism with which Private Moon fought on against overwhelming odds contributed in a large measure to breaking up a powerful enemy threat and did much to insure our initial successes during a most important operation.

NOTES:

NOTES:

NOTES:

NOTES:

NOTES:

NOTES:

NOTES: